THE ENTREPRENEURIAL SELF

Translated by Steven Black

THE ENTREPRENEURIAL SELF

Fabricating a New Type of Subject

Ulrich Bröckling

$SAGE

Los Angeles | London | New Delhi
Singapore | Washington DC

Los Angeles | London | New Delhi
Singapore | Washington DC

SAGE Publications Ltd
1 Oliver's Yard
55 City Road
London EC1Y 1SP

SAGE Publications Inc.
2455 Teller Road
Thousand Oaks, California 91320

SAGE Publications India Pvt Ltd
B 1/I 1 Mohan Cooperative Industrial Area
Mathura Road
New Delhi 110 044

SAGE Publications Asia-Pacific Pte Ltd
3 Church Street
#10-04 Samsung Hub
Singapore 049483

Editor: Chris Rojek
Assistant editor: Gemma Shields
Production editor: Katherine Haw
Copyeditor: Sharon Cawood
Proofreader: Audrey Scriven
Indexer: Leon Wolff
Marketing manager: Michael Ainsley
Cover design: Shaun Mercier
Typeset by: C&M Digitals (P) Ltd, Chennai, India
Printed and bound by CPI Group (UK) Ltd,
Croydon, CR0 4YY

Library of Congress Control Number: 2015939814

British Library Cataloguing in Publication data

A catalogue record for this book is available from
the British Library

ISBN 978-1-4739-0233-6
ISBN 978-1-4739-0234-3 (pbk)

CONTENTS

ABOUT THE AUTHOR

Ulrich Bröckling is professor for Cultural Sociology at the Albert-Ludwigs-University of Freiburg/Germany. His main areas of research include Studies of Governmentality, Theories of Subjectification, Political Sociology and Critical Management Studies.

FOREWORD TO THE ENGLISH EDITION

Being an entrepreneur is more than just a profession or even a vocation, nor is it merely a variety of economic activity or the legal status of being self-employed. An entrepreneur is something we are supposed to become. The call to act as an entrepreneur of one's own life produces a model for people to understand what they are and what they ought to be, and it tells them how to work on the self in order to become what they ought to be. In other words, the entrepreneurial self is a form of *subjectification*. As such, entrepreneurial activity is less a fact than a field of force. It is an *aim* individuals strive for, a *gauge* by which they judge their own conduct, a daily *exercise* for working on the self, and finally a *truth generator* by which they come to know themselves. This form of subjectification is not restricted to independent businesspeople and shareholders. The call to see ourselves as entrepreneurs of our own lives initiates and sustains this process of constantly shaping the self. You are only ever an entrepreneur *à venir*, only ever in a state of becoming one, never of being one.

People are addressed as entrepreneurs of their own selves in the most diverse contexts, and they are susceptible to this interpellation because orienting themselves on its field of force leads to basic social recognition. Indeed, in a marketized world, acting entrepreneurially is the very condition of participation in social life. Moved by the desire to stay in touch and the fear of dropping out of the society of competition, people answer the call to be entrepreneurial by helping to create the very reality it already presupposed.

The entrepreneurial field of force may indeed tap unknown potential but it also leads to permanent over-challenging. It may strengthen self-confidence and what psychologists call self-efficacy but it also exacerbates the feeling of powerlessness. It may set free creativity but it also generates unbounded anger. Competition is driven by the promise that the most capable will reap the most success, but no amount of effort can remove the risk of failure. The individual has no choice but to balance out in her own subjective self the objective contradiction between the hope of rising and the fear of decline, between empowerment and despair, euphoria and dejection.

That is a short summary of some of the basic theses of this book. The original German edition was first published in 2007, one year before the greatest financial crisis to shake the global economy since 1929. Are the book's arguments now obsolete? Or has its diagnosis of the rise of the entrepreneurial self become instead even more pertinent?

There is a lot to indicate that neoliberal market radicalism has at least been dampened by the events following the Lehman Brothers' bankruptcy. This applies not only to government budgeting und financial markets but also to the hegemony of entrepreneurial subjectification. Yet the call has not fallen silent. On the contrary, the crisis has increased the pressure to develop individual distinctions, 'unique selling points', in order to stay competitive. At the same time, a new figure needs to be added to that of the entrepreneurial self: the 'indebted man'.[1] While the entrepreneurial self is continually concerned with sniffing out profit opportunities, the indebted self must perpetually re-establish its credit rating. The entrepreneurial self is constantly required to demonstrate creativity, customer orientation, innovation and the will to take risks, while the indebted subject must, over and over again, make itself transparent, open up its books and make a convincing show of being able to pay back its credit. The entrepreneurial self is never finished with self-optimizing, while the indebted self can never retire from self-revelation.

The current study delineates the entrepreneurial self as an imperative role model from a Western, and more specifically from a German, perspective. Large parts of this depiction will also apply to other contemporary societies. Calls to become a certain type of subject are as susceptible to globalization as anything else. Yet there are cultural colourations, path dependencies and nuances. The 'New Spirit of Capitalism'[2] has more than just one face. In informal economies in African, Latin American and Asian countries, as well as in larger Western cities, armies of ordinary virtuosos must expend all their energies on entrepreneurial activity just to stay alive. They are propelled onward not by the old dishwasher-to-millionaire dream but by hunger. If we want to find people who closely approximate the image of the entrepreneurial self, we should look not only at the slick adventurers of new economy start-ups but also at the plastic bottle harvesters on the rubbish tips of Lagos and at the windscreen washers on the intersections of Mexico City, or, for that matter, closer to home, at the flower vendors in our bistros and bars.

I am indebted to Wolfgang Essbach, Ulrich Jaekel, Stefan Kaufmann, Susanne Krasmann, Thomas Lemke, Axel. T. Paul, Matthias Schöning and Manfred Weinberg for their encouragement, criticism and many suggestions. I thank Steven Black for his careful translation, which has rendered the academic German of the original in readable English. Warm thanks also go to Leon Wolff who assisted in the search for English editions of the cited literature and in proofing bibliographic details, and also to Barbara Handke, who established contact with SAGE Publications.

Ulrich Bröckling

Freiburg, August 2015

Notes

1. Maurizio Lazzarato (2012) *The Making of the Indebted Man: Essay on the Neoliberal Condition*, Los Angeles: Semiotext(e); Lazzarato (2015) *Governing by Debt*, South Pasedena, CA: Semiotext(e).
2. Luc Boltanski and Eve Chiapello (2005) *The New Spirit of Capitalism*, London/New York: Verso.

INTRODUCTION

At first, the concierge was intending to write a genealogy of the economic subject. But he has a fancy for anachronism. That is why he has become a concierge. Or did the anachronism consist precisely in writing a genealogy of the economic subject?[1]

As the French philosopher Gilles Deleuze plaintively remarked in the early 1990s, the notion that enterprises have a soul is 'the most terrifying news in the world'.[2] The only message to top that is the injunction that everyone should transform themselves, into the last corner of their souls, into an entrepreneur on a mission of their own. This injunction is being delivered today by countless motivation gurus and self-management trainers, as well as by economists, education experts, trend researchers and politicians of almost all stripes. The present book examines this demand, the social undertow it generates and the field of force that grows up around it. The entrepreneurial self that gives the book its title involves a set of interpretative schemes with which people today are supposed to understand themselves and their lives. It involves normative demands and role models, as well as institutional arrangements, social technologies and technologies of self according to which people are expected to regulate their behaviour. In other words, the entrepreneurial self is what is fashionably referred to in the business world as a mission statement.

The figure of the entrepreneurial self is used in precisely this sense in a key document for the German discussion, the final report from the *Kommission für Zukunftsfragen Bayern-Sachsen* (Bavarian-Saxonian Commission for Future Concerns) from 1997. Anticipating in its tone much of the reform agendas that have since been made reality, the report sets an explicit political aim. It states that 'the ideal model for the future is the individual as self-provider and the entrepreneur of their own labour. This insight must be awakened; self-initiative and self-responsibility, i.e. the entrepreneurial in society, must be developed more strongly'.[3] The 'entrepreneurial knowledge society' of the 21st century is no longer calling for 'the perfect copyists of preset blueprints' as the 'wage earner oriented industrial society' of the 20th century had required and produced. What the economy and society really need are 'creative, enterprising people with a much greater readiness and capacity than hitherto to assume responsibility for themselves and others in all matters'. The task of the state is to provide aid in this period of transition.

Politics must 'provide an ordering framework and value orientation'. Those measures intended to stimulate 'more entrepreneurial activity and responsibility' would lead 'directly to a reduction of the social welfare state'. This, incidentally, would mean 'in no way just a loss but also a win for the individual and society'. This latter insight is however ignored by large sections of the population. For which reason, in addition to politics, the economy and the media were called on to reinforce the popular will to keep up with progress. The imperative tone is coupled with the threat that Germany's 'by international standards almost unique material prosperity, paired with social equity, a higher degree of inner and outer security, high amount of leisure time etc.' could 'collapse like a house of cards' unless 'individual views and behaviour as well as collective ideals' were reoriented on entrepreneurial practice.[4] This dire and urgent tone makes the report itself already part of the field of force whose construction it is proposing.

The present study is focused on the way this field of force works, on the energies it consolidates and sets free, on the way it pulls individuals in contrary directions all at once, as well as on the methods those individuals employ for adjusting their own movements to the pull. Like the commission report, this study understands the entrepreneurial self as a programme for governing. The experts commissioned by the state were pushing to have the programme carried out. The present work concentrates instead on understanding it, on bringing into relief the programme's strategic elements, making palpable how the demand is constitutionally unfulfillable and, finally, demonstrating the logic of exclusion and guilt it consequently exposes people to. Following Michel Foucault's lectures on the history of governmentality[5] and the subsequent 'studies of governmentality',[6] the current investigation extends the concept of government beyond the sphere of state intervention to include other strategies for conditioning human behaviour. The field of force of the entrepreneurial self draws on various sources, not only on the decisions of political administration and the recommendations of their expert advisers.

The materials consulted for the study are correspondingly heterogeneous. Among others, I have analysed macroeconomic, psychological and sociological theories as well as management programmes, creativity, communication and cooperation guidebooks and popular advice books, all of which had in common that they made explicit the rationale of entrepreneurial practice and method, thus enabling readers to adapt their behaviour to it as an overall ideal model of how to live. The field of force of the entrepreneurial self is a field of discourse, but it is more than just that. The investigation relies on books, journal articles and other published writings, but a large part of the literature consists of texts intended for immediate practical application: training manuals, textbooks, success guides and similar aids are less concerned with providing convincing arguments than with guiding practice – they are rarely over-blessed with intellectual brilliance, written either in an exceedingly technical or a charismatic, invocational tone. They define a zone of the utterable and the knowable, while directed, above all, at the doable. They not only provide answers to the question 'what am I supposed to do?' but also supply detailed instructions on exactly *how* to do what one ought to do.

Of course, the survey of the entrepreneurial field of force does not permit us to state how people really move within it. Which rules and regularities they follow (including when they diverge from these rules) is of interest to the present work only insofar as their behaviour is influenced by the strategies and technologies of the entrepreneurial self and to the extent these make use of methods of quantitative and qualitative sociological research. What is being investigated therefore is not what those who are subjected to the regime and who constitute themselves as subjects via this subjugation in reality say or do, but rather a regime of subjectification. The question is not how much effective power is possessed by the imperative to be enterprising, but rather by which means the latter exercises this power. What we are concerned with is not the reconstruction of meaningful subjective worlds, behaviour orientation or shifts in the social structure, but with a grammar of governing and self-governing. Put metaphorically, the book investigates not how far people let themselves drift or how they use the current to move forward more quickly, or whether they attempt to evade it or swim against it, but rather the current itself and how it draws people in particular directions.

Concentrating on the rationale and the programmes of the entrepreneurial self poses a danger of reinforcing the sense of inevitability they endeavour to suggest. The study seeks to avert this danger by bringing into focus those programmes' inherent antinomies: autonomy and heteronomy, rational calculation and action amidst uncertainty, cooperation and competition. This approach holds open the gap between the unlimited demand and its limited fulfilment. The issue in what follows is not only what individuals are called on to do and how they are enabled to do it; the study is also about how their efforts often go wrong and how they can never entirely satisfy the requirements placed upon them.

Such a project runs at diagonals to the current disciplinary divisions within social research. More precisely, it can be attributed to a number of different departments. The study is intended primarily as a contribution to a political sociology that avoids reducing political activity to actions by the state and other big players. It is also attentive to the micropolitics of the everyday, to the structures of governance and to all the means by which individuals, public and private institutions regulate their common concerns.

Entrepreneurial practice is without doubt a specific form of economic activity and what has been referred to above as a field of force is a dynamic of assimilating all practice to the model of economic practice. The question to be further examined here is socio-economical in that it is concerned with how this practice type is made credible and made to permeate society. According to an old bon mot by the American economist

James Duesenberry, 'economics is all about how people make choices; sociology is all about how people don't have any choices to make'.[7] In contrast, the present study shows – and to this extent it is economic sociology – how the current economization of the social leaves individuals no free choice except to continuously choose between alternatives they have not themselves chosen. In other words, people have freedom forced upon them.

As an overall model, the entrepreneurial self develops a particular dynamism in the world of enterprise from which it stems. In the sociology of work and industry, as well as in the sociology of organization, it has long been discussed to what extent altered forms of organizing work and business have rendered obsolete the worker of the Fordist age, that type which the above-cited commission report cynically caricatures as 'the perfect copyists of preset blueprints', replacing him with the new type of the 'labour force entrepreneur' or 'entreproyee'.[8] The present study follows up on this discussion by investigating the way current management concepts commit employees to engage in entrepreneurial practice, deploying strategies to increase employee autonomy, responsibility and flexibility.

The entrepreneurial self is an offspring of *homo economicus*, that model of what it is to be a human, on which the science of economics bases its models of human behaviour. The description of this figure thus also falls within the anthropological branch of social science, which analyses implicit and explicit images of the human and the way such images affect behaviour. Since the study deals with at least informally sanctioned behavioural norms – the entrepreneurial self is propagated by means of the promise of success and the threat of failure – it can also be read within a sociology of norms. With its concern for the methods by which the entrepreneurial self is generated, it also contributes to a research domain that could be referred to as the sociology of social technologies and technologies of the self, and that has been to date little introduced into the discipline and at best systematically elaborated on in studies of governmentality. Sociology must here demonstrate its capacity for self-reflection, since the technologies for shaping human behaviour on the entrepreneurial model are based on sociological knowledge and methods.

Finally, mention should be made of cultural sociology. The focus is on what has come to be termed *enterprise culture*. The term does not refer to the 'us-feeling', evoked and continually stimulated by images, rituals, narratives and codes of conduct to promote employee commitment to 'their' firm and reinforce corporate identity. Nor does it refer to the inner worlds and underworlds of businesses brought to light by ethnographers of the labour world. The term 'enterprise culture' refers here to the symbolic order of that field of force that makes 'be enterprising!' the overarching maxim by which to govern the self and others, extending the model beyond the confines of business to enter all aspects of life.

The structure of the investigation

How can a research project be successfully carried out that is situated in so many different contexts at once? The book abstains from reconstructing the field of force of the entrepreneurial self from a central perspective. Instead, it gathers together a series of individual investigations that approach the regime of subjectification from different angles, favouring exemplary examinations over a systematic presentation. The coherence of the whole consists not in an architectonics in which each element is assigned a fixed place, but in the convergence of lines.

The study begins with a methodological section (Chapter 1) which outlines the research programme, responding to impulses in particular from Michel Foucault, Louis Althusser, Nikolas Rose, Gunther Teubner and Michael Hutter. This chapter contours a *genealogy of subjectification* to be undertaken in the following chapters, contrasting it with other sociological theories. Here, we will not yet be treating the entrepreneurial self specifically but rather elaborating on what is a subjectification regime in general and how it can be studied.

Chapter 2 begins by gathering evidence, following the career of the entrepreneurial self and related figures such as the 'intrapreneur' and the 'Me Inc.' in political journalism, in current sociological research, in management discourse and finally in state measures for activating self-entrepreneurship as a means of raising employability (the so-called *Hartz-Gesetze*). This is preceded by an evaluation of the theory from G. Günter Voß and Hans J. Pongratz of the transition from employee to 'entreployee',[9] which shows clearly the divergent research vectors that proceed from a parallel set of basic assumptions.

The subjectification regime of the entrepreneurial self is also a regime of knowledge whose power consists in no small part in conveying to people a truth about themselves, about the logic behind their actions and their social relations. This aspect is explored in more depth in Chapter 3, which analyses those economic theories and schools of thought that lend credibility to the regime of generalized entrepreneurship and establish the rationale of entrepreneurial practice.

Chapter 3 reconstructs how the precursors of German ordoliberalism, US human capital theorists and Friedrich August von Hayek, a leading proponent of the Austrian School of Economics, proposed the market as that agency guaranteeing an optimal (self) regulation of social exchange. According to this point of view, competition among market agents (also according to this view, entrepreneurial individuals are nothing if not market agents) is the source not only of economic but also of political reason and should therefore be kept free of all restrictions and strengthened by favourable conditions. The comparison of these three variants of neo-liberalism also illustrates their divergence.

The ordoliberal discussion tends to push the political protection of competition, while human capital theory construes human behaviour generally as action under the conditions of competition, thus construing *homo economicus* as an entrepreneurial self. Meanwhile, von Hayek emphasizes the randomness of market events, interpreting competition as an evolutionary process advancing independent of the will of individual protagonists.

Chapter 4 explores the question of what distinguishes entrepreneurial practice from other forms of human activity. Instead of seeking personality traits for entrepreneurs, as does economical psychology, we are here concerned with the kind of economical definitions of the entrepreneur as function worked out in particular by Ludwig von Mises, Israel M. Kirzner, Joseph Schumpeter, Frank H. Knight and Mark Casson. On their account, entrepreneurs are, first, alert discoverers of speculative profit opportunities; second, innovative, creative destroyers of existing means of production and distribution; third, risk takers; and fourth, coordinators of the production process optimizing resource allocation. These four basic functions converge where they transgress their own borders and struggle to outdo one another under the dictate of comparison.

Chapter 5 addresses the contract, that fundamental social institution for regulating exchange relations and by extension entrepreneurial activity. It has been observed that the principle of the contract is currently being extended to relations previously not subject to contractual regulation. At the same time, the specifically economical contract is pushing back other contractual traditions. From this perspective, it will be examined how transaction cost theory (Alchian, Demsetz and Williamson) defines questions of social organization generally as contract problems, evaluating contractual arrangements exclusively in terms of the transaction costs incurred. The decision to adopt this or that form of contractual agreement is thereby subject to calculation in entrepreneurial terms and to entrepreneurial risks. James M. Buchanan's constitutional economics provides an economic theory of the social contract according to which the state is brought about by individuals calculating utility maximization. Buchanan posits that people agree on collective rules of play in order to best pursue their own individual benefit, in particular to protect property. While these rules restrict people's freedom to act, they put them in a better position than they otherwise would be without state-guaranteed rights. Constitutional economics and its theory of the contract are based on an anthropology that grasps human beings fundamentally as the property owners of their own selves. In order to accumulate human capital, they need to divide themselves up into a number of distinct assets and an additional entity to administer these assets by exchange and cooperation with a view to profit.

The entrepreneurial self is not merely a construct derived from theories of economics. It is the telos written into current strategies of mobilizing and optimizing people; strategies or technologies with the effect of imperatives operating not only within the economic sphere but in society in general. This is shown in Chapter 6. Four key concepts are examined here: creativity, empowerment, quality management and the concept of the project. Together, they illuminate various facets of entrepreneurial activity, at the same time translating them into social technologies and technologies of the self.

Creativity (Chapter 6) is an element of innovation, the ability to recognize and grasp chances for profit and the creative destruction that makes space for new things. A chief concern in this chapter is the way the psychology of creativity conceptualizes the capacity for innovation as a human faculty, a social, normative aim as well as a learnable skill, at the same time providing appropriate techniques for developing and increasing this skill.

The entrepreneurial self is supposed to be active and self-reliant. Its confidence in its own power should be reinforced and constantly self-affirmed. This purpose is served by strategies of empowerment. Chapter 7 traces the origins of empowerment back to the emancipation struggles of grassroots social movements, as well as to their disparate fields of application and appropriation. This illuminates the paradox of the empowerment programmes, which work by attributing powerlessness to their prospective recipients and then offering to eradicate said powerlessness.

The heading *Quality* (Chapter 8) points to the way the entrepreneurial self must market its human capital in such a way as to find buyers for the skills and products it has on offer. In other words, quality means customer orientation. This will be demonstrated using the example of *total quality management* – the continual safeguarding and improvement of standards through elaborate techniques of quality control which systematically extend the model of the market to include personal relations within firms. There will also be an examination of *360-degree feedback*, which integrates employees and supervisors in a panoptical system of mutual observation and evaluation intended to set in motion a dynamic of permanent self-optimization.

Chapter 9 subsequently deals with the phenomenon of the *project*. On the one hand, this means the sequencing of work (and by extension of all of life) in temporary enterprises demanding a maximum of flexibility from the entrepreneurial self. On the other hand, the idea of the project implies a specific mode of cooperation, for example 'project teams', both permitting and at the same time imposing a high degree of self-organization. The chapter reconstructs the genesis of 'projection', departing from Daniel Defoe's *Essay upon Projects*, through to alternative projects from the 1970s, before employing Luc Boltanski and Ève Chiapello's study *The New Spirit of Capitalism* to sketch a profile of the requirements made of a project worker. The following sections use standard manuals to investigate technologies that ensure the smoothest possible project management and self-modelling under the principle 'Project Me'.

In the conclusion (Chapter 10), the study doubles back to the sense of uneasiness it started with. As the contours of the entrepreneurial self emerged more distinctly, its shadow sides also imposed itself with increasing force: the demand to optimize becomes interminable, selection by competition becomes increasingly relentless, the fear of failure becomes irresistible. This should all be reason enough to get out of the way of the field of force created by the entrepreneurial call. The sense of uneasiness grew in the course of the study as it became apparent how market mechanisms either absorb or marginalize opposing tendencies, recasting non-conformism itself as a measure of successful conformity to the entrepreneurial self. The closing chapter suggests *exhaustion, irony* and *passive resistance* as three ways of disturbing the entrepreneurial field of force. It closes with consideration of a question: How can the compulsion to be different be transformed into the art of being different *in a different way*?

Several of the considerations presented here go back to lectures and articles I have published elsewhere.[10] They have been reworked and supplemented here.

Notes

1. Ernst-Wilhelm Händler (2002) *Wenn wir sterben*, Frankfurt: Suhrkamp, p. 470.
2. Gilles Deleuze (1992) 'Postscript on the Societies of Control', *October*, 59, Winter, pp. 3–7, here: p. 7.
3. Kommission für Zukunftsfragen Bayern-Sachsen (ed.) (1997) *Erwerbstätigkeit und Arbeitslosigkeit in Deutschland. Entwicklung, Ursachen und Maßnahmen, Teil III: Maßnahmen zur Verbesserung der Beschäftigungslage*, Bonn, p. 36, www.bayern.de/wp-content/uploads/2014/09/Bericht-der-Kommission-für-Zukunftsfragen-der-Freistaaten-Bayern-und-Sachsen-Teil-3.pdf
4. Kommission für Zukunftsfragen Bayern-Sachsen (ed.) (1997) pp. 35–44.
5. See Michel Foucault (2009) *Security, Territory, Population: Lectures at the Collège de France 1977–1978*, New York: Picador; Foucault (2010) *The Birth of Biopolitics: Lectures at the Collège de France, 1978–1979*, New York: Picador. In the German editions, the two lecture series are joined under the heading *Geschichte der Gouvernementalität*, vols 1 and 2.
6. For an overview, see: Ulrich Bröckling, Susanne Krasmann and Thomas Lemke (2012) 'From Foucault's Lectures at the Collège de France to Studies of Governmentality: An Introduction', in: Ulrich Bröckling, Susanne Krasmann and Thomas Lemke (eds), *Governmentality: Current Issues and Future Challenges* (2nd edition), Abingdon: Routledge, pp. 1–34. I adopt here, and in the following, the terminology employed by Thomas Osborne who distinguishes between *studies of governmentality* and *governmentality studies*: 'The former proceed nominalistically and are basically an exercise in the history of thought. The latter resemble rather a realistic political sociology in search of just that more or less regular generalizations about our present from which the former are trying to liberate us!' The approach of the studies of governmentality is

'admittedly not indifferent to those questions of most interest to the social sciences but it has a different point of departure that must be taken into account as such. Otherwise there would result presumably a kind of symmetrical split with the sociologists complaining about the insufficient consideration of the social in the studies of governmentality and those concerned with governmentality would accuse sociology of lacking interest in questions of government. And all that despite the fact that both lines of research – leaving the carefree amalgam of governmentality studies out of the picture – do entirely different things. *Vive la difference*' (Thomas Osborne (2001) 'Techniken und Subjekte: Von den "Governmentality Studies" zu den "Studies of Governmentality"', in: *Demokratie. Arbeit. Selbst: Analysen liberal-demokratischer Gesellschaften im Anschluss an Michel Foucault, Mitteilungen des Instituts für Wissenschaft und Kunst Wien*, 56(2/3), pp. 12–16, here: p. 14).

7. James Duesenberry (1960) 'Comment on "An Economic Analysis of Fertility"', in: The Universities National Bureau Committee for Economic Research (ed.), *Demographic and Economic Change in Developed Countries*, Princeton, NJ: Princeton University Press, p. 233.

8. See Chapter 2.

9. Pongratz, H. J. and Voß, G. G. (2003) 'From Employee to "Entreployee": Towards a "Self-Entrepreneurial" Work Force?', in: *Concepts and Transformation*, 8(3), pp. 239–254.

10. (2000) 'Totale Mobilmachung: Menschenführung im Qualitäts- und Selbstmanagement', in: Ulrich Bröckling, Susanne Krasmann and Thomas Lemke (eds), *Gouvernementalität der Gegenwart*, Frankfurt: Suhrkamp, pp. 131–167; (2002) 'Das unternehmerische Selbst und seine Geschlechter: Gender-Konstruktionen in Erfolgsratgebern', in: *Leviathan*, 30, pp. 175–194; (2002) 'Jeder könnte, aber nicht alle können: Konturen des unternehmerischen Selbst', in: *Mittelweg 36*, 11(4), Aug./Sept., pp. 6–26; (2002) 'Diktat des Komparativs: Zur Anthropologie des "unternehmerischen Selbst"', in: Ulrich Bröckling and Eva Horn (eds), *Anthropologie der Arbeit*, Tübingen: Narr Dr. Gunter, pp. 157–173; (2003) 'Das demokratisierte Panopticon: Subjektivierung und Kontrolle im 360°-Feedback', in: Axel Honneth and Martin Saar (eds), *Michel Foucault: Zwischenbilanz einer Rezeption.* Frankfurter Foucault-Konferenz 2001, Frankfurt: Suhrkamp, pp. 77–93; (2003) 'You are not responsible for being down, but you are responsible for getting up: Über Empowerment', in: *Leviathan*, 31, pp. 323–344; (2004) 'Über Kreativität: Ein Brainstorming', in: Ulrich Bröckling, Axel T. Paul and Stefan Kaufmann (eds), *Vernunft – Entwicklung – Leben: Schlüsselbegriffe der Moderne*, Munich: Wilhelm Fink, pp. 235–243; (2004) 'Empowerment', 'Kontrakt', 'Kreativität', 'Unternehmer', in: Ulrich Bröckling, Susanne Krasmann and Thomas Lemke (eds), *Glossar der Gegenwart*, Frankfurt: Suhrkamp, pp. 55–62, 132–138, 139–144, 271–276; (2005) 'Projektwelten: Anatomie einer Vergesellschaftungsform', in: *Leviathan*, 33, pp. 364–383; (2005) 'Gendering the Enterprising Self: Subjectification Programs and Gender Differences in Guides to Success', in: *Distinktion: Scandinavian Journal for Social Theory*, 11, Oct., pp. 7–25; (2007) 'Regime des Selbst: Ein Forschungsprogramm',

in: Thorsten Bonacker and Andreas Reckwitz (eds), *Kulturen der Moderne. Soziologische Perspektiven der Gegenwart*, Frankfurt: Campus Verlag Gmbh, pp. 119–139; (2010) 'Human Economy, Human Capital: A Critique of Biopolitical Economy', in: Ulrich Bröckling, Susanne Krasmann and Thomas Lemke (eds), *Governmentality: Current Issues and Future Challenges*, New York: Routledge, pp. 247–268.

1

GENEALOGY OF SUBJECTIFICATION

The Subject is a Battlefield.[1]

Paradoxes of the self

Becoming a subject is a paradoxical process in which active and passive elements, autonomy and heteronomy, are inextricably intertwined. According to the version prevalent since George Herbert Mead,[2] the self brings itself about by adopting the perspective of the other, thereby generating a self-image. The self must therefore already exist at least in rudimentary form in order to perform this act of subjectification through objectification. From an anthropological point of view, the contradiction between self-constitution and antecedent constitution is a consequence of the human being's 'eccentric positionality'. The human becomes a subject because it needs to *make* itself what it already is, because it needs to lead the life that it lives.[3] What characterizes this subject is that it recognizes itself, forms itself and acts as an autonomous I. Yet it derives its ability to act from precisely those instances against which it asserts its autonomy. For the self, coming into being coincides with being subjugated.[4]

The paradox of subjectification thus interpenetrates with that of power, understood as the ensemble of forces affecting the subject. On the one hand, power predates the subject. The subject is neither just a docile victim nor a self-willed opponent of power interventions, but rather always their posterior effect. On the other hand, power can only be exercised on subjects and therefore presupposes them. Power is based on the contingency of human action and therefore must presuppose an element of freedom. If human behaviour were completely determined, there would be no need for power interventions and indeed they would be ineffectual, they would just bounce off. According to Michel Foucault, the exercise of power operates through a 'total structure of actions brought to bear upon possible actions: it incites, it induces, it seduces, it makes easier or more difficult; in the extreme it constrains or forbids absolutely; it is nevertheless always a way of acting upon an acting subject or acting subjects by virtue of their acting or being capable of action'. For the person whose action is affected in this way, 'a whole field of responses, reactions, results and possible inventions may open up'.[5]

The subject absorbs the forces it is exposed to, modifying their points of contact, directions and intensities. By so doing it bends them around and directs them at itself. As Deleuze writes, '[s]ubjectivation is created by folding'.[6] Exercise of power becomes reflexive. As Kierkegaard famously put it, 'the self is the relationship to oneself'.[7] In self-exploration, self-modelling and self-expression, the self constitutes itself as its own object, makes an image of itself and gives itself its own shape. It is here doubly bound; obtaining the status of subject means, as Foucault writes, on the one hand, 'being subject to someone else by control and dependence', while, on the other hand, it means being 'tied to his own identity by a conscience of self-knowledge'.[8] This polyvalence returns on the level of language in the double meaning of most 'self' composites. The 'self' in self-control designates both the controlling and the controlled element; self-determination can mean determining one's own self as well as having one's self determined by others.[9] The subject is both effect and pre-condition, address and author of power interventions. It is an entity that performs its own creation but whose performances are built into orders of knowledge, into plays of force and relations of domination. In this interpenetration of affecting, being affected and self-affecting lies the paradox of self-constitution: 'If the subject is *neither* fully determined by power *nor* fully determining (of power but significantly and partially both), the subjected exceeds the logic of noncontradiction, is an excrescence logic, as it were.'[10]

Paradoxes cannot be resolved, which is why they persist in the form of problems.[11] In other words, logical impossibilities perpetuate themselves as practical tasks. There can be no such thing as a subject free of contradiction. Correspondingly, the work of subjectification is as unavoidable as it is interminable. This work is recursive since the worker and her object coincide. Consequently, there is a multiplication of self-references (as is indicated not only by the frequency of the prefix 'self') into which stops can be built, although the movement cannot be permanently halted. The subject of subjectification exists only in the gerundive, as that *to be* scientifically examined, pedagogically advanced, therapeutically supported, informed, legally sanctioned, aesthetically presented, politically administered, economically made productive, etc.[12] It is neither the final principle of thinking, willing and feeling, nor the imaginational centre of the person, in which an authentic I can crystallize despite all 'alienation', nor is it the potential sovereign that must first free itself from all possible 'colonisations'. It is neither tabula rasa, in which the social powers inscribe themselves, nor the autonomous author of its own life. The subject is the focal point for all the efforts to define and control it from without and within. It is a social problem and an individual task, not a product but rather a relation of production.

This makes it necessary to radically historicize notions of what a subject is. What a subject is has not been decided once and for all, but rather can only be disclosed via the historical complexes of semantics and knowledge, the self and social technologies that have been and continue to be appealed to in its theoretical determination and practical formation.[13] Such an undertaking is aimed neither at a history-of-ideas approach to the individual nor at an historical reconstruction of the human sciences. Nor is it a variant of psycho-history or historical-genetic psychology, pursuing changes in knowledge and practices of the body, of emotion, imagination, cognition. Finally, no individual life stories or self-portraits will be delineated, as biographically oriented social research attempts to do. As informative as the results of such disciplines and self-disciplines are, the present study adopts a different focus. It follows the research programme that Nikolas Rose[14] terms, with reference to Michel Foucault, 'genealogy of subjectification'. This programme does not investigate the transformations of subjectivity, but rather the way in which the subject has been problematized in certain historical moments and the solutions that have been found. In other words, the study is not asking what a subject is but which knowledge is mobilized in order to answer this question and which methods are applied to actually shape the subject.

Subjectification, understood in this way, is more than just individualization. Inversely, the latter should in turn be decoded as a particular mode of subjectification that is historically contingent and subject to historical transformation; a mode by which individuals, when observing and describing themselves, determine what they are, not in terms of positions or affiliations but by what distinguishes them from everyone else.[15] Since its beginnings, sociology has shown that modern societies cause individualization and socialization to mutually reinforce. The more the individual is socialized, the more it is individualized, and vice versa. Sketching the consequence of these dynamics, Niklas Luhmann writes, 'being an individual becomes a duty' because, for the individual, 'the uniqueness and incomparability of his social existence becomes the premise of social exchange with him'. He 'is categorized in almost all contexts ... but so that the category always refers to an individual and the category merely regulates the extent to which his individuality is concretely investigated and needs to be actualized as the premise of further conduct'.[16] The paradox of subjectification returns here in the form of a self-relation that grasps individualization either as a process of replicating social prototypes or as an internal dialogue or struggle between several selves. The oxymoron of a series of unique things follows from the first case, while from the other results the oxymoron of a divided individual. While 'homme-copie'[17] must again and again assure himself of his own particularity, the plural self is never done with gathering its separate elements into a coherent whole.[18]

Without adopting Luhmann's theory of differentiation, the present study follows his reconstruction of historical semantics by focusing on the terminologies and complexes of knowledge by which individuals are assigned to types and compelled to individualize. However, the study is less interested in the 'cultivated semantics' of social-scientific self-description of society, concentrating instead on the unspectacular yet intrusive 'utility semantics' of training manuals, psychological advice books, management and self-management programmes, which provide concrete instructions on how to deal with people and how people should behave in order to pass as individuals.[19] At the same time, the genealogy of subjectification is concerned not only with the store of rules for making sense within a society or its functioning systems, but it also extends its focus to the institutional arrangements and expertise systems, categories of ordering and methods of sorting, learning programmes and mechanisms of sanctioning, (self) monitoring and (self) formation procedures with the help of which individualized subjects are generated and self-generate. While system theory grasps semantics as idealized and/or post hoc description of societal structures, the genealogy of subjectification analyses the complex processes of joining and translating between discourse formations, social technologies and technologies of the self. It shares with Luhmann his methodical nominalism and a regard for the equally differentiating and homogenizing effects of the regimes of self. Instead of presupposing something like individualization in order to produce descriptions of current phenomena accordingly, the genealogy traces the dispositif of knowledge and practices, which both enables and compels people to grasp themselves as autonomous persons with a distinctive identity they can seek to express authentically; that knowledge and those practices, in short, which have caused them to see and govern themselves as individuals. However, whereas system theory sees a co-evolution of individualization and a social structure of functional specialization, the genealogy of subjectification is focused on the discontinuities, on what goes on beneath a radar system that only picks up stratified and functionally differentiated forms of socialization. Instead of writing a history of the development or even the decline of the subject, it identifies disparate historical configurations in which specific ways of thinking about subjects are combined with specific ways of actually shaping them.

Along similar lines, the geneaology I am presenting here can also be distinguished from Anthony Giddens' considerations of the 'trajectories of the self' in late modernity,[20] which he diagnoses as a phenomenon of the present, as well as Ulrich Beck's related studies on individualization in the risk society. Both emphasize that contemporary forms of socialization present people with an unprecedented range of choices, while at the same time compelling them to choose between them. Beck writes:

> To modify Jean Paul Sartre's words, people are condemned to individuality. Individuality is a coercion, a paradox coercion to produce, self-design, self-stage not only one's own biography but also its involvements from outside and its networks, and this must be done throughout the changing preferences, decisions and stages of life. However, it is also done within the social-political conditional framework and stipulations of the education system (acquisition of certificates), the job market, labour and welfare regulations, the housing market, etc.[21]

Forcing people to become individuals also means they end up having to blame themselves for failing. Someone who is obliged to 'conceive himself or herself as the center of action, as the planning office with respect to his/her biography, abilities, orientations, relationships and so on'[22] cannot avoid viewing defeats as bad planning on their part. Subjectification thereby becomes an eminently political project. 'Leading your own life' in turn becomes a series of strategic decisions and tactical calculations, a 'politics of life'. The self comes to appear as a reflexive project, subjecting itself to permanent self-monitoring either on its own or with the help of professional advisors, therapists, coaches and other authorities, in order to continually re-adjust its life trajectory. Here, the chances of self-realization go hand in hand with the risk of crashing.

The genealogy of subjectification intersects with the theory of reflexive modernity at two points: in the thesis that, today, the government of the self is dictated to by self-government and, second, in its concern for the paradox of an obligation to be free. However, Beck and Giddens focus on how individuals seek to master their everyday lives in the fields of possibility provided for them while attempting to assemble their own biographies. Meanwhile, the analysis of regimes of subjectification is concerned with the way these fields of possibility get constituted, the lines of force that traverse them, the way individuals' options are mobilized, restricted or canalized; in short, how they conduct their conduct, and how they are led, 'conducted', to do so. Beyond that, the genealogy is sceptical of epoch labels like 'late modernity', 'reflexive modernity' and 'risk society', which attempt to subsume the present under a single dominant principle. The research programme being pursued here is directed not at 'society' or 'the self' but rather investigates the rationales and technologies that make society as a unit and individualized subjects as agents at all conceivable, and generate them in reality. Instead of reconstructing regimes of the self from a central perspective, it retraces their origins in a set of interrelations. The contours of contemporary subjectification, as thus disclosed, cannot be reduced to a coherent principle of integration, to a dominant ideology or an organizing centre. Instead, they emerge into view as the effect of manifold micro-techniques and ways of thinking that come to consolidate into macrostructures and wider discourses. *Society* and *the self* are the result not the starting point.

Interpellation of the subject and the subject of interpellation

Since talk of the subject always implies a regime of subjectification, a description of the subject is always also a prescription. This fact corresponds to an 'impossible' temporal structure that merges 'always already' with 'not yet'. Louis Althusser embraced this paradoxical demand made on people to become what they already are in the concept of interpellation. In his famous primal scene, a policeman hails or interpellates a passerby in the street: 'Hey, you there!' The hailed individual turns around, becoming a subject in this turning of the body, because 'he has recognized that the hail was "really" addressed to him, and that "it was really him who was hailed" (and not someone else)'.[23] The policeman's call evokes a spontaneous sense of guilt that can only be evoked in the first place because it was always already there. Recognizing this guilt and becoming a subject is one and the same act. Replace in the example the authoritative voice of the policeman as the representative of state power with other voices and the model illustrates the programme of formation and self-formation. Regimes of subjectification confront the individual with specific expectations, which he can try to reject, undermine or fulfil, but which he can never entirely satisfy. And they can only confront him as long as he always already feels basically insufficient: 'Self recognition in the call presupposes assent to subjectification and indicates at the same time that the scene has always already occurred'.[24]

We are perhaps inclined to see the origins of this feeling of guilt and insufficiency in a need for recognition, ascribable to a human dependency on the society of others. Because the 'struggle for recognition' is never-ending and always entrains traumatic experiences of disavowal and rejection, the individual is forced to adapt his relation to himself to the expectations others have of him. This adaptation does not equate to conformity – a distinction that again makes manifest the paradox of subjectification, this time as the paradox of freedom: 'Subjugation, the fact that the human passion for self-preservation makes us vulnerable to those who promise us our bread, also bears the possibility of revolt'.[25]

Despite the subtlety with which Althusser's parable condenses the way the subject is subject to a prior, social mediation, it leaves out two facts: the individual is not only hailed but is also himself a hailer of others; second, his desire for orientation in finding himself can in no way be fulfilled. Franz Kafka captured this in a short parable that can be read as the complement to Althusser's scene. Kafka appropriately entitled the piece 'A commentary'. Althusser was interested in interpellation and the readiness to understand the social determination of the self as self-determination. Kafka meanwhile describes both the inevitability and the futility of all efforts to be oneself:

It was very early in the morning, the streets clean and deserted, I was on my way to the station. As I compared the tower clock with my watch I realized it was much later than I had thought and that I had to hurry; the shock of this discovery made me feel uncertain of the way, I wasn't very well acquainted with the town as yet; fortunately, there was a policeman at hand, I ran to him and breathlessly asked him the way. He smiled and said: "You asking me the way?" "Yes," I said, "since I can't find it myself". "Give it up! Give it up!" said he, and turned with a sudden jerk, like someone who wants to be alone with his laughter.[26]

Kafka's miniature would seem at first to be a lesson in non-recognition. A different reading suggests itself in the light of Althusser's interpellation scene. Now, the story would be about subjectification as a task, as *Aufgabe* in the double meaning of something you have to do, the task, and something you stop doing or literally give up, abandonment. The newly awakened I seeks its way, unquestioningly, as a matter of course – subjectification as *Aufgabe* in the first meaning (task). Then it discovers that its own time and the system's time are not synchronized, that the individual and society are not calibrated to one another and that the I is unfamiliar to itself. This realization triggers uncertainty and dread. The I turns to an authority figure able to show him the way but who instead confronts him with the futility of his efforts, introducing the second meaning of *Aufgabe* (abandonment) with his derisive 'give it up, give it up'.

Althusser's subject is always already socialized and experiences being a self as the compulsion to orient itself on the role models provided. Meanwhile, Kafka's I must spend its whole life exploring and forming itself, well aware that it is doomed to fail because the social imperative to become a subject can never be fulfilled. Neither in Althusser nor in Kafka does there exist an external standpoint from which to deduce criteria for the right use of freedom. Nevertheless, neither of them depicts an entirely pre-determined scenario. In relation to 'work on the self', this means that even though there exists no space that is not covered by social demands, there do exist spaces of play for the individual. Thus, although no paths lead to the true self, there are infinitely many paths that can be taken while vainly seeking it. The drama of subjectification first becomes really palpable in these two sequences of moves: the policeman hailing and the one hailed doing an about-turn, the I seeking help and the policeman turning around. No one can avoid becoming a subject and no one finally succeeds in it.

This brief literary excurse should also have clarified the differences between a genealogy of subjectification and the theory of recognition.[27] In contrast to the latter, the genealogy does not seek a normative basis for critiquing abusive, repressive and exploitative conditions; it forwards no ideal of successful recognition. Instead, it reverses the problem, asking which mechanisms cause people to comprehend their efforts to become subjects in terms of a struggle for recognition and which strategies they employ. In other words, we are not asking which norms would assure recognition, but rather how recognition itself can become a norm and which practices and discourses secure its acceptance as a norm.

Government of the self

Like Althusser, Michel Foucault grasps subjectification as a conditioning process, in which social shaping and self-shaping merge. While Althusser describes this process on the linguistic model of signification, Foucault is primarily interested in the mechanisms of heteronomy and autonomy in the sets of relations between mindset, conditioning strategies and technologies of the self that make humans into subjects and with which they make themselves into subjects. Foucault is focused on the 'formability of human capabilities',[28] studying them by means of a 'speculative empiricism', a hypothetical 'as if' approach, which assumes that humans are capable of being infinitely formed. Starting from this methodological pre-supposition, he reconstructs those power mechanisms and truth regimes by which humans have been shaped or have shaped themselves in the past. This troika of shaping, being shaped and self-shaping, which he analysed in his earlier work in regard to their discursive orders and disciplinary apparatuses, is given the term 'government' by Foucault in the late 1970s.

Subjectification is for Foucault a task for government in the anachronistic sense in which he used the term generally:

> This word must be allowed the very broad meaning which it had in the sixteenth century. 'Government' did not refer only to political structures or to the management of states; rather it designated the way in which the conduct of individuals or of groups might be directed: government of children, of souls, of communities, of families, of the sick. It did not only cover the legitimately constituted forms of political, economic subjection, but also modes of action, more or less considered and calculated, which were destined to act upon the possibilities of action of other people. To govern, in this sense, is to structure the possible field of action of others.[29]

To this should be added: and one's own activity, since 'whoever wants to be able to govern the state must first know how to govern himself'.[30]

At the same time, the focus is less on the real practices of governing others and governing self as on the *art* of government, 'government's consciousness of itself'.[31] The main concern is the knowledge inherent in the practices, specifically the practices of subjectification, the systematization and 'rationalization' of a pragmatics of government. The disparate ways of problematizing the subject and steering oneself and others are thus implicated in the rationalities and technologies of governing human beings for which

Foucault coined the term governmentality. He also spoke of the 'conduct of conduct', where to conduct in the double sense of the French *(se) conduire* 'is at the same time to "lead" others (according to mechanisms of coercion which are, to varying degrees, strict) and a way of behaving within a more or less open field of possibilities'.[32]

Subjectification unfolds in a strategic field where the individual is exposed to deliberate, targeted efforts to condition her, while at the same time conditioning herself in a deliberate and targeted way. For this reason, we must first concentrate on the epistemic configurations and practices that invest the self-relation with form and direction. We follow Foucault's method when he writes:

> Here we are taking as a homogeneous domain of reference not the representations that men give of themselves, not the conditions that determine them without their knowledge, but rather what they do and the way they do it. That is, the forms of rationality that organize their ways of doing things (this might be called the technological aspect) and the freedom with which they act within these practical systems, reacting to what others do, modifying the rules of the game, up to a certain point (this might be called the strategic side of these practices).[33]

This does not mean reducing the subject to a rationally controlled and self-controlling entity, which would mean neglecting the fact that its motivations and actions are only ever partly conscious to itself, which consequently sets limits on control. Like psychoanalysis, the genealogy of subjectification recognizes that the I is not the master of its own house. Yet in contrast to psychoanalysis, the genealogy is not aimed at draining an inner Zuyderzee,[34] as was Freud, nor providing the other with a free space outside of the hall of mirrors that is the imaginary, as Lacan aimed to do. Instead, it reconstructs those forms of knowledge and methods with which people are supposed to be able to know, explore and govern themselves and their unconscious. We 'know' our unconscious only as far as such knowledge is communicated, i.e. as far as it is spoken and made coherent in specific social settings by means of specific techniques of self-exploration. The psychoanalytic hermeneutic is thus not a tacit premise; it is itself a prominent object of genealogical investigation.

This applies no less to other variants of the search for a hidden truth of the subject. That the self is an inner space to be explored, developed and cultivated is not self-evident. It is the effect of a specific regime of control over the governing and self-governing. The genealogy does not drop the distinction between inside and outside, but instead of cave-diving or interior designing the soul, it asks which bodies of knowledge and methods have occasioned people to determine their self-relation by means of this topology. It investigates how an interior constitutes itself without presupposing it as having always already existed. This is what is meant by designating the self as fold – the self as a more or less fleeting, more or less stable form of the self relating to itself. A fold is a relation of inside to outside in which each can only be conceived of in terms of the other. The inside is merely an outside turned on itself, and vice versa.

To understand subjectification as strictly relational, a third term needs to be added to the inside–outside binary. Following a consideration by Norbert Ricken, the regimes of the self can be regarded as always operating on the basis of the *given* (human corporeality, life story, historical and cultural situation); second, they confront individuals with *tasks* (e.g. with myriad imperatives to individualize and self-optimize); and third, they are repeatedly brought up against incidents of the *withdrawal* of something beyond the reach of auto-formation and hetero-formation:

> Subjectivity then means not only being unable to comport oneself to oneself and to others 'completely' and transparently (because it is impossible to present oneself fully to oneself), but also comporting oneself precisely to this removal of self and other. This throws subjectivity into relief as a *difference* that cannot be resolved into an *identity*, but rather is characterized by ruptures, antagonisms and 'blind spots'.[35]

Consequently, the genealogy is not limited to the reconstruction of an historical ontology and deontology of the self, but also traces its limits, blurred lines, unintended effects and contradictions.

In so doing, the genealogy dismisses the idea of a self-identical self. The subject interacts with the models of self-interpretation and self-modelling imposed on it, inventing itself in vastly different ways depending on the context. The ways in which the subject sees and modifies itself are as diverse as the forms of truth and types of power plays it is embedded in. Subjectification is self-invention in the plural, not in the singular:

> You do not have the same type of relationship to yourself when you constitute yourself as a political subject who goes to vote or speaks at a meeting and when you are seeking to fulfil your desires in a sexual relationship. Undoubtedly there are relationships and interferences between these different forms of the subject; but we are not dealing with the same type of subject. In each case, one plays, one establishes a different type of relationship to oneself.[36]

Real fictions

The genealogy is 'not a history of subjectivity as such, but rather an analysis of the events in the history of the technologies of subjectivity'.[37] It therefore cannot be known how many people really come under the influence of specific governing and self-governing programmes and to what extent their behaviour is thus conditioned. The genealogy does not study whether

programmes have effects but which reality they generate. Instead of investigating causes and effects, it concentrates on describing the mode of operation
and rationale of subjectification regimes. The main question is not 'why and
wherefore?' but 'how?'.

How do subjectification programmes infiltrate behaviour and the sense
of self? Two legal sociologists, Michael Hutter und Gunther Teubner, have
adopted a system theory approach to give an explanation that can be usefully
applied to the genealogy. Their point of departure is the disagreement between
economists and jurists on the one side and sociologists and psychologists on
the other over the ontological status of *homo economicus* and *homo juridicus*.
Hutter and Teubner dismiss the position that these figures are mere theoretical
constructs from economics and jurisprudence, which must hold prognostically
but cannot claim real content. At the same time, they dismiss the contrary position that sees in them a concentration of empirically verifiable human motives
and behaviours. Their thesis is that *homo economicus* and *homo juridicus* are 'real
fictions' that supply the economic and legal systems with the agents they need
in order to operate. These autonomous subsystems address the surrounding
psychic systems as persons, using them as semantic tools for transforming their
communication into activities attributable to agents. The psychic systems in
turn can be addressed in this way because they deploy a personal construction
for the continuation of sense. These fictions of human agency, *homo economicus*
and *juridicus*, thus stabilize 'the connection between communication in economy and law and the psychical operations going on at the same time'.[38] By
means of the semantic tool of personhood, social systems prey on the inner
dynamics of psychic systems, exploiting 'the self constitution of souls toward
their own self constitution'.[39] Hutter and Teubner describe this procedure as an
interaction of conditioning and self-conditioning:

> By choosing an idiosyncratic construction of personhood and thus creating
> internal perturbations, the social systems make themselves only at small
> selected points dependent on the continual, much richer psychic processes.
> This strictly selective social perception of the psyche is in turn only perceived
> psychically. The thought processes of the psyche are thus conditioned by the
> social subsystem, but only indirectly, because the psyche socializes itself. The
> self observation of psychic systems is oriented on the concept of person-
> hood formed in the social system. In other words, the economy exploits the
> human 'need to possess' in order to create future opportunities for payment;
> the law exploits the human 'need for strife' in order to create future oppor-
> tunities for norm production. At the same time, a self-socialization by the
> participating psyches takes place. At the same time again, a self-colonization
> of the psyches takes place, in which the 'ownership drive' and the 'desire for
> strife' are newly constituted by the fascination for communication based on
> money and norms. The medium 'money' and the medium 'legal norms' create
> their own appropriate forms of reason.[40]

Each social subsystem uses its specific rationale to 'see' and personify specific human qualities, 'seeing' and personifying only these. Each 'invents its own social psychology', fabricating the agents it needs to be addressees by presupposing their existence.[41]

Hutter and Teubner start from the observation of functionally differentiated (and continually differentiating), autopoietic, closed subsystems. In contrast, the present investigation of the entrepreneurial self sees market mechanisms encroaching on other social areas. To put it in system theory terms, what is being posited here is an asymmetrical interpenetration between the economic system and the other functional systems. Despite this difference, the theory of the person as an institutional fiction and a parasitic social-psychical structure has the advantage of accentuating the discursive nature of subject construction (fictions must be told), while at the same time tracing this construction back to basic social institutions. The rational agent and the entrepreneurial self are not merely effects of discourse; they are the guises of an extremely practical imperative dictating how humans are to see themselves as people and how they are to act in order to participate in the marketplace. There is much to be learnt about selling things and selling oneself and every act of selling teaches something new. Finally, of further use for the genealogy is the observation from system theory that the various real fictions (or, put in terms of a Foucauldian analysis of power relations, the specific rationalities of regimes of subjectification) only ever actualize excerpts of possible human action, expanding them out to universals, turning the social ontology of the subject into an essentialist anthropological determinant. By turning limited, institutional constructions of personhood into absolutes, regimes of the self damage untapped human potentials, while instantiating an ideal according to which individuals are moulded.

Programmes, appropriations, resistance

The gap between the promises made by programmes of governing and self-governing and their delivery is an integral part of how they work. Such programmes are not automatic stimulus–response systems. Instead, they generate suction, making certain forms of behaviour more likely than others. For this reason, what is here referred to as a regime of subjectification cannot be reduced to a moral code. It not only focuses on a canon of rules of what should and should not be done, but also defines the forms of knowledge in which individuals recognize the truth about themselves, the mechanisms of control and regulation with which they are confronted, the specialists whose advice and instructions they trust, as well as the social and self technologies which permit individuals to effect by their own means or with the help of others a certain number of operations on their own bodies and souls, thoughts, conduct, or ways of being, so as to transform themselves in order to attain a certain state of happiness, purity, wisdom, perfection, or immortality.[42]

Regimes of subjectification constitute fields of force affecting the way institutions are structured and administered, labour and insurance agreements, technical apparatuses and architectural structures, media production and the routines of everyday life. These lines of force enter into such complex interactions that every attempt to fix a general definition of the subject is doomed to fail because these mutually criss-crossing, amplifying, impeding and deflecting forces are continually re-configuring. For this reason alone, the genealogy of subjectification undertakes local analyses rather than attempting to contain everything in a large-scale system.

Although the methodical focus is on the rationales and strategies within programmes of subjectification, we will not be neglecting the contingent processes by which these regimes are appropriated and rejected, the ruptures and resistance that oppose them. We will not only be looking at a normatively deficient and smoothed-over reality. Programmes never translate seamlessly into individual behaviour; appropriating their rules always entails modifying them. The individuality of human behaviour insinuates itself in the form of opposing movements, inertia and techniques of neutralization. Regimes of forming the self and others do not provide a blueprint that needs simply to be followed. They require continual trial and error, invention, correction, criticism and adaptation.[43] In the 'norming of the I by the I',[44] there are always opportunities to refuse social norms of subjectivity, yet the radical refusal of a particular order of selfhood also refers to it by virtue of negating it. The extent to which a programme has failed can only be measured in terms of its aims. In order to describe resistant moments in the subject, you have to know what they are directed at. Conversely, the opposing forces that challenge, undermine, slow down and, in extreme cases, block programmes for governing the self and others are themselves contributing to those programmes' construction and modification: 'Resistance is not merely the counterstroke to power; it also directs and shapes it. Furthermore, just as resistance can be seen as a certain manifestation of failure, so too can failure be seen as serving to direct and shape the process of governing'.[45]

As resistance against the moulding of the self also becomes rationalized, attempting to counteract the subjectification regime via subversive strategies and tactics, it establishes its own form of governing and self-governing, a counter-regime whose workings and rationale would need to be studied in the same way as the regime it combats. Methodologically, this obliges us to dispense with the split perspective. Instead of merely analysing *either* the effects on the individual *or* the opportunities for resistance, the study must instead trace the broader structure that results from their convergence.

The mechanisms and materials of the subjectification regime and the types of resistance it provokes are as various as its aims. Work on the self can pursue any number of aims, but it is indispensible to have one, or even several. Without such guidance, the individual could be led in any direction. In this respect too, regimes of subjectification are not compact, consistent units. Contradictory targets for moulding and self-moulding conflict and/or combine in a variety of blends.

Different aims are represented by different groups of experts with their own specific knowledge resources, forms of legitimation and cultures. Regimes of subjectification require subjectification 'regents'. The regents lend the programmes authority, define the tasks, disseminate the technologies required to fulfil them, provide motivation and sanctioning, feedback and evaluation of results. The classic specialists – pastors, teachers, doctors – have been supplemented by countless advisors, evaluators, therapists and trainers. These 'experts of subjectivity' and their preventative, curative or correctional but always normalizing interventions 'transfigure existential questions about the purpose of life and the meaning of suffering into technical questions of the most effective ways of managing malfunction and improving "quality of life"'.[46] This development has been tightly intertwined with professionalizing processes and an elaboration and heightened reflexivity of method. The regimes of subjectification are themselves subject to the 'scientification of the social', described by the historian Lutz Raphael as a signature mark of the 20th century that continues to increase in the 21st.[47] The genealogy of the human sciences at least partially bleeds into that of subjectification. The figure of the expert extends the paradox of self-constitution into performative contradiction. The expert walks on stage with the appellative gesture of an authority that knows better than his audience members what the latter really need, while at the same time encouraging them to mistrust any outside conditioning, constantly preaching at them to 'become yourself!'. In order to find out who you are, you obviously need someone else to help you. Every piece of good advice entails the humiliating judgement that you are in need of it. Professional help constitutes you as this needy subject. Today, Kafka's policeman would formulate his 'give it up, give it up' in more optimistic tones as a coaching offer.

The present as problem

The genealogy of subjectification follows Foucault's methodological principle of ascending analysis. To do this we must

> begin with its infinitesimal mechanisms, which leave their own history, their own trajectory, their own techniques and tactics, and then look at how

these mechanisms of power – which have their solidity and, in a sense, their own technology – have been and continue to be invested, colonized, used, inflected, transformed, displaced, extended and so on by increasingly general mechanisms and forms of overall domination.[48]

The starting point consists of local investigations. These concern the real behaviour and self-interpretations of particular people only as far as these behaviours and interpretations trigger, result from or interfere with efforts to govern them. Programmes of governing will be analysed, programmes intended to guide action, but which fail to coincide with it in reality. Examining curricula, textbooks or classroom architecture is not the same as reconstructing individual learning processes. The genealogy of subjectification in no way forgoes empirical research, but the empirical material it refers to consists neither of regularities and probabilities nor of incalculable moments of individual behaviour but rather of attempts to affect this behaviour. We are not asking what a pupil does or does not do, but rather which institutions and people (including the pupil herself) attempt to get her to do certain things and abstain from others.

In this respect, the approach has an affinity with the research programme of a social science hermeneutics. The latter describes the social construction of the self based on observing and interviewing social agents and other means of obtaining self-interpretations and accounts of behaviour patterns, extrapolating from these data an interpretation of their *life-world* orientations. Meanwhile, the genealogy analyses the multiple control and self-control mechanisms regulating the social agents' conception of themselves and their behaviour. It therefore also interprets, but shifts the perspective away from the agents and toward the efforts to control their actions. It interprets programmes of governing set down in practices, texts, images and other artefacts; interpretations of meaning that attempt to influence other interpretations of meaning, behaviours that attempt to influence other behaviours.

There is a similar difference in the sociological analysis of everyday rituals of interaction and role play of the type exemplified by Erving Goffman.[49] Like Goffman, the genealogy of subjectification presupposes that the self is self-generating. It also analyses the effects of institutional contexts and societal conventions on individual self-presentation. Both approaches deal with strategies of conditioning and self-discipline, 'making up people'.[50] The focus, however, is different. Goffman is chiefly interested in the implicit framing of everyday behaviour, whereas the genealogy of subjectification interrogates the explicit rules that seek to move individual performances in a specific direction. The objects of study are not scripts but rather guidebooks on the art of acting.

The work of genealogy is essentially the reconstruction of the past in order to deal with problems in the present. The investigation of the historical dispositif and of the governing of self and others is a critical project, if we understand the 'cultural form' of critique, together with Foucault, as 'the art of not being governed *like that*, by that, in the name of those principles, with such and such an objective in mind and by means of such procedures, not like that, not for that, not by them'.[51] Of course, this type of critique has no fixed location. It is not content to simply replace being passively governed with active self-governing. The genealogy does not pretend to know whether there is a place beyond the government of the self, but it nevertheless insists on making visible the impositions placed on individuals by the regimes of subjectification. To quote Foucault once again – this time the sublime Foucault – what is at stake

> is seeking to give new impetus, as far and wide as possible, to the undefined work of freedom ... it will separate out, from the contingency that has made us what we are, the possibility of no longer being, doing, or thinking what we are, do or think.[52]

In formal terms, the research programme outlined here can and must be deployed in a combination of two ways. The first way is to compare various regimes of subjectification and elaborate on their discontinuities and oppositions. This approach tends to follow Foucault's work on disciplinary societies, the history of madness and the analyses of antique and early Christian concepts of self-governing. The second is to examine a specific configuration and dissect the relations of force that contribute to it, the stores of knowledge and technologies it has recourse to, the rationale that ensures its acceptability, and, finally, the resistance it provokes and that provokes it in turn. The present study follows this second route, investigating a model of subjectification in which a large number of current practices of government and self-government are concentrated: the model of the entrepreneurial self. This is the thesis to be made explicit in what follows.

Notes

1. Paolo Virno (2004) *A Grammar of Multitude*, Los Angeles/New York: Semiotext(e), p. 78.
2. See George H. Mead (1934/1962) *Mind, Self, and Society from the Standpoint of a Social Behaviorist*, Chicago: University of Chicago Press, pp. 173ff.
3. Helmuth Plessner (1985) *Die Stufen des Organischen und der Mensch* (3rd edition), Berlin: Suhrkamp, pp. 288ff., here: p. 310. See also Marjorie Grene (1966) 'Positionality in the Philosophy of Helmuth Plessner', in: *The Review of Metaphysics*, 20, pp. 250–277, here: pp. 274ff.
4. See Judith Butler (1997) *The Psychic Life of Power: Theories in Subjection*, Stanford, CA: Stanford University Press, p. 17.
5. Michel Foucault (1983) 'Subject and Power', in: Hubert L. Dreyfus and Paul Rabinow, *Michel Foucault: Beyond Structuralism and Hermeneutics*, Chicago: University of Chicago Press, pp. 208–226, here: pp. 219f.

6. Gilles Deleuze (1988) *Foucault*, Minneapolis: University of Minnesota Press, p. 104.
7. Søren Kierkegaard (1849/1941) *The Sickness Unto Death*, Princeton, NJ: Princeton University Press, p. 14.
8. Foucault (1983) 'Subject and Power', p. 212.
9. Mariana Valverde (1996) points out that many theories – in particular psychological ones – attempt to resolve paradoxes of the subject or the self by indexing the contradictory sides to differing psychical forces or entities: 'The distinction between the self that controls and the (immature, lower) self that is controlled presupposed by the term, self-control' is in some ways a naturalized distinction between two things, between passion and reason, but could also be regarded as a spatial division between two psychic spaces' ('Despotism and Ethical Liberal Governance', in: *Economy and Society,* 25, pp. 357–372, here: p. 369).
10. Butler (1997) *The Psychic Life of Power*, p. 17.
11. An important reason why paradoxical notions are currently proliferating is that neither can the societal contradictions be dialectically resolved nor does it any longer appear credible to describe the effects of capitalist modernization as phenomena of ambivalence; to accept them, recognize them and withstand them as such.
12. Georg Simmel (1917/1984) *Grundfragen der Soziologie* (4th edition), Berlin/New York: Walter de Gruyter, pp. 83f., located more precisely this gerundive form of the subject historically. According to Simmel, it first comes to dominate in the enlightenment and in its ideal of perfectibility: 'In the 18th century the feeling becomes extremely powerful that the I that we already are is yet to be made. We are not purely and absolutely identical with it but rather in veiled and distorted form due to our historical–social fortunes. This normalisation of the I by the I is morally justified because the ideal I, in the higher sense more real, is the general human I and, by attaining it, true equality among all people is also attained.'
13. On the concept and reality of self technologies, see Luther H. Martin, Huck Gutman and Patrick H. Hutton (eds) (1988) *Technologies of the Self,* Amherst, MA: University of Massachusetts Press.
14. See Nikolas Rose (1996) *Inventing Our Selves: Psychology, Power, and Personhood*, Cambridge: Cambridge University Press, p. 23.
15. See Niklas Luhmann (1989) 'Individuum, Individualität, Individualismus', in: *Gesellschaftsstruktur und Semantik,* Vol. 3, Frankfurt: Suhrkamp, pp. 149–258, here: p. 215.
16. Luhmann (1989) 'Individuum, Individualität, Individualismus', p. 252.
17. According to Luhmann (1989, p. 221, note), the term is borrowed from Stendhal.
18. On the various possible theories of a multiple self, see Jon Elster (1986) 'Introduction', in: *The Multiple Self,* Cambridge: Cambridge University Press, pp. 1–34, as well as the other chapters in the volume.
19. Niklas Luhmann (1980) 'Gesellschaftliche Struktur und semantische Tradition', in: *Gesellschaftsstruktur und Semantik: Studien zur Wissenssoziologie der modernen Gesellschaft,* Vol. 1, Frankfurt: Suhrkamp, pp. 9–71, here: p. 19.

20. Anthony Giddens (1991) *Modernity and Self-Identity: Self and Society in the Late Modern Age*, Stanford, CA: Polity Press, pp. 70ff.
21. Ulrich Beck (1993) *Die Erfindung des Politischen: Zu einer Theorie reflexiver Modernisierung*, Frankfurt: Suhrkamp, p. 152.
22. Ulrich Beck (1992) *Risk Society: Towards a New Modernity*, London: Sage, p. 135.
23. Louis Althusser (1971) *Lenin and Philosophy and Other Essays*, London: New Left Books, p. 163.
24. Sven Opitz (2004) *Gouvernementalität im Postfordismus: Macht, Wissen und Techniken des Selbst im Feld unternehmerischer Rationalität*, Hamburg: Argument, p. 82.
25. Judith Butler (2003) 'Noch einmal: Körper und Macht', in: Axel Honneth and Martin Saar (eds), *Michel Foucault: Zwischenbilanz einer Rezeption*, Frankfurt: Suhrkamp pp. 52–67, here: p. 67.
26. Franz Kafka (1983) 'Give it up!', in: *The Complete Stories*, New York: Penguin.
27. See, above all, Axel Honneth (1995) *Struggle for Recognition: The Moral Grammar of Social Conflict*, Cambridge: Polity.
28. Osborne (2001) 'Techniken und Subjekte', p. 12.
29. Foucault (1983) 'Subject and Power', p. 221.
30. Foucault (2009) *Security, Territory, Population*, New York: Palgrave Macmillan p. 94.
31. Foucault (2010) *The Birth of Biopolitics: Lectures at the College de France (1978–1979)*, New York: Palgrave Macmillan, p. 2. In the very next sentence, Foucault distances himself from the concept of *consciousness of itself*, turning instead to 'the way in which this practice that consists in governing was conceptualized both within and outside government, and anyway as close as possible to governmental practice'.
32. Foucault (1983) 'Subject and Power', p. 221.
33. Michel Foucault (1984) 'What is Enlightenment?', in: Paul Rabinow (ed.), *The Foucault Reader*, New York: Penguin, pp. 32–50, here: p. 48.
34. 'It's [psycho-analysis'] intention is, indeed, to strengthen the ego, to make it more independent of the super-ego, to widen its field of perception and enlarge its organization, so that it can appropriate fresh portions of the id. Where id was, there ego shall be. It is a work of culture – not unlike the draining of the Zuider Zee' (Sigmund Freud (1964) 'New Introductory Lectures on Psycho-Analysis and Other Works (1932–1936)', in: *The Standard Edition of the Complete Psychological Works of Sigmund Freud*, Vol. XXII, London: W. W. Norton, pp. 5–182, here: p. 80).
35. Norbert Ricken (2004) 'Die Macht der Macht – Rückfragen an Michel Foucault', in: Norbert Ricken and Markus Rieger-Ladich (eds), *Michel Foucault: Pädagogische Lektüren*, Wiesbaden: Springer, pp. 119–143, here: p. 139.
36. Michel Foucault (1994) 'The Ethics of the Concern for Self as a Practice of Freedom' (interview with H. Becker, R. Fornet-Betancourt and A. Gomez-Müller, 20 January 1984), in: *Ethics, Subjectivity and Truth: The Essential Works*

of Michel Foucault 1954–1984, Vol. 1, New York: Allen Lane, pp. 281–301, here: p. 290.

37. Osborne (2001) 'Techniken und Subjekte', p. 13.

38. Michael Hutter and Gunther Teubner (1994) 'Der Gesellschaft fette Beute: Homo juridicus und homo oeconomicus als kommunikationserhaltende Fiktionen', in: Peter Fuchs and Andreas Göbel (eds), *Der Mensch – das Medium der Gesellschaft*, Frankfurt: Suhrkamp, pp. 110–145, here: p.116.

39. Hutter and Teubner (1994) 'Der Gesellschaft fette Beute', p. 118.

40. Hutter and Teubner (1994) 'Der Gesellschaft fette Beute', p. 119.

41. Hutter and Teubner (1994) 'Der Gesellschaft fette Beute', p. 121.

42. Michel Foucault (1988) 'Technologies of the Self', in: Luther H. Martin et al. (eds), *Technologies of the Self*, Amherst, MA: University of Massachusetts Press, pp. 16–49, here: p. 18.

43. See Peter Miller and Nikolas Rose (1990) 'Governing Economic Life', in: *Economy and Society*, 19, pp. 1–31, here: p. 14.

44. Simmel (1917/1984) *Grundfragen der Soziologie*, New York: Walter de Gruyter, p. 84.

45. Jeff Malpass and Gary Wickham (1995) 'Governance and Failure: On the Limits of Sociology', in: *Australian and New Zealand Journal of Sociology*, 31(3), pp. 37–50, here: p. 43.

46. Rose (1996) *Inventing Our Selves*, Cambridge: Cambridge University Press, p. 151.

47. Lutz Raphael (1996) 'Die Verwissenschaftlichung des Sozialen als methodische und konzeptionelle Herausforderung für eine Sozialgeschichte des 20. Jahrhunderts', in: *Geschichte und Gesellschaft*, 22, pp. 165–193.

48. Michel Foucault (2003) *Society Must be Defended: Lectures at the College de France (1975–76)*, New York: Penguin, p. 30.

49. See, in particular, Erving Goffman (1971) *The Presentation of Self in Everyday Life*, Harmondsworth: Penguin; Goffman (1971) *Relations in Public: Microstudies of the Public Order*, New York: Allen Lane; Goffman (1967) *Interaction Ritual: Essays on Face-to-Face Behavior*, New York: Pantheon; Goffman (1974) *Frame Analysis: An Essay on the Organization of Experience*, Boston: Northeastern University Press. For a comparison of Goffman and Foucault's different research perspectives, see Ian Hacking (2004) 'Between Michel Foucault and Erving Goffman: Between Discourse in the Abstract and Face-to-Face Interaction', in: *Economy and Society*, 33, pp. 277–302.

50. See Ian Hacking (1986) 'Making up People', in: Thomas C. Heller, Morton Sosna and David E. Wellbery (eds), *Reconstructing Individualism: Autonomy, Individuality, and the Self in Western Thought*, Stanford, CA: Stanford University Press, pp. 222–236.

51. Michel Foucault (1997) 'What is Critique?', in: Sylvère Lotringer and Lysa Hochroth (eds), *The Politics of Truth*, New York: Semiotext(e), pp. 41–81, here: p. 45.

52. Foucault (1984) 'What is Enlightenment?', p. 46.

2

TRACING THE CONTOURS OF THE ENTREPRENEURIAL SELF

Ich-AG [from the English Me Incorporated] The notion of one's own person as a joint-stock company. The term indicates the decisive social transformation around the turn of the millennium. People regard themselves increasingly as entrepreneurs of their own lives, electing to assume responsibility for themselves rather than making others responsible for them. This development is confluent with the forced withdrawal of the state from its comprehensive security function. In addition, the transformation of the culture of work toward more self-reliance and entrepreneurship fosters the self-image as Me-Incorporated. A core component, as in a real joint-stock company, is the importance of working on one's own person: 'I must increase the market value of my Me-shares'.[1]

The entrepreneurial self has no name and no address. Specimens can be found neither in offices nor in start-ups. Nor is it what empirical social research refers to as a 'modal personality', the statistical construct of the average subject combining the most common personality traits in a given group. Nor is it the newest social type, distilled from interviews or psychoanalytic case histories. It is neither a character mask from Marxian ideology critique, nor is it a script from the sociology of interactionism. The term 'entrepreneurial self' does not denote an empirically observable entity but rather a way of addressing individuals as people, of altering them and causing them to alter themselves in a particular way. It is a *real fiction* in the sense employed by Hutter and Teubner (see Chapter 1): a highly effective *as if*, initiating and sustaining a process of continual modification and self-modification of subjects by mobilizing their desire to stay in touch and their fear of falling out of a social order held together by market mechanisms. The entrepreneurial self is a subject in the gerundive – not something that exists but something that ought to be brought into existence.

The figure of the entrepreneurial self is concentrated in both a normative model of the human and a multitude of contemporary technologies of self and social technologies of and society whose common aim is to organize life around the entrepreneurial model of behaviour. The figure is not only a set of rules of conduct; it also defines the forms of knowledge in which individuals recognize the truth about themselves, the control and regulation mechanisms they are subject to and the practices by which they condition themselves. In other words, the discourse of the entrepreneurial self does not so much tell people what they are; rather, it tells them what they have to become, and they can only become it because they have always already been addressed in terms of it.

Entrepreneurial self or entreployee?

What distinguishes the entrepreneurial self from Max Weber's 'ideal type' is precisely this appellative, prescriptive, subject-constituting character. According to Weber's theory of social science, in order to find the ideal type in relation to a specific point of interrogation, especially characteristic elements need to be extracted from the material of a socio–historical context and raised to the level of a 'unified *analytical* construct'.[2] One such current ideal type is the 'labour force entrepreneur' or 'entreployee', whom the German sociologists G. Günter Voß and Hans J. Pongratz regard as 'a new basic form of the commodity of labour'. According to the authors, this type supplements if not replaces the formerly prevalent 'professionalised Fordian mass worker', embodying 'as leading type [the] most progressive form of subjective productive power'.[3] In contradistinction, the entrepreneurial self is not a heuristic category capable of guiding an analysis of social structure. Instead, it is the micropolitical rationale or logic, on which contemporary technologies of governing and self-governing converge. To reformulate the distinction already made above: it is not a tool for describing reality but for changing it.

Voß' and Pongratz' diagnoses coincide in many ways with the sets of demands made on the entrepreneurial self: first, workers are required to increase self-organization and self-monitoring; second, there is a growing coercion of workers to economize their own work capabilities and productivity; and third, everyday life in general is increasingly conducted on the model of enterprise.[4] However, the two sociologists of labour concentrate on changes to job orientation, exploring in this context the paradox phenomenon of 'hetero–organised self-organisation'.[5] In contrast, the present analysis of the entrepreneurial call is focused less on the 'subjectification of work'[6] than on *the work of subjectification.*

For the entrepreneur of her own labour force, the line blurs between wage earning and leisure, work life and private life, and the pressure to economize seeps into all aspects of daily life. Accordingly, Voß, Pongratz and other exponents of this approach broaden the labour-sociology perspective to take in the sociology of daily life. Once again, the interrogations run on parallel lines but there is an overt difference in focus: the approach employed by the authors mentioned investigates which strategies and arrangements people employ to cope with everyday life and which pressures they are subject to. The approach of the present study is to concentrate on the rationale and rationalizations, the programmes and technologies that pretend to come to people's aid by telling them how to live their lives.

Voß und Pongratz have since revised their thesis of change in the socially dominant types of labour force in the context of an empirical study. They no longer postulate that the old has been replaced by the new, but rather that both types co-exist. Summarizing their results, they write:

> the loosening of normal work standards has two mutually countervailing effects. On the one hand, it is the dialectical extension of the type of the labour force entrepreneur and on the other hand it is the strategic deployment of elements of a proletarian model of labour especially well suited for 'simple' tasks.[7]

Accordingly, features characteristic of the labour force entrepreneur such as self-controlling, self-economizing and self-rationalizing are increasingly apparent in burgeoning job areas like information and communication technologies, as well as in education, consultancy and the so-called new economy, while the other segments of the job market are still dominated by the long-term employee type. The precarious labour force entrepreneur variant constitutes the growing army of small-scale freelancers eking out a living as 'Me Incorporated' with or without the aid of government supplements and with no realistic prospect of attaining the prosperity once associated with the figure of the entrepreneur.

The following elucidations are not an attempt to test the reach of the call to the entrepreneurial and to compare it with other calls. Instead, the focus is on elaborating on the rationale of this form of subjectification as well as on several of the key technologies that embody it. This form of subjectification affirms the diagnosis made by the theory of the labour force entrepreneur that, at the present time, imperatives to behave enterprisingly condition people's relations to themselves and to others. In contrast again to Voß and Pongratz, the present study is more focused on how theories and programmes mobilizing the entrepreneurial self are disseminated and how they gain credibility across political, social and academic divides.

The triumph of the entrepreneur

Unquestioned credibility is a kind of historical a priori for thought and action. We realize that we can think and act differently when we see how the tacit presuppositions of our thought and action are woven into an historical context, when we return to the points of crisis at which previous unquestioned assumptions became questionable and new ones developed. How do we account for the current convergence of a number of regimes of subjectification on the entrepreneurial self? Where is the historical point of entry for the 'triumph of the entrepreneur'?[8]

In 1984, the French writer and editor of the magazine *Esprit*, Paul Thibaud, published an article under this title. He submits the diagnosis that

[t]he ideological ground itself is in motion; it is the things themselves that instruct us, not just material events (irrepressible unemployment and its results), but mental drifts, unforeseen conclusions to which we are led, previously self-evident claims which suddenly can no longer be advocated: that the economy, for instance, is just a set of means at the service of society.

Thibaud attributed this shift of values to a crisis of the social–democratic era. According to his thesis, this era once obeyed the idea of disrobing the economy of its violent aspects and making it serve as the guarantor of a universal right to employment. The welfare state promised societal security at the cost of social discipline and standardization. Society appeared built on a set of rights defining the way individuals were educated, paid and engaged in leisure activities. Within this framework, it was up to people themselves which aims they pursued and which values they held. In 1968 at the latest, the utopian promise of a hygienic society had fallen out of favour and from the social–democratic project there remained little more than an individualism that exhausted itself in modest private hedonism within the latitude provided by the welfare state.

Thibaud understood the re-emergence of the entrepreneurial spirit as an immediate consequence of this process of erosion. After hedonistic individualism won the battle against puritan morals, it lost its revolutionary, romantic and exalted features and took to the art of the possible. This meant redirecting energies that 1968 had previously channelled into messianic political ideologies. The individual pursuit of happiness was transferred to consumption, which no longer promised the serial satisfaction of standardized needs in a Fordian mass culture, but lured instead with adventure and self-realization and rendered material inequality inaudible under a hymn to difference. The consumerist came together with the entrepreneurial imperative. Consumers were to accumulate 'pleasure capital', showing themselves as innovative, risk-loving and decisive, as though leading an enterprise to market victory. In the process, they could train behavioural dispositions that had succeeded in other areas of life:

From an entrepreneur of one's own pleasure, one can become an entrepreneur as such. This disproves, at least in part, Bell's thesis concerning the contradiction of capitalist culture: that it is puritanical and disciplinarian on the side of production, pleasure-seeking and seductive on the side of consumption. Between pleasure-seeking individualism and enterprising individualism, there will henceforth be less contradiction than solidarity; and the passage from one attitude to the other is smooth. So this individualism, denounced as impracticable, ends up by finding in itself a kind of salvation, instilling civic prudence and a spirit of initiative.[9]

There was no longer an irresolvable contradiction between self-realization and economic success. Now the two were complementary.

According to Thibaud, this transformation corresponded to altered modes of production that in their own way also contributed to a renaissance of the entrepreneurial spirit. The myth of the self-made man celebrated its resurrection:

As needs and life-styles are differentiated, production becomes more diversified and mobile. The sense of commerce, of sale, of conception – especially the anticipation of new needs – the fact of being attuned to a nascent social mood become opportunities as much as technology and organization … [E]very day we are told the story of someone who, 'starting with nothing,' had the genius to discover in his contemporaries the 'latent need' of an object or a service which, in our routineness, we would not have imagined.[10]

Thibaud emphasized that entrepreneurial culture did not mean the end of state intervention. He accurately depicted the transition from the welfare state to the activating state before it had occurred in fact: 'The new relations between economy and society will not be defined – as certain demagogues claim – by returning to wildcat capitalism, but rather by developing policies that integrate society into economy, policies of mobilization, integration, negotiation, which increasingly involve non-management groups in the functioning of the economy.'[11] The integration of society into economy that Thibaud describes involves an inversion of means and ends. The economy is no longer an instrument in the service of society and its political institutions. From now on, society and its institutions will be made to obey the imperatives of the economy. Thibaud concludes by outlining some of the effects of this transformation. The social-democratic era had tried to solve the problems arising from the rule of the economy by means of legal measures and social insurance. This problem now returns as a moral one: the problem of the superfluous masses, 'those who are marginalized, i.e., all kinds of persons who are declared useless, whom the hard-pressed welfare state leaves in the dirt and for whom other policies must be conceived'.[12]

The most remarkable thing about Thibaud's essay is its early recognition of the advent of the entrepreneur before the figure had fully come into view. The rise to power of Margaret Thatcher in Great Britain in 1979 and Ronald Reagan in the USA in 1981 had marked the break with post-war Keynesian economics. The general Keynesian consensus is what Thibaud refers to as the social-democratic era. A tenet of Thatcherism and Reagonomics was that individual citizens should become the entrepreneurs of their own lives.

The postulate of individual responsibility was hoisted to the top of the political agenda and underwrote the dismantling of social welfare safety systems.[13] Conservative lobbies in the UK and the USA had been calling for a radical free market turn since the 1970s. Their demand was not for the state to withdraw altogether but rather for it to establish a general 'enterprise culture', an active programme leaving no area of life untouched. A document from the British Centre for Policy Studies states that '[e]nterprise culture is defined as the full set of conditions that promote high and rising levels of achievement in a country's economic activity, politics and government, arts and sciences, and also the distinctively private lives of the inhabitants'.[14]

US president Reagan blew the same trumpet, declaring in a 1985 article a new 'entrepreneurial age' and calling on his fellow countrymen and women to reinvent the future, as had their ancestors between the Civil War and the Great Depression. Appealing to putatively typical national strengths – 'To be enterprising is not uniquely American, but entrepreneurialism seems to be found more in the nature of our people than just about anywhere else' – Reagan promised his government would do everything in the way of tax cuts and thinning state bureaucracy to get the enterprising spirit off the launch pad.[15] As comic as the self-satisfied bathos of such expressions may appear, such appeals by government to the entrepreneurial spirit already have the same effect of stimulation as the economic measures they are meant to legitimize. If such rhetoric is considered necessary, it is because the free market and its protagonists – the entrepreneurs of their own selves – do not move under their own steam alone but rather by the force of permanent mobilization.

Sociological analyses

In Germany, where the social-democratic project was abandoned later and less abruptly, the topos of the 'entrepreneur of her own labour' emerged for the first time, as far as can be ascertained on the basis of the present evidence, in 1984.[16] One of the circumstances of its demise was an analysis of the subjective strategies for coping with mass unemployment. Wolfgang Bonß, Heiner Keupp and Elmar Koenen identified the following reactions to unemployment: in addition to a 'mimetic, defensive reaction triggered by fear' and a 'tactical realism of the labour market', the basic experience of which was a 'sudden disappointment at the fact that securing employment could not be guaranteed by professional skill, practical understanding, intelligence and the mobilisation of all the economic and social resources belonging to the average man', they added to this a further reaction:

> the hope of exploiting the chaotic situation in the labour market by mobilizing capacities for action, turning the seller of his own labour into the 'entrepreneur of his own labour.' This fiction, heavy with practical consequence, consists in

> regarding oneself as the focal point of the logic of the labour market. That means making oneself virtually into the active subject of a rationality that uses the labour market to its own end. This 'entrepreneur' possesses nothing beyond his own labour force, yet he can offer a series of (partly artificial) differentiable skills, yet he can offer a series of skills that can be differentiated (sometimes artificially), mainly by resorting to basic and auxiliary abilities, for example possessing a driver's licence, work experience, social skills like 'confidence', 'leadership qualities', previous knowledge, sales training, administration experience, knowledge of foreign languages, stenographic or typing skills, skills in text or data processing.[17]

Imagining oneself as an entrepreneur turns the sense of powerlessness over real or threatened unemployment into an active posture and produces the rugged individual making it on her own in the wilderness of the labour market.

Bonß, Keupp and Koenen's remarks turn out to be especially farsighted given the fictional and yet seriously consequential character of this self-mobilizing, in which simulation and stimulation blend indistinguishably. The act of imagining oneself as an efficient agent instead of a defenceless plaything of market forces morphs indiscernibly into actually comporting oneself coherently and assertively as a market subject. This fiction undoubtedly occasions real effects. But it is another story to what degree people assume this fiction, how hard it is to sustain it and which opposing experiences they must overlook in order to keep up appearances.

In German social science, discussion of the general spread of entrepreneur-type behaviour has mostly been from the point of view of the sociology of labour, especially the sociology of industry.[18] The discussion came to a controversial head[19] with the critical entreployee theory of Voß and Pongratz, while the report of the *Zukunftskommission Bayern-Sachsen*, quoted in the introduction and co-authored by prominent sociologist Ulrich Beck, recommended the entrepreneurial self to political decision makers as a model for the future.

Similar to Voß and Pongratz, the Milan-based sociologist Sergio Bologna, an activist in the radical left-wing *potere operaio* in the 1970s, defines what he calls the 'new autonomy', the entrepreneurial form of work and life in contradistinction to the type of the Fordist mass worker. Whereas the latter was integrated in a hierarchical factory regime that regulated internal and external cooperation, autonomous workers have to organize their business relations themselves, meaning part of their work is taken up with communication. For such freelancers, the usual separation between workplace and private life is dissolved. Living space and workplace, free time and work time merge indiscernibly, overstepping by a broad margin the Fordist-era 40-hour work week. While employees leave the market as soon as they enter the factory, freelancers are at the market all the time. The gain in self-determination is paid for by a loss of economic security:

They can go for long periods without earning anything, living off savings to cope with the 'vacant times.' The notion of risk is inscribed upon the mentality of independent work, which is why its performance always has an aspect of advertising, by which means the independent worker tries to secure either the prolongation of the business relationship to the employer or initiate new relationships ... The fear of 'vacancy' prevents the independent worker from enjoying the fruits of his labour.[20]

Bologna points out that in the 1970s and 1980s self-employment was often a free choice made to evade the disciplinary pressure of the factory, rather than being imposed by economic necessity. In hindsight, despite their anti-capitalist thrust, the diverse forms of counter-culture after 1968 became a laboratory for entrepreneurial behaviour. For the new self-employed, the harmonizing of life and work, once proclaimed by the alternative movement, gets translated into an extension of work into all areas of life. For the genealogy of the entrepreneurial self, it is important to be aware of these counter-cultural roots of the new autonomy. This awareness guards against the fallacious view that the entrepreneurial demand is a form of repression. This view fundamentally overlooks the especially perfidious way the new regime of capital accumulation beats subjectivity into being. The type of the entrepreneurial self, of whose emergence Bologna could not be directly aware, could only rise to dominance by responding to a broad wish for autonomy, self-realization and non-alienated work. Without the utopian energies and the struggles of the new social movements, without their experiments with non-hierarchical organization, without the widespread refusal to be pressed into the Fordist mould, the role model of the entrepreneurial self would never have attained such attractive force.

Several British sociologists, discussing the upheavals of the Thatcher era under the title 'enterprise culture', have taken up Michel Foucault's concept of governmentality, providing an outline of the entrepreneurial self with the aid of his analyses of neoliberalism. The first step in this direction was taken by Colin Gordon[21] in his introduction to his reader, *The Foucault Effect* from 1991. Gordon offers an explanation of some fragmentary remarks of Foucault's on the construction of the subject within *human capital theory*,[22] applying them to contemporary issues around the general acceptance of mass unemployment and the rationale of benefit programmes. He writes:

The idea of one's life as the enterprise of oneself implies that there is a sense in which one remains always continuously employed in (at least) that one enterprise, and that it is a part of the continuous business of living to make adequate provision for the preservation, reproduction and reconstruction of one's own human capital. This is the 'care of the self' which government commends as the corrective to collective greed ... What some cultural critics diagnose as the triumph of auto-consuming narcissism can perhaps be more adequately understood as a part of the managerialization of personal identity and personal relations which accompanies the capitalization of the meaning of life.[23]

Gordon also concludes that the entrepreneurial self as a form of subjectification is a recurrence of *homo economicus* in inverted form. This reanimation presupposes human practice as fundamentally dictated by free choice for the purpose of maximizing utility. Whereas classical liberal thinkers like Smith, Hume and Ferguson were convinced that humans would follow their nature and act as rational economic subjects if political factors did not hinder them, the entrepreneurial self must instead be permanently recreated and activated by the state. This type of subjectification is not the freeing up of latent forces but rather a permanent effort of pushing and forming; not laissez-faire but behaviour modification, in all areas of life.[24] Governmentality studies focus less on changes in the domain of work than on the spread of entrepreneurial demands and self-interpretations in other spheres of life. Governmentality is especially concerned with the political strategies and psychological techniques deployed for governing individuals and causing them to govern themselves. *Enterprise* is not understood here as a specific type of organization but rather as a type of activity that can apply to firms, public institutions and private organizations as well as to their members, and finally to all and any individuals and all situations in life. Summarizing the rationale behind the prevalent programmes and popular cultural offers, Peter Miller and Nikolas Rose write that

> [i]ndividuals had to be governed in light of the fact that they each sought to conduct their lives as a kind of enterprise of the self, striving to improve the 'quality of life' for themselves and their families through the choices that they took from the marketplace of life.[25]

The objection was voiced that enterprise culture had not taken hold in everyone's heads; that many continued to adhere to values like equality and solidarity rather than join in the song of praise to excellence and competition. Paul du Gay and Graeme Salaman met this objection by pointing to the deep roots of enterprise discourse in everyday life:

> [E]ven if people do not take enterprise seriously, even if they keep a certain cynical distance from its claims, they are still reproducing it through their involvement in the everyday practices within which enterprise is inscribed. Thus enterprise should not be viewed as a 'pure' discourse as that term is often (mis)understood – i.e. as a combination of speech and writing – but always and only as a dimension of material practices, with material conditions of emergence and effectiveness.[26]

In addition, Nikolas Rose has established that in the call to the entrepreneurial self economic success and self-realization are not contradictory but rather interdependent and mutually reinforcing. They both follow the imperative of infinite growth: people ought not only to maximize their self-control, self-esteem, self-awareness and health but also their work performance and their wealth. They will be better equipped to do this in proportion as they more actively assume responsibility for their own lives. If they are unable to cope with the strain of it all, they should seek professional help. The enterprising ethos and the values of therapy, especially in humanistic psychology, seem only at first glance opposed to one another. They converge in the regime of the self where it drives people to 'work on themselves' and take their lives in hand. The regime provides the self with a series of tools for dealing with a range of challenges, for seizing control of its own activities, setting targets, making plans to fulfil its needs, relying throughout on its own forces.[27] In short, enterprising selves are not manufactured with the strategy *discipline and punish* but rather by activating their powers of self-motivation.

Intrapreneuring

In their concise theoretical treatment, Bonß, Keupp and Koenen emphasized the role of auto-fiction. The exponents of governmentality studies, on the other hand, focused on the political rationale, the technologies of self and the significance of psychological advice and expertise. The effects of self-shaping, they claim, correspond to a number of normative interpretations and institutional practices that address individuals as entrepreneurs of their own selves, thereby recommending that they orient themselves on this model. The proliferation of the entrepreneurial discourse was due less to publications and sociological analyses and still less to government statements and other political utterances. It came instead from a text genre that dominated the book market in the early 1980s: management literature. Books like Tom Peters' and Robert H. Waterman's (1982) *In Search of Excellence*, which has in the meantime sold more than five million copies and become the bestselling management book of all time, and Gifford Pinchot's (1985) *Intrapreneuring*, together with a plethora of other titles,[28] praised entrepreneurial virtues and supplied details of how the entrepreneurial spirit could be made to emanate down to employees, showering its benevolent effects on them from within.

Peters and Waterman, for example, identify as a distinguishing feature of leading American companies a 'simulated enterprise factor'. For the purpose of raising innovative potential, the authors recommend creating a 'limited autonomy position', which they define as 'a position that has substantial entrepreneurial champion-like qualities, but is actually quite constrained and exists in a much broader setting than one might expect'.[29] The loosening of company hierarchies, the establishment of free spaces and incentives and, above all, internal competition can create an environment in which 'creative fanatics' flourish, those enthusiastic and at the same time practical 'champions' whose innovations are so necessary to competing on the market:

'All the activity and apparent confusion we were observing revolves around fired–up "champions" and around making sure that the potential innovator, or champion, comes forward, grows, and flourishes – even to the extent of indulging a little madness'.[30] The emphasis, however, is on the *little* in 'a little madness': 'Since business is a "get–things–done" institution, creativity without action-oriented follow-through is a barren form of behaviour. In a sense, it is irresponsible'.[31] Peters and Waterman make no secret of the fact that the enterprise virtues their 'champions' should aspire to are entirely in the service of company success. When the authors invoke the 'enterprise in the enterprise', they do not mean the normal employee but rather middle managers. Nor should even their self-determination be unlimited. The tether is lengthened, not cut: 'It involves socializing the managers to believe they are would-be champions, yet at the same time maintaining very substantial control where it counts.'[32] The 'simulated enterprise factor' is built on the paradox of externally controlled autonomy.

Simulations have a reality of their own. They feign something that does not exist in itself but by feigning it they bring it into reality. Employees are not entrepreneurs but getting them to act as though they are turns the model into a general norm, which will influence their behaviour. Gifford Pinchot's invention of the 'intrapreneur', the 'intracorporate entrepreneur', aims to harness the power of norms to change reality. The intracorporate entrepreneur is distinguished by a readiness to take risks and the drive to innovate – attributes that inject energy into enterprises instead of paralysing them as do bureaucratic 'analysis and control systems'. Enterprises can here make use of the fact, Pinchot continues, that entrepreneurial ambition is not being driven mainly by the profit motive. 'Intrapreneurs' are rather 'primarily motivated to satisfy a personal need for achievement'.[33] Pinchot explains this motivation with a deep lunge into popular psychology. Since the book is primarily addressing a US audience, it frames entrepreneurial spirit as a specifically American virtue:

> Our childhood fantasies still have more to do with taming the frontier and breaking free from tyranny than with advancing steadily toward the heights of vast organizations. Unlike the Japanese or most European nations, we lack a homogeneous culture and the manners for deference to authority. This makes it very difficult for most of us to accept the role of respected cog in a vast industrial machine. But we do have a spirit of self-reliance, adventure, and willingness to try new things. The result is that while we are poor at regimentation, we have a full measure of the entrepreneurial spirit.[34]

Pinchot, whose weapon of choice, like that of Peters and Waterman, is anecdotal evidence, is concerned to show not only that enterprising personalities make good subordinates, despite their rugged individualism, but also that companies absolutely need them in key positions. However, specific organizational measures need to be taken to retain intrapreneurs in the company and increase their vigour. Pinchot stresses the importance of free election of tasks, not changing supervisors mid-project, the autonomy to make decisions within set frameworks, having sufficient resources and generous time frames, abandoning the 'home-run philosophy' and petty territorial struggles, risk affinity, failure intolerance, interdisciplinary teams and independence in the choice of internal and external partners. These

> freedom factors are a way of managing, based on looking at a problem from the bottom up, not from the top down. They are derived from considering what the people who actually do the work need in order to get on with their jobs … The presence or absence of these freedom factors determines how effective intrapreneurs can be in your corporate culture.[35]

Finally, the inventor of the term 'intrapreneur' equips his creation with a toolkit for building up the 'intraprise' from the idea to the business plan and from internal networking to team making and leading.

The bestsellers of Peters and Waterman and Pinchot mark the transition from the role model of the 'organization man'[36] to the entrepreneurial self. The organization man is not a model for ordinary people to follow but rather for employees in leading positions. The recommendations are directed at large companies who want to break up ossified structures by simulating entrepreneur functions (see Peters and Waterman) or by integrating entrepreneur types in the company (see Pinchot).

How to set up Me Inc.

Advice literature from the 1990s finally pushed this rationale of the entrepreneurial self to its logical extreme, no longer propagating merely the entrepreneur within the enterprise but now presenting the individual *as* the enterprise: *You & Co.*[37] or the *Life Entrepreneur.*[38] The success and self-management tractates[39] that boomed in this decade were only partly about efficient methods for organizing time and work while coping with stress. They were, above all, modern wisdom teachings, instructing readers on how to lead the good life, providing an all-embracing model for subjectification with practical exercises for attaining *self-optimization*.

The guidebooks frame personality development and enterprise management as an organic, coherent whole. In order to fulfil the imperative of one such advice book, entitled *Self-Management: Become the Entrepreneur of Your Own Life*,[40] the same procedure must be followed as for setting up any new business. According to another success guidebook, the task for the entrepreneurial individual is to define herself as a product and then undertake thorough market research. This means grasping herself as an autonomous unit, not as part of a greater whole. She should see herself as surrounded by a market, even when she is the employee of a company.[41] Identifying yourself as a commodity is only the first step. The coupling of the individual and the enterprise goes further. The entrepreneurial self is not only the unification of product and producer, boss and subordinate, but also of buyer and seller. The individual can only realize her enterprising potential by applying the principle of intrapreneurship to herself and splitting herself down the middle. As the 'customer of her own self', she is her own queen, a creature whose needs want to be recognized and fulfilled by the 'provider of her own self'. If the provider ignores the needs of her internal business partner, the latter will punish her with a lack of motivation, exhaustion or other forms of energy loss. On the other hand, if the exchange works, everyone's a winner. So it is just as important to know your own desires as it is to know your strengths and weaknesses. According to William Bridges, the author of *Creating You & Co.: Learn to Think Like the CEO of Your Own Career*, the entrepreneurial self has to ask itself four questions: (1) What do I really want at this point in my life? (desires); (2) What am I really good at? (abilities); (3) What kind of person am I and in what kinds of situations am I most productive and satisfied? (temperament); (4) What advantages do I have: what aspects of my life history or life situation could I turn to my advantage? (assets).[42] The analysis of the D.A.T.A. (Desires, Abilities, Temperament, Assets) 'helps you to position yourself not as a job applicant but as the best way to get something done, the best way to get a problem solved, or the best way to capitalize on a ripe opportunity'.[43]

On this logic, the individual remains the entrepreneur of her own self even if she loses her job. The I cannot be laid off. The management of life ceases only with death. Thus, the self-administration of individual human capital extends way beyond working life and knows neither closing time nor the private sphere. Self-management is supposed to activate the potential of the whole person, not just her ability to work. Being an entrepreneur is not about how much you earn; it's about attitude to life. Christian Lutz, an author identifying as a researcher of a scholarly object termed 'the future', gives the following definition:

> By 'life entrepreneurs' we mean people who feel the same responsibility for their own lives as they would for a business. In their responsible dealings with a dynamic environment they develop their own abilities and use them to develop further and to shape their environment. In the course of this process the work of self-description produces appropriate filters and value criteria. In other words, life is perceived as the potential for the further development of which one feels solely responsible; one deepens the consciousness of the fact that development is only possible in synergy with a dynamic environment and that this in turn implies responsibility and responsiveness in the form of openness towards the environment's expectations.[44]

Michel Foucault defined discipline in reference to the trained body as 'no longer simply an art of distributing bodies, of extracting time from them and accumulating it, but of composing forces in order to obtain an efficient machine'.[45] For the self-entrepreneur, self-interrogation and self-training serve the same purpose. Self-management programmes are not adapted to a standardized set of personality features but rather to the standard of individuality, the point being that distinction is the key to a competitive edge in the marketplace. You should cultivate non-conformity because it distinguishes you from others and this provides economic advantages; you should *Commodify Your Dissent!*[46] To the extent that the individual makes herself an unmistakable *Brand me*® she has prised herself loose of the masses and can trump her competitors, provided the personal label guarantees real quality and satisfies the customers, whether they be potential employers or partners. The subject, as found in European philosophy, declared dead and buried by some, lives on as the trademark. All men and women are equal, but only in the need to be different from one another. The norm of individuality shows itself not only in the cult of uniqueness and the duty to be different but, above all, in the faith in individuals' unlimited ability to shape their own lives. The self-management conviction that anyone can be anything they want to be is vaguely subtended by a radical psychological constructivism:

> Our life is what our thinking makes it. We should take this statement by Marcus Aurelius to heart – every day. We all know that there is no such thing as objective reality. Everyone sees things and events through their own subjective lenses and interprets them according to their own patterns of thought.[47]

The hasty syllogism that the presence of perspective in thinking means that thought is omnipotent, turns out to be useful auto-suggestively. Donning the right glasses automatically increases your effective powers. In motivational terminology, '[b]ehaviour regulation geared towards performance and social needs requires a perception of reality with a slight positive distortion'.[48] Psychological techniques like neuro-linguistic programming (NLP), the method base for a number of self-management programmes, function by repeatedly combining external stimuli with specific sensations and ideas. 'Mental training' is supposed to make it possible to re-programme bad habits of thought and behaviour and 'learn to use your brain in more functional ways'.[49] Success thus becomes a consequence of how the individual is configured; the NLP-trained self-enterpriser becomes the director of her own 'cerebrally suitable success film'.[50] The approach's technicity is reminiscent of the heroic era of behaviourism, unburdened by questions of truth and value. Since all models are simply hypothetical, all that should really matter is choosing those that 'assist you when undertaking goal-oriented work in finding the most direct route'.[51] In other words, to *become* an entrepreneur of your own self, you simply *imagine* yourself as an enterprise and subject the whole company and all its departments to a quality check along the lines of:

> Are all of your personality elements fully engaged? Is every part at work in
> its proper place where it can attain maximal results? Are the parts working
> well together or is there competition and contention over jurisdiction? Is
> there reason to be concerned that some parts have handed in their 'inner
> letter of resignation'? Do all the parts even know each other or do you
> feel like the victim of a bundle of disparate fragments? Are all the parts
> *enjoying* the work, are they all *healthy*? Do they feel adequately respected
> and acknowledged?[52]

The questions already imply the answers: 'Aims are not achieved by inner
trials of strength or self-overcoming, but rather by the dynamics of a cohesive,
frictionless, syntonic personality system'.[53] To eliminate 'success roadblocks',
such as those resulting from a conflict between 'career [and] happiness parts',
the recommendation is to convene an internal round table sitting conference, electing a 'creative part' moderator, to seek possibilities for improving
collaboration. In this model of personality, identity is corporate identity, the
'certainty of having a strong team consisting of a manifold of "true selves"'.[54]

Some doubt may persist here as to whether the antagonistic tendencies
in the soul will really be reconciled by this method. On the other hand, a
person torn between career and joie de vivre follows the entrepreneurial
programme by being permanently in motion. When conflicting demands
are being made of people, it is a reliable indicator for the call to the entrepreneurial self. The list of key skills the self-help literature both dictates to
readers and promises to provide them with is predestined to impose impossible tasks on even the most ambitious self-optimizer. This excess of demand
is part of the programme. It keeps the individual in a state of constant tension because she has to move in multiple directions at once. She must work
untiringly for the firm while also taking care of her limited reserves. The
programmes glide seamlessly between a grammar of severity and a grammar
of care. The self-entrepreneur must decide intuitively or tactically which
key to play in, but must finally be skilful in both.

This simultaneous mobilization of opposing forces is echoed in the way
the self-help guides combine opposing strategies, propagating a rational and
at the same time charismatic form of self-control. On the one hand, the
entrepreneurial self should be a calculating administrator of its own life, on
the other hand a source of motivational energy, untiringly striving for new
achievements, and a firework spitting out innovative ideas. There is an obvious
contradiction in this demand to optimize self-discipline and enthusiasm all at
once. The disciplinary control and training are aided by checklists, contracts
and feedback systems, techniques for releasing forces of passion, affirmation,
auto-suggestion and self-outdoing. The one type of personal effort points the
ship in the right direction and the other supplies the propulsion.

This regime of self-discipline is distinguished from earlier models in that
the traditional disciplinary subject was always just beginning, whereas the

self-entrepreneur is never finished.[55] Both further education and the need for personal growth become continuous and permanent. The imperative to self-optimize implies the need to make comparisons, which in turns entails a general state of competition. A person can only maintain their position temporarily and in relation to their competitors, so no one can afford to rest on their laurels because they are in a game where the conditions of victory are continually shifting. Today's secret to success is tomorrow's recipe for disaster.

The inner sense of coherence among personality parts goes with a coherent outward presentation. For the self-entrepreneur, there is no shame in selling oneself. On the contrary, it is the only way to build self-esteem. The self-entrepreneur is her own permanent assessment centre, well aware that it is not enough to merely possess abilities; the crucial thing is to come across as the authentic expression of an individual personality. But self-marketing would miss its mark if it were mere role play. You must actually become what you want to come across as. For this reason, there is no point in trying to tear off the masks, execrating self-management as alienation. If you were to tear off the masks, the faces would go with them. The only form of self-alienation left would be the unhappy consciousness that distinguishes between outer appearance and inner being, objective commandment and subjective desire.

The tacit claim of the advice literature is that the omnipresence of the market leaves the individual with the choice between plunging head first into the competition and being left behind. People are autonomous economic entities, who should pursue happiness on their own initiative and at their own risk, and whose success therein will be in proportion as they relate to themselves in a market-like fashion. 'The Market's Will be Done', as Tom Peters profanely puts it.[56] The market is a kingdom of contingency, a fluid mix where loopholes and niches suddenly appear and as quickly disappear, more often than not filled by a competitor. Every attempt to arrest the flux is doomed to fail. To be successful, you must mimetically adapt to the environment, or, better still, outdo it in dynamism, seizing the day before someone else does.

The equalization of the individual and the enterprise that runs through management literature aims at producing synergy. When enterprises attempt to gain a competitive edge by elevating their employees to the status of self-enterprisers; when state agencies, educational institutions and NGOs improve efficiency by re-organizing like an enterprise, then the individual increases her chances of being made use of by acting like a labour force or like a relationship and leisure manager. Inversely, the 'humanistic' ideals of the autonomous life and inner balance that converge in the concept of the 'active personality with its harmoniously interacting parts'[57] promote the development of those qualities that companies demand of their employees, that employment agencies demand from their 'clients', universities from their students and volunteer associations from their members. Personal growth coincides with an accumulation of human capital; working on the self comes to coincide with job training.

The management and self-management literature displays unashamedly the rationale of the entrepreneurial self and the mechanisms by which it is generated. For this reason, we will continue to refer to this literature in the following chapters (and despite its lack of inner coherence and the difficulty of measuring its real effects on readers). Since the entrepreneurial self only exists in the gerundive, since it is a melange of prescription and description, it can be nowhere better studied than in what can be termed its *construction manuals*. These generate the undertow, the pull, the magnetic force which *is* the entrepreneurial self.

After the new economy

Entrepreneurship discourse boomed in the 1990s with the rise of the new economy. However, it did not die off after the crash in 2001 and the attacks of 9/11. Instead, it changed its tone: the mood became more austere and the dreams more modest. This is especially evident in changes to the term *Ich-AG*, the German equivalent of Me Inc. Getting off the launch pad as a glittering fashion accessory, the word peaked as a political programme for combatting unemployment and finally crashed as *Unwort des Jahres* (the 'worst word of the year'), chosen by a commission of linguists to draw attention to 'factually inappropriate and inhumane phrasings in public language usage'.[58] The rags–to–riches dream has lost its power to convince and the post–hippy coolness of the dotcom generation has frayed. To be successful, you now don't have to be the 'client' of an employment agency. Finally, the dark side of entrepreneurial self-optimizing has also become visible: the constant fear of not having done the right thing or not enough of it, the feeling of insufficiency, is as much a part of the entrepreneurial self as mercantile skill or the courage to take risks. A popular slogan among German 'Ich-AGs' was that *Selbständige* (freelancers, literally *self-standing*) are so called because they literally work *constantly* (*ständig*). No amount of effort guarantees security but a lack of harsh self-discipline can ensure failure. The call to the entrepreneurial self also reaches people aware enough that they are economically superfluous, so much so that the promise of success sounds more like a taunt. The set of values and practices propagated in training courses for the long–term unemployed and aid measures for youth, in teaching programmes at special schools, in self-help groups and in politically engaged charities are at a basic level analogous to what executives are taught at exclusive coaching workshops, personality seminars, motivation week-ends, and in self-help books on management and careers. The same values are invoked: self-responsibility, creativity, initiative, assertiveness, 'team' skills. There is the same activating rhetoric, the same imperative to optimize and the same faith in the power of faith in the self. In all these instances, the market is the final judge.

Notes

1. Trendbüro (ed.) (2001) *Duden Wörterbuch der New Economy* (Duden Dictionary of the New Economy), Mannheim: Bibliographisches Institut, p. 79.
2. Max Weber (1949) '"Objectivity" in Social Science and Social Policy', in: *The Methodology of Social Sciences*, Glencoe, IL: Free Press, pp. 49–112, here: p. 90.
3. Hans J. Pongratz and G. Günter Voß (2003) 'From Employee to "Entreployee": Towards a "Self-Entrepreneurial" Work Force?', in: *Concepts and Transformation*, 8(3), pp. 239–254.
4. Hans J. Pongratz and G. Günter Voß (2003) 'From Employee to "Entreployee"', in particular pp. 240ff.
5. Hans J. Pongratz and G. Günter Voß (1997) 'Fremdorganisierte Selbst-organisation', in: *Zeitschrift für Personalforschung*, 7, pp. 30–53.
6. See Manfred Moldaschl and G. Günter Voß (eds) (2002) *Subjektivierung von Arbeit*, Munich/Mering: Hampp.
7. Hans J. Pongratz and G. Günter Voß (2003) *Arbeitskraftunternehmer: Erwerbsorientierungen in entgrenzten Arbeitsformen*, Berlin: Auflage (Forschung aus der Hans-Böckler-Stiftung, Bd. 47), p. 242.
8. Paul Thibaud (1985) 'The Triumph of the Entrepreneur', in: *Télos*, Nr. 64, Summer, pp. 134–140, here: p. 134. [Original: 'Le triomphe de l'entrepreneur', in: *Esprit*, Dec. 1984, pp. 101–110]
9. Thibaud (1985) 'The Triumph of the Entrepreneur'.
10. Thibaud (1985) 'The Triumph of the Entrepreneur', p. 138.
11. Thibaud (1985) 'The Triumph of the Entrepreneur', p. 140.
12. Thibaud (1985) 'The Triumph of the Entrepreneur'.
13. With her infamous phrase '[t]here is no such thing as society', Prime Minister Thatcher encapsulated the point succinctly. As she elaborated, 'I think we've been through a period where too many people have been given to understand that if they have a problem, it's the government's job to cope with it. "I have a problem, I'll get a grant." "I'm homeless, the government must house me." They're casting their problem on society. And, you know, there is no such thing as society. There are individual men and women, and there are families. And no government can do anything except through people, and people must look to themselves first. It's our duty to look after ourselves and then, also to look after our neighbour. People have got the entitlements too much in mind, without the obligations. There's no such thing as entitlement, unless someone has first met an obligation' (Margaret Thatcher, Interview with *Women's Own* Magazine, 31.10.1987).
14. Cited in Paul Morris (1991) 'Freeing the Spirit of Enterprise: The Genesis and Development of the Concept of Enterprise Culture', in: Russell Keat and Nicholas Abercrombie (eds), *Enterprise Culture*, London: Routledge, pp. 21–37, here: p. 23. For a social science examination of enterprise culture, also see Roger Burrows (ed.) (1991) *Deciphering the Enterprising Culture*, London: Cengage; Malcolm Cross and Geoff Payne (1991) *Work and the Enterprise Culture*, London: Falmer; Paul Heelas and Paul Morris (eds) (1992)

The Values of the Enterprise Culture: The Moral Debate, London: Routledge; Colin Gray (1998) *Enterprise and Culture*, London: Routledge.

15. Ronald Reagan (1985) 'Why this is an Entrepreneurial Age', in: *Journal of Business Venturing*, 1, pp. 1–4, here: pp. 1, 3.

16. In more general terms, the insight that in a capitalist economy the worker acts as the free vendor of their power to work is a truism of political economy. As the German economist Lujo von Brentano explained in 1907, 'every worker who sells his labour to an employer is also an entrepreneur ... He transforms his labour power by transforming food into labour, by training special abilities, by releasing the collected tension through force of will to render it effective in the production process. He is also a producer, because he endows pre-existent material and energy with a different form, thus investing it with greater utility. He offers this to the buyer of labour power as an autonomous good and does this on his own account and at his own risk. He is the entrepreneur of labour services. The granting of his freedom, by making him responsible for himself, has made him into this entrepreneur and precisely in this capacity he demonstrates his freedom' (Lujo von Brentano (1907) *Der Unternehmer: Vortrag gehalten am 3. Januar 1907 in der Volkswirtschaftlichen Gesellschaft in Berlin*, Berlin: Simion, pp. 19, 26f.). What is new is that the worker no longer acts as an entrepreneur by selling his labour power; in addition, its buyers demand that he show entrepreneurial initiative and responsibility within the labour time he has bartered for.

17. Wolfgang Bonß, Heiner Keupp and Elmar Koenen (1984) 'Das Ende des Belastungsdiskurses? Zur subjektiven und gesellschaftlichen Bedeutung von Arbeitslosigkeit', in: Wolfgang Bonß and Rolf G. Heinze (eds) (1984) *Arbeitslosigkeit in der Arbeitsgesellschaft*, Frankfurt: Suhrkamp, pp. 143–188, here: pp. 182f.

18. See e.g. Martin Baethge (1991) 'Arbeit, Vergesellschaftung, Identität: Zur zunehmenden normativen Subjektivierung der Arbeit', in: *Soziale Welt*, 42, pp. 6–19; Harald Wolf (1999) *Arbeit und Autonomie: Ein Versuch über Widersprüche und Metamorphosen kapitalistischer Produktion*, Münster: Westfälisches Dampfboot.

19. Stefan Kühl (2000) 'Grenzen der Vermarktlichung: Die Mythen um unternehmerisch handelnde Mitarbeiter', in: *WSI-Mitteilungen*, 53, pp. 818–828; Christoph Deutschmann (2001) 'Die Gesellschaftskritik der Industriesoziologie: ein Anachronismus', in: *Leviathan*, 29, pp. 58–69.

20. Sergio Bologna (1997/2006) *Die Zerstörung der Mittelschichten: Thesen zur neuen Selbständigkeit*, Graz/Vienna: Nausner and Nausner, p. 38. (The term 'new autonomy' (neue Selbständigkeit) used above is extracted from this title.)

21. Colin Gordon (1991) 'Governmental Rationality: An Introduction', in: Graham Burchell, Colin Gordon and Peter Miller (eds), *The Foucault-Effect: Studies in Governmentality*, Chicago: University of Chicago Press, pp. 1–51. The anthology presented Foucault's lecture 'Governmentality' to an Anglophone public for the first time, as well as including articles mainly by former Foucault collaborators. In retrospect, it can be seen as the initiating publication for studies of governmentality.

22. On Foucault's lecture *The Birth of Biopolitics* (2010), which contains his analyses of German ordoliberalism and human capital theory (especially that of Gary S. Becker), see Chapter 3, this volume.
23. Gordon (1991) 'Governmental Rationality', p. 44.
24. Gordon (1991) 'Governmental Rationality', p. 43. See also Graham Burchell (1996) 'Liberal Government and Techniques of the Self', in: Andrew Barry, Thomas Osborne and Nikolas Rose (eds), *Foucault and Political Reason: Liberalism, Neo-liberalism and Rationalities of Government*, London: University of Chicago Press, pp. 19–36.
25. Peter Miller and Nikolas Rose (1995) 'Production, Identity, and Democracy', in: *Theory and Society*, 25, pp. 427–467, here: p. 455.
26. Paul du Gay and Graeme Salaman (1992) 'The Cult(ure) of the Customer', in: *Journal of Management Studies*, 29, pp. 615–633, here: p. 630.
27. Nikolas Rose (1998) 'Governing Enterprising Individuals' in: *Inventing Our Selves: Psychology, Power, and Personhood*, Cambridge: Cambridge University Press, pp. 150–168. See also the chapter 'Enterprising Selves', in: Pat O'Malley (2004) *Risk, Uncertainty and Government*, London: Routledge-Cavendish, pp. 68ff.
28. Thomas J. Peters and Robert H. Waterman (1982) *In Search of Excellence: Lessons from America's Best-Run Companies*, New York: Harper; Gifford Pinchot III (1985) *Intrapreneuring: Why You Don't Have to Leave the Corporation to Become an Entrepreneur*, New York: Joanna Cotler. An overview of the cult of the entrepreneur in management literature from the 1980s is given by Patrick Wright (1987) 'Excellence', in: *London Review of Books*, 21 May, pp. 8–11. An analysis of both the managerial and the sociological discourses on enterprise is undertaken from an organization theory perspective informed by post-structuralism in Daniel Hjorth (2003) *Rewriting Entrepreneurship – for a New Perspective on Organisational Creativity*, Copenhagen: Samfundslitterature Press.
29. Peters and Waterman (1982) *In Search of Excellence*, p. 212.
30. Peters and Waterman (1982) *In Search of Excellence*, p. 202.
31. Peters and Waterman (1982) *In Search of Excellence*, p. 202.
32. Peters and Waterman (1982) *In Search of Excellence*, p. 213.
33. Pinchot (1985) *Intrapreneuring*, p. xvi.
34. Pinchot (1985) *Intrapreneuring*, p. 3.
35. Pinchot (1985) *Intrapreneuring*, pp. 196f.
36. See William H. Whyte (1956) *The Organization Man*, New York: Clarion.
37. See William Bridges (1998) *Creating You & Co.: Learn to Think Like the CEO of Your Own Career*, Cambridge, MA: Da Capo.
38. Christopher Gergen and Gregg Vanourek (2008) *Life Entrepreneurs: Ordinary People Creating Extraordinary Lives*, San Francisco, CA: John Wiley & Sons.
39. Regarding this literature, see Heidi Marie Rimke (2000) 'Governing Citizens through Self-Help Literature', in: *Cultural Studies*, 14, pp. 61–78; Paul Lichterman (1992) 'Self-Help Reading as a Thin Culture', in: *Media, Culture and Society*, 14, pp. 421–447.
40. See Rolf Wabner (1997) *Selbstmanagement: Werden Sie zum Unternehmer Ihres Lebens*, Niedernhausen/Ts: Falken.

41. Bridges (1998) *Creating You & Co.*, p. 140.
42. Bridges (1998) *Creating You & Co.*, pp. 31ff. See also William Bridges (1994) *JobShift: How to Prosper in a Workplace Without Jobs*, New York: Da Capo.
43. Bridges (1998) *Creating You & Co.*, p. 31.
44. Christian Lutz (1995) *Leben und Arbeiten in der Zukunft (Life and Work in the Future)*, Munich: Langen/Müller, p. 57.
45. Michel Foucault (1977) *Discipline and Punish*, New York: Vintage Books, p. 164.
46. See Thomas Frank and Matt Weiland (eds) (1997) *Commodify Your Dissent: Salvos from the Baffler*, New York: W. W. Norton & Co.
47. Marie-Louise Neubeiser (1992) *Management Coaching*, Dusseldorf/Vienna: Orell Füssili, p. 161.
48. Michael Kastner (1999) *Syn-Egoismus: Nachhaltiger Erfolg durch soziale Kompetenz*, Freiburg: Herder, p. 285.
49. Richard Bandler (1985) *Using Your Brain – For a Change: Neuro-Linguistic Programming*, Moab, UT: Real People Press, p. 9.
50. Cora Besser-Siegmund and Harry Siegmund (1991) *Coach Yourself: Persönlichkeitskultur für Führungskräfte*, Düsseldorf: ECON-Verlag, pp. 73ff.
51. Besser-Siegmund and Siegmund (1991) *Coach Yourself*, p. 95.
52. Besser-Siegmund and Siegmund (1991) *Coach Yourself*, p. 130.
53. Besser-Siegmund and Siegmund (1991) *Coach Yourself*, p. 16.
54. Besser-Siegmund and Siegmund (1991) *Coach Yourself*, p. 132. Such notions of a multiple self strongly suggest comparison with the psychiatric discourse on 'multiple personalities'. The entrepreneurial self is supposed to represent an association of competing and cooperating elements, while patients with multiple personality suffer precisely from the dissociation between parts acting as independent personalities caused by extreme trauma. One of the two phenomena – the rise of the illness or the rise of the discourse on it – could be assignable to the analogy between the underlying conceptions of the subject. At any rate, the therapies for multiple personality do attempt, if not integration, then at least a liveable co-existence among the partial personalities by supporting the patients in moderating their separate voices and committing them to rules of communication. See Ian Hacking (1995) *Rewriting the Soul*, Princeton, NJ: Princeton University Press.
55. Deleuze (1992) 'Postscript on the Societies of Control', p. 5.
56. Tom Peters (1992) *Liberation Management*, New York: Alfred A. Knopf, p. 528.
57. Besser-Siegmund and Siegmund (1991) *Coach Yourself*, p. 144.
58. See www.unwortdesjahres.net/.

PART 1

The Rationality of the Entrepreneurial Self

3

THE TRUTH ABOUT THE MARKET: VARIANTS OF NEO-LIBERALISM

But apart from this contemporary mood, the ideas of economists and political philosophers, both when they are right and when they are wrong, are more powerful than is commonly understood. Indeed the world is ruled by little else. Practical men, who believe themselves to be quite exempt from any intellectual influences, are usually the slaves of some defunct economist. Madmen in authority, who hear voices in the air, are distilling their frenzy from some academic scribbler of a few years back.[1]

Entrepreneurs only exist where there are markets; entrepreneurial activity is aimed at market success. The claim advanced in this study – that individuals are addressed today in a variety of contexts as enterprising selves and are admonished to act accordingly – implies that these contexts are regulated by market mechanisms or that there exists at least the expectation that they should be. In other words, the enterprising self can only become a prevalent form of subjectification when the market acts as a privileged site of social integration or at least when it claims to do so.

This expansion of market mechanisms to potentially all areas of social relations, including the relation to self, is at the heart of Michel Foucault's analysis of neo-liberal governmentality. Foucault, however, is not asking which social orders are conducted in market form and by means of which institutional practices. Instead, he analyses in the texts of the German ordoliberals and the Chicago School a rationale of governing that deploys the market as 'a sort of permanent economic tribunal confronting government'.[2] Foucault shows how these economists introduce a new form of governmental reason, equidistant from classical liberalism, Keynesianism and national socialist and Soviet totalitarianism. It is readily apparent that neoliberal theories possessed a significant force that has continued to grow since Foucault held his lectures at the *Collège de France* in the late 1970s. Indeed, the fact of their significance was the main impulse to write this book. Neither Foucault's analyses nor the present book forward an argument about the application of neoliberal programmes (or whether that application is impossible or unsuccessful), the relations of forces in which they may have attained discursive hegemony or the intellectual networks, theoretical and political careers of their protagonists.[3] In what follows we are only concerned with the *principles of neo-liberal governmentality* as enunciated in the programmes.

The present account follows Foucault's reconstruction of German ordoliberalism and US human capital theory. Especially in reference to the latter, we will go deeper into Foucault. The third section considers Friedrich August von Hayek, a thinker whose version of neoliberal thinking Foucault covered only marginally in the lectures. The following is largely a reading of Foucault's reading. There are two reasons for this partial neglect of the primary sources. First, Foucault's lectures on the history of governmentality were first printed in 2004 and have been only sparsely subjected to scholarly evaluation.[4] Second, and more importantly, we are not attempting a thorough exhibition of neoliberal positions. Instead, we are concentrating on one aspect, which Foucault elaborates on as the ultimate object of neoliberal governmental rationality and which we will adopt and expand: *How does the discourse of neo-liberal economics enthrone the enterprise as the universal model of societal organization and the self-entrepreneur as the universal model of human subjectivity?*

A government of freedom

Neither liberalism in its classical 18th- and 19th-century forms nor 20th-century neoliberalism have a unified idea nor a unified political practice. Their coherence consists in a motion of recoil. Foucault regards the art of liberal government as a basically critical project predicated on the suspicion that 'there is too much governing going on ... The whole question of critical governmental reason will turn on how not to govern so much. The objection is no longer the abuse of sovereignty but to excessive government'.[5] The leading thread for this self-imposed restriction on the part of governmental reason is provided by political economy – 'a sort of general reflection on the organization, distribution, and limitation of powers in a society'.[6] Foucault shows how this reflection is performed differently in the neoliberal era than it was in classical liberalism.

The 18th-century proponents of political economy already judged government practice differently than did their predecessors, the theoreticians of sovereignty and national interest, by considering the *effects* of government rather than its natural legitimacy: 'In other words, political

economy does not discover natural rights that exist prior to the exercise of
governmentality; it discovers a certain naturalness specific to the practice
of government itself';[7] a naturalness which government practice must follow in order to avoid harm. The site where this truth about the nature of
government manifests itself is the market, which, according to Foucault,
changes from the locus of adjudication to 'a site of veridiction'.[8] The object
of this veridiction is government itself. 'On the one hand, the market
appeared as something that obeyed and had to obey "natural", that is to say,
spontaneous mechanisms', and on the other hand as the agent discovering
the 'natural', the 'normal' or the 'good' price expressive of the true value
of the products.[9] Both elements are intertwined. Finding the truth of the
market means disclosing its nature. In turn, in order to draw out its true
nature, the market must be made real in practice, since it can only utter its
truth when its natural mechanisms are not falsified by outside interference.

The new art of governing is thus performed as a government of freedom,
a freedom that government does not prescribe but rather presupposes and
manages. Instead of the classical liberal 'be free', the message is now: 'I am
going to produce what you need to be free. I am going to see to it that you
are free to be free.'[10] Governing according to this maxim means relinquishing all measures that would tether the invisible hand, which in turn implies
placing all political interventions under suspicion. Foucault's interpretation
of liberal governmentality is not exhausted by this critical approach, but
also takes account of the regimes of discipline and control established in the
name of freedom. The theory and practice of liberal government is both a
permanent exercise of doubt as well as a specific use of power. The growth
of new freedoms is accompanied by an increase in efforts to discipline their
exercise. In order to secure a space for the free play of natural market forces,
individual and group interests need to be counter-balanced by measures
such as civil law, social security, tariffs, anti-trust laws, compulsory schooling and military service, and the internment of those deemed insane and
criminal. Yet these security measures run the risk of undermining what they
should be securing:

> [I]f this liberalism is not so much the imperative of freedom as the manage-
> ment and organization of the conditions in which one can be free, it is clear
> that at the heart of this liberal practice is an always different and mobile
> problematic relationship between the production of freedom and that which
> in the production of freedom risks limiting and destroying it.[11]

From this point of view, freedom is not a universal measuring rod against
which to measure reality:

> Freedom is never anything other — but this is already a great deal — than an actual
> relation between governors and governed, a relation in which the measure of
> the 'too little' existing freedom is given by the 'even more' freedom demanded.[12]

In objecting to the excess of government, liberalism both diagnoses current government and attempts a cure for the crisis of governmentality, not least of all the crisis of liberal governmentality itself. The history of liberalism is a history of the struggles against 'not enough' freedom for 'still more' freedom. The neo-liberal theories growing up in the 1930s were a reaction to the 1929 crisis. They developed alternative models to the Soviet and national socialist versions of plan economies as well as to Keynes' programme of counter-cyclical public spending to increase aggregate demand. According to the neoliberals of ordoliberalism and the Chicago School, economic depression and the resulting government hypertrophy are due not to market failure, which does not exist, but rather to interventions in the market. They draw the further conclusion that it is not enough to regard the market as a corrective and as the outer limit of state intervention, as did classical liberalism in its fight against state absolutism. According to Foucault, the ordoliberal viewpoint is to

> ask the market economy itself to be the principle, not of the state's limitation, but of its internal regulation from start to finish of its existence and action. In other words, instead of accepting a free market defined by the state and kept as it were under state supervision ... the ordoliberals say we should completely turn the formula around and adopt the free market as organizing and regulating principle of the state, from the start of its existence up to the last form of its interventions. In other words: a state under the supervision of the market rather than a market supervised by the state.[13]

That means bidding farewell to a basic principle of classical liberal governmentality: laissez-faire. It is the conviction of the ordoliberals that unfettered competition should replace exchange as the principle of the market. Moreover, unfettered competition does not emerge of its own accord when the government gives free rein to market dynamics. This notion involves an institutional in place of a naturalist theory of economics. Some force (market freedom) that has always been simmering below and need only be released from government restriction to bubble over becomes a final objective that can never be fully reached, requiring not passivity but active effort: 'Pure competition must and can only be an objective, an objective thus presupposing an indefinitely active policy.'[14] The market does not produce a self-stabilizing harmony left to its own devices, but must instead be constantly stabilized from without. It is not the 'correctional facility' celebrated by classical liberalism but must itself be continually corrected in order not to 'degenerate'. What the ordoliberal theory of political economy demands is no longer, as in Adam Smith's time, to afford the market a space free of administrative influence within a given political order, but rather a restructuring of society according to the principle of competition. The market and the state are no longer two separate spheres whose independence the state is to guarantee by monitoring the border between them. Ordoliberalism instead demands 'a sort of complete superimposition of market mechanisms, indexed to competition, and governmental policy. Government must accompany the market economy from start to finish ... One must govern for the market, rather than because of the market'.[15]

Continual intervention replaces mere abstention. The neoliberal state is both active and activating. This interventionism is opposite to the Keynesian variety. Instead of compensating for the negative social effects of competition, it eliminates the factors interfering with competition. It is not directed against market economy but rather is the condition of its possibility. Its categorical imperative is, in Foucault's phrasing: 'So we do not touch the laws of the market but act so that institutions are such that these laws, and only these laws, really are the principle of general economic regulation and, as a consequence, of social regulation.'[16]

If the purpose of laws is to enforce the laws of the market, then government may not attempt to exercise economic and social control over the details of the economic process. Its only task is to provide a formal framework in which economic agents can pursue their individual aims as unrestrainedly as possible. Ordoliberal politics is thus defined as diametrically opposed to plan economy. The aim is not the control of resources but rather the establishment of the rules of play within which the economic order can best develop itself.[17] This order should be protected not least of all against monopolies. As Alexander von Rüstow writes: 'the first and most essential among those social, institutional conditions that truly underlie the beneficial functioning of market mechanisms is the prevention of all hindering competition and the rigorous restriction of market freedom to pure performance competition.'[18]

The ordoliberals are firmly opposed to a leveller-type politics of redistribution. They regard welfare state measures aimed at rebalancing access to consumer goods as incommensurable with market principles. At most, they admit minimal income redistribution from the biggest earners to those incapable of earning who can take part in the market only with state help.[19] As Foucault writes, social market economy 'involves only the marginal transfer from a maximum to a minimum; it is absolutely not the establishment of or regulation around an average'.[20] The purpose of social politics is to avoid exclusion and promote active inclusion in competition.

There is another important difference to classical liberalism. When the German version of neoliberalism wants to establish the market as a regulative principle, the aim is less a society of general exchange of goods than universal competition: 'Not a supermarket society, but an enterprise society.'[21] This shifts the liberal art of government away from the equivalence principle that levels qualitative differences. The regime of exchange value has long established itself; now the challenge is to make room for the diversity of entrepreneurial initiative. The agenda is not the commodification of all areas of life but rather the expansion of competition. Economic subjects should encounter one another not as trade partners but as competing entrepreneurs.

The purpose of ordoliberal regulation is thus 'the generalization of forms of "enterprise" by diffusing and multiplying them as much as possible, enterprises which must not be focused on the form of big national or international enterprises or the type of big enterprises of a state'.[22] Individuals should find themselves lodged

> within the framework of a multiplicity of diverse enterprises connected up to and entangled with each other, enterprises which are in some way ready to hand for the individual, sufficiently limited in their scale for the individual's actions, decisions, and choices to have meaningful and perceptible effects, and numerous enough for him not to be dependent on one alone.[23]

The objective here could be said to be to apply the subsidiary principle to the economy, or, as Foucault writes, paraphrasing Wilhelm Röpke, 'shifting the center of gravity of governmental action downwards'.[24]

Despite their apologia of the market, the ordoliberals are doubtful that the spread of economic mechanisms is a good thing. They see competition as the best ordering principle in the sphere of economics, but only in this sphere. According to them, to prevent society collapsing into 'hungry hordes of vested interests', compensatory measures must be met in other social areas. As Röpke writes:

> [w]e have no intention to demand more from competition than it can give. It is a means of establishing order and exercising control in the narrow sphere of a market economy based on the division of labor, but not a principle on which a whole society can be built. From the sociological and moral point of view it is even dangerous because it tends more to dissolve than to unite. If competition is not to have the effect of a social explosive and is at the same time not to degenerate, its premise will be a correspondingly sound political and moral framework.[25]

Economic imperialism

The American neoliberalism studied by Foucault, at least the human capital theory version of Gary S. Becker und Theodore W. Schultz, is not at all interested in this kind of partition. The ordoliberals were for a staggered economy consisting of basic entrepreneurial elements and their political programme provides the necessary institutional prerequisites of such an economy. Meanwhile, the economists of the Chicago School see the logic of competition as the root of human activity itself and are consequently less concerned with social institutions than with individual behaviour.[26] The main feature of human capital theory is its 'economic imperialism',[27] the extension of economic explanations to areas of life formerly not counted among the economic.

This expansion of the economic domain brings a new type of discourse into play. In contrast to the openly prescriptive argumentation of the ordo-liberal originators of social market economics, human capital theory insists on the descriptive character of its investigations. The proponents of human capital theory claim not to be addressing how people *ought* to act individually and collectively but rather how they are already actually acting. Correspondingly, human capital theory places itself at a greater distance from everyday politics than West German post-war liberalism. Foucault writes:

> I think this is why American liberalism currently appears not just, or not so much as a political alternative, but let's say as a sort of many-sided, ambiguous, global claim with a foothold in both the right and the left. It is also a sort of utopian focus which is always being revived. It is also a method of thought, a grid of economic and sociological analysis.[28]

The ordoliberal programmes for the nascent Federal Republic of Germany were a response to a specific historical situation, whereas human capital theory goes further by claiming universal validity and volunteering to explain human behaviour in its entirety.

This throwing open of the borders, as well as the behavioural theory that goes far beyond mere 'methodological individualism',[29] is one of the main reasons for Foucault's interest in what Gary S. Becker has called the 'economic approach to human behavior'.[30] Foucault sees Becker's writings as exemplifying the rationale of neo-liberal governmentality in its most radical and hence clearest form, providing the distilled essence of the entrepreneurial self. As in his reading of ordoliberalism, Foucault sees here a shift from the principle of trade to that of competition. Human capital theory casts the human being as *homo economicus*; not a partner in trade as in classical economics but the 'entrepreneur of himself ... being for himself his own capital, being for himself his own producer, being for himself the source of [his] earnings'.[31]

The claim that employees are also entrepreneurs is not new. The decisive innovation of human capital theory is to treat consuming as an enterprising act. The consumer is henceforth not just a passive receiver of goods but also an active producer.[32] Purchasing goods or services is not the concluding economic act but an input, an investment of resources, in particular of the scarce resource of time, toward a maximum output of satisfaction. By adding consumption time to labour time as elements of economics, human capital theory is able to encompass all human activity in its analyses. The individual is an economic institution whose existence, like that of an enterprise, depends on a series of choices. Whatever someone does, she could just as easily do something else within the same time frame. We must therefore assume that she will choose what she most prefers. The human being in human capital theory is, above all, an entity concerned constantly with the business of making decisions.

Becker's 'economic approach', applied 'relentlessly and unflinchingly' to all human behaviour, 'assumes that individuals maximize welfare as they conceive it, whether they be selfish, altruistic, loyal, spiteful, or masochistic'.[33] The human creature is a rational agent of choice occupied wholly with the allocation of limited resources in a situation of competition. Human practice is a choice between alternatives of greater and lesser appeal and is fundamentally self-serving. Each action has its price (though this price may or may not be expressible in monetary terms), since choosing one thing means foregoing another. The cost of an act of choice consists in having to do without the next best alternative choices.[34] Economic theory does not extend to naming the preferences people have and explaining their origins. For Becker, a second decisive presupposition is that there exist historically constant elementary preferences such as 'health, prestige, sensual pleasure[, b]enevolence, or envy'. The third premise concerns the existence of markets 'that with varying degrees of efficiency coordinate the actions of different participants – individuals, firms, even nations – so that their behavior becomes mutually consistent'. This refers not only to monetary markets:

> Even without a market sector, either directly or indirectly, each commodity has a relevant marginal 'shadow' price, namely, the time required to produce a unit change in that commodity; in equilibrium, the ratio of these prices must equal the ratio of the marginal utilities.[35]

This presupposes in turn that supply and demand regulate how agents maximize utility and balance their preferences.

These basic assumptions are for Becker not empirically validated claims about human nature but rather heuristic constructs, the elements of a hypothetical anthropology, a methodological 'contrivance for the sake of reducing complexity'. The assumption that humans act rationally 'contains no statement about reality, but rather is the formulation of an analytic *scheme* that guides the generation of statements about reality'.[36] By equating the human with *homo economicus*, human capital theory can grasp it only to the extent that it behaves accordingly. This rational schema also provides Becker with a governmentalist approach. If the individual is permanently pursuing maximal gain, then its behaviour can be influenced by altering the relative costs of the different options. Since she is constantly making decisions, *homo economicus* is someone 'who is eminently governable'.[37] This economic notion of human susceptibility to discipline already carries the seeds of its practical application. If all conduct can be described in a cost-benefit analysis, then people have no choice but to make choices in all their activities. The theoretical approach identifying people as benefit-maximizing subjects acting in a market already begins to make them into this kind of subject and pressures them into making themselves into it.

The premise of human capital implies simply that knowledge and abilities, health, outward appearance, social prestige, work ethics and personal habits are to be regarded as scarce resources requiring investment in order to be developed, maintained and increased. According to Becker's ally Theodore W. Schultz, '[t]he human agent becomes ever more a capitalist by virtue of his personal human capital, and he seeks political support to protect the value of that capital'.[38] Even someone who possesses no goods possesses time and will invest it to maximum benefit according to his preferences, for example to maintain good health, as Schultz explains, elucidating the foundation of human capital theory thus:

> gross investment in human capital entails acquisition and maintenance costs, including child care, nutrition, clothing, housing, medical services, and care of oneself. The service that health capital renders consists of 'healthy time' or 'sickness-free time' which contributes to work, consumption, and leisure activities … Longer life results in more years of participation in the labor force, and brings about a reduction in 'sick time.' Better health and vitality in turn lead to more productivity per man-hour at work.[39]

Becker interprets the decision whether to marry or not, whether to have children and how within the same scheme. On this reading, people marry 'when they expect to be better off than if they remained single, and they divorce if that is expected to increase their welfare'.[40] 'For most parents, children are a source of psychic income or satisfaction, and, in the economist's terminology, children would be considered a consumption good' – a consumer good with a somewhat longer period of use than others, or even as the means of production for further income, providing financial security for parents in old age. Whether or not potential parents decide to have one or more children depends on whether the expected benefits outweigh the costs. An additional cost factor is children's 'quality':

> A family must determine not only how many children it has but also the amount spent on them – whether it should provide separate bedrooms, send them to nursery school and private colleges, give them dance or music lessons, and so forth. I will call more expensive children 'higher quality' children, just as Cadillacs are called higher quality cars than Chevrolets. To avoid any misunderstanding, let me hasten to add that 'higher quality' does not mean morally better. If more is voluntarily spent on one child than on another, it is because the parents obtain additional utility from the additional expenditure and it is this additional utility which we call higher 'quality'.[41]

As the entrepreneurs of their own selves, individuals are 'abilities machines', writes Foucault, summarizing Becker and Schultz's notions of education as a form of human capital investment. These machines require careful planning, maintenance and continual adjustment to market demands. This cannot be started too early. Before the individual begins to develop her competencies, her parents and other social institutions must already have invested in her:

> We know that the number of hours a mother spends with her child, even when it is still in the cradle, will be very important for the formation of an abilities-machine, or for the formation of a human capital, and that the child will be much more adaptive if in fact its parents or its mother spend more rather than less time with him or her. This means that it must be possible to analyze the simple time parents spend feeding their children, or giving them affection as investment which can form human capital.[42]

The logic of accumulation is naturally not only concerned with care for the infant, but also with using the time spent caring and the phases outside of active caring as efficiently as possible. A whole industry has since grown up, with backup support from neuro-science, around providing 'active' play material for infants as objects of human capital investment.[43]

Becker pre-empts moralist attacks on his economic approach by reminding us of its heuristic power. Nor does his hypothetical anthropology lack empirical evidence. His theory is accused of coldness, but the theory answers that it is human beings themselves who are cold when looked at economically. The kind of private eugenics that has since become commonplace confirms Becker's analysis of fertility. Quality management ensures that the lower the number of children a family has and the higher the costs of educating them, the more important is the quality of the raw material and the more probable it is that foetuses with prenatal diagnoses of anomalies or handicaps will be aborted.

The biopolitical dimension of neoliberal governmentality referred to in the title of Foucault's lectures is particularly manifest here. Before the corresponding technologies had become prevalent, Foucault had already spoken of a logic of selection flowing inexorably from the combination of genetic diagnostics and the economization of the individual:

> as soon as a society poses itself the problem of the improvement of its human capital in general, it is inevitable that the problem of the control, screening, and improvement of the human capital of individuals, as a function of unions and consequent reproduction, will become actual, or at any rate, called for. So, the political problem of the use of genetics arises in terms of the formation, growth, accumulation, and improvement of human capital.[44]

With its principle of optimization, human capital theory deepens political economy into bio-political economy. This is shown not only in questions of family planning. It characterizes the individual as the capitalist or sovereign of her own self, whose dealings with her mind and body are the expression of investment and disinvestment decisions. With every action she maximizes her utility, exercising, as Foucault puts it, the right over herself 'to take life or let live'.[45] As is bluntly put by Becker, 'most (if not all!) deaths are to some extent "suicides" in the sense that they could have been postponed if more resources had been invested in prolonging life'.[46] The ruling principle here is 'it's your own fault!': if you get sick, it's because *you* didn't take care of your health; if you suffer an accident or are the victim of crime, it's because *you* didn't take appropriate precautions. Whatever act a person performs, they choose from among competing preferences:

> Good health and a long life are important aims of most persons, but surely no more than a moment's reflection is necessary to convince anyone that they are not the only aims: somewhat better health or a longer life may be sacrificed because they conflict with other aims. The economic approach implies that there is an 'optimal' expected length of life, where the value in utility of an additional year is less than the utility foregone by using time and other resources to obtain that year. Therefore, a person may be a heavy smoker or so committed to work as to omit all exercise, not necessarily because he is ignorant of the consequences or 'incapable' of using the information he possesses, but because the lifespan forfeited is not worth the cost to him of quitting smoking or working less intensively.[47]

The sovereign decision over life and death separates out into countless micro-decisions with which the individual shortens or prolongs their life. Each cigarette is a little self-pronounced death sentence, every round of jogging a little potential reprieve.

When following this argumentation more closely, the language of hardness comes to the surface as no less important than the concern for health, care and education. When life becomes an economic function, disinvestment means death. This applies equally to a society's treatment of its whole population as to particular groups such as parents, parents-to-be and children, both born and unborn. It applies also to the individual's treatment of themselves. The human capitalist of their own life constitutes their self both as a subject and an object of individual choices. As an active subject, they are in charge of their own life and the consequences of their actions are registered as opportunity costs. As the passive object of their own actions, they are reduced to mere existence, dependent on being invested in by their own self.[48] As the sovereign master of their self, they cannot afford to tolerate residual pockets of resistance to utility maximization within their empire. Subjugated to their own yoke, they cannot decide what to fear more: the imperative to self-optimize or the move to disobey it and thereby lose themself entirely.

Because so much is at stake, the individual will attempt to be as well informed as possible in order to make the right decisions, which also involves balancing costs and benefits, i.e. weighing up time spent and information gained. It only emerges later which resource allocation brings the highest return on investment. No one has all the information, so market success is influenced by chance, which means that a relative information advantage can be decisive. The drive for knowledge is thus also an economic function, making neoliberalism an art of government that relies on systematic information management and professional expertise. Like any other activity aimed beyond immediate satisfaction, the acquisition of knowledge is an investment in one's own human capital, an allocation of personal resources with the purpose of improving the efficiency of later resource allocation. In this way, an education programme is part of the process of becoming a *homo economicus*.

Above all, everyone must learn to continually monitor their investments, adjusting them as needed. Behaving enterprisingly doesn't just mean investing one's own resources in the maximization of utility, but also 'the ability to reallocate resources in response to new events is pervasive'.[49] The development of enterprising competencies is subject to the law of supply and demand. These skills will spread in proportion to the returns on innovation and the learning effort they require. Accelerated social change makes markets more dynamic, which in turn forces people to adopt new paths and broaden their enterprising abilities. This means the demand for entrepreneurship grows in proportion to the energy of the economy. Schultz defines this demand as a function of economic imbalance. He writes: 'Human agents who perceive and evaluate such disequilibria with a view of deciding whether or not it is worthwhile for them to reallocate their resources, including the allocation of time, are entrepreneurs.'[50] At best, the result is a feedback loop with expanding markets raising enterprising spirits and activities, which in turn raises market activity. The main lesson the market teaches is the tautology that the best conditions for learning to thrive and survive on the market are found where market laws reign.

Competition as a method of discovery

Friedrich August von Hayek was also convinced of the superiority of market mechanisms. Yet while the ordoliberal discussion is focused on securing an institutional basis for competition, and while the economic imperialism of human capital theory sees competition as the key determinant of human behaviour, Hayek, in contrast, views competition as an evolutionary process, breaking its path independent of, and frequently against, the will of its agents. This anti-rationalist and anti-utilitarian approach puts Hayek's version of neoliberalism at odds with both the ordoliberal will to actively design the economy and with the thesis of rational choice in human capital theory. On the other hand, he shares with both a rejection of the naturalist bent in classical liberalism. Freedom is for Hayek neither an innate character nor the result of reasoned planning, as it was for the ordoliberals. It is rather an 'artefact of civilization',[51] seized from nature in the course of cultural evolution. However, it is not derived from a utilitarian individual striving for gain, as human capital theory would have it. According to Hayek, 'the pleasure which man is led to strive for is of course not the end which evolution serves but merely the signal that primitive conditions made the individual do what was usually required for the preservation of the group, but which under present conditions may no longer do so'.[52] The task for theory is 'to discover the significance of rules we never deliberately made, and the obedience to which builds more complex orders than we can understand'.[53]

The market and competition develop, according to Hayek, as a result of a mechanism of selection operating behind participants' backs. The ordo-liberals sought to aid the reason of the market by deliberate intervention, while human capital theory presupposed that individuals are capable of optimizing resource allocation on their own. For Hayek meanwhile, the economic order and the kind of comportment it makes necessary result from the evolutionary pressure to adapt:

> competition will make it necessary for people to act rationally in order to maintain themselves. It is based not on the assumption that most or all the participants in the market process are rational, but, on the contrary, on the assumption that it will in general be through competition that a few relatively more rational individuals will make it necessary for the rest to emulate them in order to prevail.[54]

In other words, the rationale of the market is not the effect but rather the cause, the motor, of human reason. The neoliberal defences of competition are all grounded in a version of social Darwinism. Yet Hayek goes further in this direction than Becker and Schultz and even more so than Röpke, Eucken and the other ordoliberals. However, his theory of cultural evolution does not postulate the natural selection of individual traits but rather the development and modification of collective rules of conduct, 'in short, the whole cultural inheritance which is passed on by learning and imitation'.[55]

Hayek backs up his claim of the superiority of the market order with communication theory. According to his argument, no entity other than the market has enough information and the capacity to process it in such a way as to optimize resource allocation and thereby balance supply and demand, although this remains an imperfect balance that must be continually readjusted. The difficulty of this task is not the complexity of information – a problem that could be solved by a planning agency with electronic data processing. The 'calculating machine' of the market is irreplaceable because the information is subjective. The economic process is made up of innumerable individual decisions that take on objective existence in the form of prices. Prices communicate 'in a single signal all the information distributed among a manifold of individuals'.[56] They manifest a 'systemic or holistic knowledge',[57] which is available for use by everybody and which would be unavailable without the market. Prices guide individuals searching for goods by telling them 'where it is worthwhile to search'.[58] Prices indicate scarcity and scarcity translates to profit potential, thus showing economic subjects the way. In other words, the market is smarter than its individual participants, so the latter had better follow its lead. Moreover, they have to keep on following. The knowledge generated by competition is not a static entity than can be acquired and stored for later reference. Because the market is in constant flux the news always arrives too late. Whether or not a decision was judicious can only be ascertained once it has produced profits on the market.

Hayek defines the market less as veridiction than as an information process. He regards competition as 'a procedure for discovering facts which, if the procedure did not exist, would remain unknown or at least would not be used'.[59] This relates to the question of 'which goods are scarce, however, or which things are goods, or how scarce or valuable they are',[60] and to the 'quantities or qualities of the goods to be produced and sold',[61] as well as to which forms of organization and which technologies are used in the production and distribution. Expressed in the language of cybernetics, the market is a self-sustaining and self-regulating system of feedback processes. Competition guides individuals by computing the sum of their calculations into prices, thereby providing

> that unity and coherence of the economic system which we presuppose when we think of it as one market. It creates the views people have about what is best and cheapest, and it is because of it that people know at least as much about possibilities and opportunities as they in fact do. It is thus a process which involves a continuous change in the data and whose significance must therefore be completely missed by any theory which treats these data as constant.[62]

This discovery process would be superfluous if its results could be predicted. Nor can it secure 'that for it as a whole the more important comes before the less important'[63] in order to really make optimal use of it: '[A]ll we can expect by employing an appropriate discovery procedure is that it will increase the prospects of unspecified persons, but not the prospects of any particular outcome for any particular persons'.[64]

A spontaneous order can be modified by deliberate intervention but, according to Hayek, this will have negative consequences: 'Progress by its very nature cannot be planned'.[65] His main objection to all forms of socialism, Keynesianism included, is that they attempt to plan progress. From the fact that future states of competition cannot be foreseen, he deduces

> that we naturally cannot improve signals whose determinate causes we do not know. We can perhaps introduce circumstances into the market that were unfortunately not considered by the signals and then wait and see if the market responds with other signals after taking these neglected signals into account. But the idea that we can improve a signal, the meaning of which we do not know, is absurd.[66]

Hayek nevertheless believes evolution needs a push, a presupposition leading to the oxymoronic ventures 'planning for freedom'[67] and 'planning for competition'.[68] He demands that the state abstain from all intervention in competition, limiting itself to 'the creation of an appropriate permanent legal framework' for well-functioning economic competition.[69] Employing an image of the state oiling the clockwork but not moving the hands or altering the mechanism,[70] he regresses from the cybernetics metaphor to one from classical mechanics, revealing the theological underpinnings to his thinking. The world as clockwork is unthinkable without a divine clockmaker. We humans shouldn't mess around with His machine because we cannot fully fathom the design. Inserted into the immanence of history, the Creator God lives on as the force of cultural evolution, revealing His mind to humankind in the market's spontaneous order. To rephrase this with a variation on Hegel: *the world market is a court of judgement*.

Hayek shares with the ordoliberals the conviction that a market economy needs the rule of law to flourish. He also shares their preference for indirect influence, with the task of the state being to 'create the conditions under which a benevolent order produces itself'.[71] On the other hand, he disagrees with the ordoliberal active promotion of competition, insisting on principled mistrust of any and all political influence. His worry is

> not that the state, when it is restricted to enforcing general rules, would not be able to do *enough* to maintain competition, but rather ... that it would be forced to do *too much* to maintain it ... In a certain sense, the enforcement of general rules has proved not to be too ineffective but rather *too* effective, because the rules do not permit a distinction between desirable restrictions on competition and those regarded under certain circumstances as damaging.[72]

More radical than other neoliberals, Hayek presents his programme as a critique of big government with a new evolutionist justification of laissez-faire. He adheres to dichotomies: unconscious evolution vs. rational construction, spontaneous order vs. organization, freedom vs. coercion – adamantly refuting socialism by means of economic theory. He thereby commits himself to a 'performative' contradiction. Abolishing regulations is itself a positive state intervention in an allegedly spontaneous order. At the same time, an already existing plan economy can be seen as issuing from a process of cultural evolution. Hayek is more upfront than the majority of neoliberal thinkers about the fact that competition not only produces victors but that success is at least as contingent on luck as on effort. A society of competition is not a meritocracy and does not generate equality. Its general rules of play, enshrined in the rule of law, should hinder cheating but cannot stop people from crashing.[73] Hayek writes:

[i]t ought to be freely admitted that the market order does not bring about any close correspondence between subjective merit or individual needs and rewards. It operates on the principle of a combined game of skill and chance in which the results for each individual may be as much determined by circumstances wholly beyond his control as by his skill or effort. Each is remunerated according to the value his particular services have to the particular people to whom he renders them, and this value of his services stands in no necessary relation to anything which we could appropriately call his merits and still less to his needs.[74]

The attempt to derive rules of personal conduct from this description of market mechanisms leads into a trap in which the individual is held in a state of constant tension: luck and skill are inseparably interwoven so he can never be certain if his success is due to chance, or his failure to lack of effort. He must continue to exert all his energy without ever knowing if it will be worth the effort. The contingency of the market means there is no relief from the pressure to permanently self-mobilize.

At the same time, the divine wisdom of the market provides a higher justification for our earthly fate. Since '[t]he remunerations which the market determines are, as it were, not functionally related with what people have done, but only with what they ought to do',[75] those who are rewarded with success can bathe in the moral certainty that justice has been served. The losers, by contrast, must suffer both the damage and the disgrace of having fallen short of the competitive requirements. Whatever they have done, their failure proves it was not what they should have done. The setbacks, which the protagonists experience as catastrophes, are from the point of view of the big calculating machine mere signals, enabling participants to readjust their investment decisions and further the evolution process. 'It is one of the chief tasks of competition to show which plans are false'[76] is Hayek's laconic comment on the principle of market selection. Mistakes are a necessary part of the learning process, even if they mean personal disaster.

Hayek is more interested in the evolutionary power of markets as a whole than in the active contributions of those taking part. He accordingly pays less attention to the figure of the entrepreneur. If he refers to her at all, it is as the product, not the motor of cultural evolution. Entrepreneurial spirit is for Hayek an exemplary form of 'systematic rational thinking', while competition is the only appropriate environment for 'breeding' the 'great entrepreneurs' and their 'gifts'. Entrepreneurship requires the right incentives to come about: 'It is no use being more rational than the rest if one is not allowed to derive benefits from being so'.[77] This involves strictly prohibiting egalitarian aspirations. For Hayek, entrepreneurial spirit doesn't mix well with social welfare and redistribution. The spirit can only fully develop when differences of power are not levelled under the pressure of egalitarian ideology. Entrepreneurs are natural ruler types, executing the rationale of the market by pursuing their own interests:

The intellectual growth of a community rests on the views of a few gradually spreading, even to the disadvantage of those who are reluctant to accept them; and though nobody should have the power to force upon them new views because he thinks they are better, if success proves that they are more effective, those who stick to their old ways must not be protected against a relative or even absolute decline in their position. Competition is, after all, always a process in which a small number makes it necessary for larger numbers to do what they do not like, be it to work harder, to change habits, or to devote a degree of attention, continuous application, or regularity to their work which without competition would not be needed.[78]

This is perhaps the quintessence of Hayek's evolutionary economics: the freedom of some is won at the cost of the defeat of others.

Vanishing points of neoliberal governmentality

The current economic theories under the neoliberal label are anything but homogeneous. We have seen divergence in decisive points between the ordoliberals, human capital theory and Hayekian spontaneous order. The distinctions would multiply were we to incorporate further versions, such as Milton Friedman's[79] *monetarism*, his son David Friedman's[80] *anarchocapitalism* or Murray N. Rothbard's *libertarian market radicalism*.[81] They are not included in the present study because they are less relevant to the figure of the entrepreneurial self. Institutional economic approaches like James M. Buchanan's and Gordon Tullock's[82] *public choice theory* and Oliver E. Williamson's *transaction cost economics*, as well as others belonging to the neoliberal family, will be discussed in .Chapter 5 with regard to the framing of contractual arrangements of economic transactions. Neoliberal theories range between moderate and radical, laissez–faire and politically activist positions, between the heuristic hypothetical anthropology of a utility–optimizing *homo economicus* and evolutionary conceptions of a human nature brought to its economic senses by markets. This polyphony makes it possible to justify widely differing politics by reference to one or another version. Neoliberal governmentality is in no way a finished political programme. The different versions are most powerfully held together by the common rationale of market mobilization.

There are also several accords in the details of the various theories. All take as their methodological assumption the scene of an individual making a decision. The neoliberal concept of freedom avoids both the existential drama of how to become yourself and the problem of emancipation from social coercion, focusing instead on the practical choice among a series of alternatives. Humans are moved by their preferences to make rational choices. They seek relative benefits, acting neither randomly nor mechanically, arriving at decisions on the basis of information (albeit incomplete information) and adapting to a constantly changing situation. Because they learn in order to maximize utility, their behaviour can be systematically influenced by incentives.[83] People can be governed because they can be conditioned; it is more efficient to govern them indirectly by incentives than by direct force.

Competition is the most effective mechanism for increasing humans' ability to learn and thereby to improve conditions for all, if not in equal measure. This provides a second common assumption of neoliberal thought: competition is the ideal tool for conditioning people, because it channels the innate addiction to self-aggrandisement rather than attempting to suppress it. Social cohesion is achieved by people's individual choices with the help of prices. Competition totalizes with its principle of universal comparability, while at the same time individualizing with its imperative to be different. Everyone has to compare themselves with everyone else in the pursuit of their goals and they can only increase their benefits to the degree that they distinguish themselves from their competitors by bringing something unique to the table. Competition can only unfold its stimulating effects when left unhindered and undistorted by outside intervention. For this reason, the same rule applies to competition as to individual utility maximization: neither is given once and for all, but must be constantly generated, secured and optimized. This is the essence of neoliberal governmentality: governing means promoting competition, while self-governing means promoting one's own competitiveness. This process is sustained by a feedback loop of conditioning: the more competition there is, the greater the opportunity for adjusting behaviour to increase competitiveness. In other words, only competition makes people competitive.

Competition is a dynamic process. As the place where competition goes on, the market is not a realm of peaceful pursuit of mutual interests by exchange, but rather an intricate and perpetual series of windows of individual opportunity opening and closing again. The mark of the entrepreneur is to see them coming. If the thrust of neoliberal government is toward generalizing competition, modelling society as a whole on the market, then it will ineluctably come to mould subjectivity on the figure of the entrepreneur.

Notes

1. John Maynard Keynes (1936) *The General Theory of Employment, Interest and Money*, London: Macmillan, p. 383.
2. Foucault (2010) *The Birth of Biopolitics*, p. 247.
3. See Dieter Plehwe, Bernhard Walpen and Gisela Neunhöffer (eds) (2006) *Neoliberal Hegemony: A Global Critique*, New York: Routledge.
4. The commentaries presented here are based on the recordings and transcripts of the lecture. See Gordon (1991) 'Governmental Rationality'; Burchell (1996) 'Liberal Government and Techniques of the Self'; Thomas

Lemke (2001) '"The Birth of Biopolitics": Michel Foucault's Lecture at the Collège de France on Neo-liberal Governmentality', in: *Economy and Society*, 30, pp. 190–207; Mitchell Dean (1999) *Governmentality: Power and Rule in Modern Society*, London: Sage, pp. 40–59; Ute Tellmann (2003) 'The Truth of the Market', in: *Distinktion*, 7, pp. 49–63.

5. Foucault (2010) *The Birth of Biopolitics*, p. 13.
6. Foucault (2010) *The Birth of Biopolitics*.
7. Foucault (2010) *The Birth of Biopolitics*, p. 15.
8. Foucault (2010) *The Birth of Biopolitics*, p. 32.
9. Foucault (2010) *The Birth of Biopolitics*, p. 31.
10. Foucault (2010) *The Birth of Biopolitics*, p. 63.
11. Foucault (2010) *The Birth of Biopolitics*, pp. 63–64.
12. Foucault (2010) *The Birth of Biopolitics*, p. 63.
13. Foucault (2010) *The Birth of Biopolitics*, p. 116.
14. Foucault (2010) *The Birth of Biopolitics*, p. 120.
15. Foucault (2010) *The Birth of Biopolitics*, p. 121. Walter Eucken, one of the early thinkers on ordoliberalism, makes the point that the 'positive economic constitutional politics' he propagates has less to do with protecting the market from the state than with using the state to protect the market against interest groups hostile to the market: 'The state cannot limit itself to permitting all men to do business, to removing obstacles to investment, licenses, banalités, ensuring economic freedom and right of abode, and avoiding state import bans; in other words, avoiding state closure measures and leaving the process of natural selection up to the price system of total competition. Instead, it is necessary to prevent the closure of markets by private power groups. What is the good of a state declaration of economic freedom when it is overturned in fact by the politics of power groups? What is the meaning of economic freedom when a rolling mill cannot be opened because the current economic syndicate deploys its political power to prevent it? Every obstacle to competition, every barrier of any sort; discounts for regular customers, exclusivity contracts, and cut prices against outsiders with the aim of destroying or scaring off, must be forbidden' (Walter Eucken (1959) *Grundsätze der Wirtschaftspolitik*, Reinbek: Rowohlt, p. 165).
16. Foucault (2010) *The Birth of Biopolitics*, p. 167.
17. Foucault (2010) *The Birth of Biopolitics*, pp. 171–174. Foucault is referring here to the position advanced by Friedrich August von Hayek in his book *The Road to Serfdom* (1944).
18. Alexander von Rüstow (1945/2001) *Das Versagen des Wirtschaftsliberalismus*, Marburg: H. Küpper, p. 113.
19. 'De-massification and de-proletarisation' and 'domestication of the current urban and industrial nomad' were the corresponding slogans. For Wilhelm Röpke, the aim was 'to eliminate the proletariat as a free class of short term wage earners and create instead a new class of workers who will become fully fledged citizens of a free society through property, reserves, embeddedness in nature and community, a share in responsibility, and fulfilling and

meaningful work' (Wilhelm Röpke (1950) *Ist die deutsche Wirtschaftspolitik richtig? Analyse und Kritik*, Stuttgart; reprinted in: Wolfgang Stützel et al. (eds) (1981) *Grundtexte zur Sozialen Marktwirtschaft: Zeugnisse aus zweihundert Jahren ordnungspolitischer Diskussion*, Stuttgart: Fischer, pp. 49–62, here: p. 59).

20. Foucault (2010) *The Birth of Biopolitics*, p. 143.
21. Foucault (2010) *The Birth of Biopolitics*, p. 147.
22. Foucault (2010) *The Birth of Biopolitics*, p. 148.
23. Foucault (2010) *The Birth of Biopolitics*, p. 241.
24. Foucault (2010) *The Birth of Biopolitics*, p. 148. Also see Röpke (1950) *Ist die deutsche Wirtschaftspolitik richtig?* p. 59.
25. Wilhelm Ropke (1950) *The Social Crisis of Our Time*, London: Hodge. Cited in Foucault (2010) *The Birth of Biopolitics,* p. 262.
26. This is not true of Milton Friedman's monetarism. Friedman, one of the most prominent representatives of the Chicago School, alongside Becker and Schultz, is bracketed out by Foucault in his lectures on US neoliberalism.
27. An attribute that Gary S. Becker accepts as a characterization of his research project: 'Economists can talk not only about the demand for cars, but also about matters such as the family, discrimination, and religion, and about prejudice, guilt, and love. Yet these areas have traditionally received little attention in economics. In that sense, it's true: I am an economic imperialist. I believe good techniques have a wide application. Adam Smith and many others believed that as well. On the other hand, my economic imperialism doesn't have anything to do with crude materialism or the view that material status is the sum total of a person's value. That view has much more in common with Marxist analysis' (Gary Becker (1993) 'Economic Imperialism' [Interview], in: *Religion & Liberty*, 3(2), www.acton.org/pub/religion-liberty/volume-3-number-2/economic-imperialism [15.03.2015]). See also Gerard Radnitzky and Peter Bernholz (eds) (1987) *Economic Imperialism:The Economic Approach Applied Outside the Field of Economics*, New York: Pwpa; Edward P. Lazear (2000) 'Economic Imperialism', in: *Quarterly Journal of Economics*, 115(1), pp. 99–146.
28. Foucault (2010) *The Birth of Biopolitics*, p. 218.
29. On the concept of methodological individualism, see Lars Udehn (2002) *Methodological Individualism: Background, History and Meaning*, New York: Routledge; Steven Lukes (1968) 'Methodological Individualism Reconsidered', in: *British Journal of Sociology*, 19, pp. 119–129.
30. See Gary S. Becker (1976) *The Economic Approach to Human Behavior*, Chicago: University of Chicago Press. The title expresses the programme clearly and distinctly. Popular introductions to the Economic Approach are provided by Richard B. McKenzie and Gordon Tullock (1978) *The New World of Economics: Explorations into the Human Experience*, Homewood, IL: Richard D. Irwin; and by David Friedman (1996) *Hidden Order: The Economics of Everyday Life*, New York: Harper Business.
31. Foucault (2010) *The Birth of Biopolitics*, p. 226.
32. Foucault (2010) *The Birth of Biopolitics*, p. 226. Foucault relies here on a summary of Becker's thought by the French economics writer Henri

Lepage (*Tomorrow, Capitalism: The Economics of Economic Freedom*, La Salle, IL: Open Court, 1982, Chapter 8); Becker's theory of the allocation of time and consumer behaviour is in Part 4: 'Time and Household Production' in *The Economic Approach to Human Behavior*, pp. 87–150.

33. Becker (1976) *The Economic Approach to Human Behavior*, pp. 4, 7; Gary S. Becker (1997) *The Economic Way of Looking at Life*. Nobel Lecture, December, in: *Nobel Lectures: Economics 1991–1995*, ed. Torsten Persson, Singapore: World Scientific, p. 38.

34. See Richard B. McKenzie and Gordon Tullock (1978) *The New World of Economics: Explorations into the Human Experience*, Homewood, IL: Richard D. Irwin.

35. Becker (1976) *The Economic Approach to Human Behavior*, pp. 5f.

36. Ingo Pies (1998) 'Theoretische Grundlagen demokratischer Wirtschafts- und Gesellschaftspolitik: Der Beitrag Gary Beckers', in: Ingo Pies and Martin Leschke (eds), *Gary Beckers ökonomischer Imperialismus*, pp. 1–29, here: pp. 9, 19.

37. Foucault (2010) *The Birth of Biopolitics*, p. 270.

38. Theodore W. Schultz (1982) *Investing in People: The Economics of Population Quality*. Berkeley, CA: University of California Press, p. 76.

39. Schultz (1982) *Investing in People*, pp. 13f.

40. Becker (1997) *The Economic Way of Looking at Life*, p. 46.

41. Becker (1976) *The Economic Approach to Human Behavior*, pp. 172f.

42. Foucault (2010) *The Birth of Biopolitics*, p. 229.

43. See Majia Holmer Nadesan (2003) 'Engineering the Entrepreneurial Infant: Brain Science, Infant Development Toys, and Governmentality', in: *Cultural Studies*, 16, pp. 401–432.

44. Foucault (2010) *The Birth of Biopolitics*, p. 228. I have explored this aspect more thoroughly elsewhere: see Bröckling (2010) 'Human Economy, Human Capital: A Critique of Biopolitical Economy'.

45. Foucault (2003) *Society Must be Defended*, p. 241.

46. Becker (1997) *The Economic Approach to Human Behavior*, p. 10.

47. Becker (1997) *The Economic Approach to Human Behavior*, pp. 9f.

48. On the juxtaposition of the sovereign that stands above the political order and those who are thrown back on their 'bare life' and excluded from the social order, see Giorgio Agamben (1998) *Homo Sacer: Sovereign Power and Bare Life*, Stanford, CA: Stanford University Press. For a critique of Agamben's blindness toward economics, see Bröckling (2010) 'Human Economy, Human Capital', pp. 248f., 264.

49. Theodore W. Schultz (1981) *Investing in People*, Berkeley, CA: University of California Press, pp. 25f.

50. Theodore W. Schultz (1980) 'Investment in Entrepreneurial Ability', in: *Scandinavian Journal of Economics*, 82, pp. 437–448, here: p. 443. See also Theodore W. Schultz (1975) 'The Value of the Ability to Deal with Disequilibria', in: *The Journal of Economic Literature*, XIII, pp. 827-846.

51. Friedrich August von Hayek (1982) *Law, Legislation and Liberty, Vol. 3: The Political Order of a Free People*, London: Routledge, p. 163.

52. Hayek (1982) *Law, Legislation and Liberty, Vol. 3*, p. 163.

53. Hayek (1982) *Law, Legislation and Liberty, Vol. 3*, p. 163.
54. Hayek (1982) *Law, Legislation and Liberty, Vol. 3*, p. 75.
55. Friedrich August von Hayek (1960) *The Constitution of Liberty*, London: University of Chicago Press, p. 59. Hayek contradicts elsewhere the attribute 'Darwinist': 'Even if one were inclined to emphasise the analogies to biological evolution, the theory of cultural evolution would have to be termed Lamarckian, not Darwinist, since it rests entirely on the transmission of acquired properties, which is completely negated by Darwinism at least in the modern version.' Hayek concedes however that, although genetic and cultural inheritance operate differently, the criterion of selection is the same: the reproductive advantage ((1996) 'Die überschätzte Vernunft', in: *Die Anmaßung von Wissen: Neue Freiburger Studien*, Tübingen: Mohr Siebeck GmbH, pp. 76–101, here: p. 85f.).
56. Friedrich August von Hayek (1996) 'Sozialismus und Wissenschaft', in: *Die Anmaßung von Wissen*, pp. 151–165, here: p. 159.
57. John N. Gray (1986) *Hayek on Liberty* (2nd edition), New York: Wiley-Blackwell, p. 38.
58. Friedrich August von Hayek (2002) 'Competition as a Discovery Procedure', in: *The Quarterly Journal of Austrian Economics*, 5(3), pp. 9–23, here: p. 13.
59. Hayek (2002) 'Competition as a Discovery Procedure', p. 9.
60. Hayek (2002) 'Competition as a Discovery Procedure', p. 13.
61. Hayek (1982) *Law, Legislation and Liberty, Vol. 3*, p. 78.
62. Friedrich August von Hayek (2014) 'The Meaning of Competition', in: *The Market and Other Orders: The Collected Works of F. A. Hayek, Vol. XV*, Chicago: University of Chicago Press, pp. 105–116, here: p. 115f.
63. Friedrich August von Hayek (1967/69) 'Principles of a Liberal Social Order', in: *Studies in Philosophy, Politics and Economics*, London: Routledge, pp. 160–177, here: p. 164.
64. Hayek (2002) 'Competition as a Discovery Procedure', p. 14f.
65. Hayek (1960) *The Constitution of Liberty*, p. 41.
66. Hayek (1996) 'Wissenschaft und Sozialismus', in: *Die Anmaßung von Wissen*, pp. 267–277, here: p. 272.
67. Friedrich August von Hayek (1939) *Freedom and the Economic System*, Public Policy Pamphlet No. 29, (ed. Harry D. Gideons), Chicago: University of Chicago Press, p. 10.
68. Hayek (1944), *The Road to Serfdom*, p. 31.
69. Friedrich August von Hayek (2001) 'Marktwirtschaft und Wirtschaftspolitik', in: *Wirtschaft, Wissenschaft und Politik: Aufsätze zur Wirtschaftspolitik* (Gesammelte Schriften in deutscher Sprache, Abt. A: Aufsätze, Vol. 6), Tübingen, pp. 3–14, here: p. 5f.
70. 'We would not call it interference if we oiled a clockwork, or in any other way secured the conditions that a going mechanism required for its proper functioning. Only if we changed the position of any particular part in a manner which is not in accord with the general principle of its operation,

such as shifting the hands of a clock, can it properly be said that we have interfered. The aim of interference thus is always to bring about a particular result which is different from that which would have been produced if the mechanism had been allowed unaided to follow its inherent principles. If the rules on which such a process proceeds are determined beforehand, the particular results it will produce at any one time will be independent of the momentary wishes of men' (Hayek (1982) *Law, Legislation and Liberty, Vol. 2: The Mirage of Social Justice*, London: Routledge, pp. 128f.).

71. Friedrich August von Hayek (2001) 'Strukturpolitik und Wettbewerbswirtschaft', in: *Wirtschaft, Wissenschaft und Politik*, Tübingen: Mohr Siebeck, pp. 15–29, here: p. 18.

72. Hayek (2001) 'Marktwirtschaft und Wirtschaftspolitik', p. 11.

73. Hayek (1982) *Law, Legislation and Liberty, Vol. 2*, p. 127.

74. Hayek (1967/69) 'Principles of a Liberal Social Order', p. 172.

75. Hayek (1982) *Law, Legislation and Liberty, Vol. 2*, p. 116.

76. Hayek (1982) *Law, Legislation and Liberty, Vol. 2*.

77. Hayek (1982) *Law, Legislation and Liberty, Vol. 2*, pp. 381f.; Hayek (1982) *Law, Legislation and Liberty, Vol. 3*, pp. 75f.

78. Hayek (1982) *Law, Legislation and Liberty, Vol. 3*, pp. 76f.

79. For a summary, see Milton Friedman (1962) *Capitalism and Freedom*, La Salle, IL: University of Chicago Press.

80. See David Friedman (1989) *The Machinery of Freedom: Guide to a Radical Capitalism* (2nd edition), La Salle, IL: University of Chicago Press.

81. See, above all, Murray N. Rothbard (1978) *For a New Liberty: The Libertarian Manifesto*, New York: MacMillan; Rothbard (1982) *Ethics of Liberty*, Atlantic Highlands: Humanities Press. In addition to these somewhat essayistic works, see Rothbard's main theoretical work: (1962) *Man, Economy, and State*, 2 vols, Princeton, NJ: D Van Nostrand.

82. See James M. Buchanan and Gordon Tullock (1962) *The Calculus of Consent: Logical Foundations of Constitutional Democracy*, Ann Arbor, MI: The University of Michigan Press; James M. Buchanan (1975) *The Limits of Liberty: Between Anarchy and Leviathan*, Chicago: University of Chicago Press.

83. See Gebhard Kirchgässner (2010) *Homo Oeconomicus: The Economic Model of Behaviour and its Applications in Economics and Other Social Sciences*, New York: Springer, Chapter 2.

THE FOUR FUNCTIONS
OF THE ENTREPRENEUR

'You know what anarchists have always believed.'

'Yes.'

'Tell me,' she said.

'The urge to destroy is a creative urge.'

'This is also the landmark of capitalist thought. Enforced destruction. Old industries have to be harshly eliminated. New markets have to be forcibly claimed. Old markets have to be re-exploited. Destroy the past, make the future'.[1]

It is generally agreed that entrepreneurial activity is economic activity. But not all economic activity is entrepreneurial. An obvious way of defining entrepreneurial activity as opposed to other types of practice is by consulting economics. Of particular relevance to a genealogy of the entrepreneurial self are those economic theories, mostly dating from the first half of the 20th century, that opposed the currently dominant neo-classical models of total competition with a dynamic understanding of market processes, featuring the entrepreneur as the dynamic agent. Of especial note here are the works of Ludwig von Mises, his student Israel M. Kirzner, also Joseph Schumpeter, Frank H. Knight, and, more recently, Mark Casson.[2] The common point of departure for these otherwise heterogeneous studies is the search for an economic explanation of profit.

Economics does not approach entrepreneurs as representing an historical ideal[3] or attempt to delineate a set of properties.[4] It is interested in them as a macroeconomic category: 'The entrepreneurs, capitalists, landowners, workers, and consumers of economic theory are not living men as one meets them in the reality of life and history. They are the embodiment of distinct functions in the market operations'.[5] A comparison of the relevant literature turns up accounts of the functions of enterprising activity that can be put into four basic categories: (1) entrepreneurs resourcefully take advantage of chances for profit; (2) they innovate; (3) they confront the insecurities of the economic process; and (4) they coordinate production and marketing.[6]

These functional definitions imply three distinctions to anterior functions. First, there are non-entrepreneurial *economic* functions, such as those of capitalists, land owners, employers, inventors and managers. The entrepreneur is often combined with these functions in the same person, but their significance in the economy is wholly distinct. Second, the entrepreneurial function is not restricted to the activities of independent businesspeople. Schumpeter goes further to affirm that it is not even contingent on the existence of the capitalist economic system. Enterprising activity can be undertaken by 'organs of a socialist community, lords of a feudal manor or the chieftains of a primitive tribe'.[7] The 'imposition of new combinations', as Schumpeter defines the function of the entrepreneur, is a type of behaviour fundamentally open to all, but is at the same time 'no career and generally no permanent state'.[8] Further, the function need not be embodied in a single human being; it can also be in an organization: 'Every social environment has its own ways of filling the entrepreneurial function'.[9] Third, the entrepreneur of the macroeconomists is not to be confused with the cold, calculating cost-benefit optimizer allocating scarce resources to the purpose of maximizing profit. This rationalist notion overlooks the unavoidable knowledge gap that conditions human behaviour, and therefore can explain neither the dynamics of the market nor profit. Entrepreneurial activity begins precisely where cost-benefit calculation stops and new possibilities for profit are discovered and exploited for the first time.

The entrepreneur as speculator

According to Ludwig von Mises, this speculative trait is constitutive of *homo agens*. By extending macroeconomics to a general *praxeology*, he at the same time defines human action in its entirety according to economic categories. Action is therefore by definition reasonable: 'The ultimate end of action is always the satisfaction of some desires of the acting man'.[10] The acting man sees a state that he views as more favourable than the given state, and his action is directed toward realizing the state desired. The most general pre-conditions for action are therefore dissatisfaction with the given state and the assumption that it can be removed or ameliorated by one's own actions. Which specific preferences the individual pursues are outside of the purview of the praxeology: 'It is not its task to tell people what ends they should aim at. It is a science of the means to be applied for the attainment of ends chosen, not, to be sure, a science of the choosing of ends'.[11] Of crucial importance is the presupposition that *all* activity is a choice between varyingly attractive alternatives and essentially egoistic ones, although this need not exclude being altruistic if it provides personal satisfaction. But since no choice is sure of success it is always a wager: 'Every action refers to an unknown future. It is in this sense always a risky speculation'.[12] Consequently, being a human being means being an entrepreneur.

Making the entrepreneurial function a general anthropological constant feeds into the process by which the market becomes the medium of all social integration. In a market economy characterized by private ownership of the means of production and by division of labour, everyone, according to Mises,

> acts on his own behalf; but everybody's actions aim at the satisfaction of other people's needs as well as at the satisfaction of his own. Everybody in acting serves his fellow citizens. Everybody, on the other hand, is served by his fellow citizens. Everybody is both a means and an end in himself, an ultimate end for himself and a means to other people in their endeavors to attain their own ends. This system is steered by the market. The market directs the individual's activities into those channels in which he best serves the wants of his fellow men ... Each man is free; nobody is subject to a despot. Of his own accord the individual integrates himself into the cooperative system. The market directs him and reveals to him in what way he can best promote his own welfare as well as that of other people. The market is supreme. The market alone puts the whole social system in order and provides it with sense and meaning.[13]

Such songs of praise are still in the style of Smith and the invisible hand, but Mises soon gives an activist turn to the classical liberal credo. The social synthesis provided by the market does not turn itself on automatically as soon as all obstacles are removed. It requires constant initiative and the willingness to take risks on the part of the protagonists, whom Mises characterizes as the comparative form of *homo agens* – 'those who have more initiative, more venturesomeness, and a quicker eye than the crowd, the pushing and promoting pioneers of economic improvement'.[14] Mises continues:

> The driving force of the market process is provided neither by the consumers nor by the owners of the means of production – land, capital goods, and labor – but by the promoting and speculating entrepreneurs. These are people intent upon profiting by taking advantage of differences in prices. Quicker of apprehension and farther-sighted than other men, they look around for sources of profit.[15]

The super-entrepreneurs are the more human humans, typifying the speculative aspect of human behaviour, the model of human perfection attained by self-perfection.

Although 'the innate and acquired inequality of men differentiates their adjustment to the conditions of their environment',[16] the humanizing effects of the market spirit are available to everyone, provided they are willing to act accordingly. Everyone who seizes opportunity is an entrepreneur:

> Each individual is free to become a promoter if he relies upon his own ability to anticipate future market conditions better than his fellow citizens and if his attempts to act at his own peril and on his own responsibility are approved by the consumers. One enters the ranks of the promoters by spontaneously pushing forward and thus submitting to the trial to which the market subjects, without respect for persons, everybody who wants to become a promoter or to remain in this eminent position. Everybody has the opportunity to take his chance. A newcomer does not need to wait for an invitation or encouragement from anyone. He must leap forward on his own account and must himself know how to provide the means needed.[17]

No one can ever rest on their laurels, since the tribunal of the market can neither condemn nor exonerate them once and for all. Taking a well-earned rest would result in losing ground.

Israel M. Kirzner, a pupil of Mises', takes up the latter's anthropological theory that 'men are not only calculating agents but are also alert to opportunities'.[18] Kirzner reinforces here Mises' emphasis on the speculative side of enterprising behaviour. The main type of opportunity is arbitrage – a price difference for the same commodity in different markets. The profit made by the entrepreneur is the result of the ability of the

> pure entrepreneur ... to discover and exploit situations in which he is able to sell for high prices that which he can buy for low prices ... It comes from discovering sellers and buyers of something he values most highly. The discovery of a profit opportunity *means the discovery of something obtainable for nothing at all.*[19]

The distinguishing feature of the entrepreneur is therefore his 'alertness': 'Entrepreneurship does not consist of grasping a free ten-dollar bill which one has already discovered to be resting in one's hand; it consists in realizing that it is in one's hand and that it is available for the grasping'.[20]

Alertness means being quicker than others, and, above all, 'spontaneous, undeliberate learning'. The information advantage needed for arbitrage profit is not dependent on 'deliberate search efforts' but on 'spontaneous discovery'.[21] '[E]ntrepreneurial alertness ... the ability to learn without deliberate search is a gift individuals enjoy in quite different degrees',[22] and therefore cannot be learnt or trained. Whether or not someone possesses alertness can only ever be known after the fact, once the person has turned out successful or otherwise. Kirzner nevertheless views the paradoxical task of promoting spontaneity as feasible, introducing what system theory calls context management and education theory since Maria Montessori refers to it as a prepared learning environment: only the market itself can provide the space of discovery; a space that must be designed (here Kirzner shows himself as an arch-liberal *political* economist) to reward alertness. Profit opportunities can only be recognized if they are allowed to subsist, instead of being eroded by taxes or blocked by state regulation:

> Since individuals obviously differ in their entrepreneurial alertness, it is clear that opportunities for social improvement will tend to be exploited most fruitfully if institutional arrangements can be patterned so as to translate such opportunities into opportunities that will be encountered by those whose entrepreneurial alertness is the most acute, the most sensitive, and the most accurate.[23]

The selection of entrepreneurs on the marketplace should not occur naturally but requires continuous incentive. Laissez-faire is not enough; alertness needs active stimulation. This too is a never-ending project.

The entrepreneur as innovator

Like Mises and Kirzner, Joseph Schumpeter also depicts the entrepreneur as someone breaking loose from familiar routines and blazing trails on their own. On the other hand, Schumpeter's entrepreneur is not so much an alert risk-taker as a creative destroyer and innovator. According to his now canonical definition, the function of the entrepreneur is

> to reform or revolutionize the pattern of production by exploiting an invention or, more generally, an untried technological possibility for producing a new commodity or producing an old one in a new way, by opening up a new source of supply of materials or a new outlet for products, by reorganizing an industry and so on.[24]

Whereas Kirzner and Mises' entrepreneur used an already existing imbalance to gain arbitrage profit, thereby causing changes that in theory lead toward balance, Schumpeter's innovator-entrepreneur 'disturbs the even flow of production and of the market by creating new ways of doing things and new things to do'.[25]

For Schumpeter, the crucial quality from an economic viewpoint was not inventiveness but the ability to establish 'new combinations' in production and distribution. For this reason, he emphasizes the role of power in entrepreneurial activity. Enterprise is a 'special case of the social phenomenon of leadership'.[26] The entrepreneur is distinguished from ordinary humanity by knowledge and understanding, but also, and more importantly, by force of will:

The leader type is characterized for one thing by a special way of looking at things. Less by intellect than by will (and, to the extent that he is character-ized by intellect, not merely by breadth or elevation but rather precisely by a particular narrowness), by the power to grasp very particular things and see them as real. Also by the capacity to go it alone and go before the others, to not feel uncertainty and resistance as opposing grounds, and so essentially by his effect on others; what we can call 'authority', 'gravity', 'command'.[27]

Schumpeter lionizes the entrepreneur into *the* hero of modernity. He is

exceptionally free of tradition and affiliation, he is the true severer of all connections, equally alien to the system of super-individual values as to the class he comes from and the class he is entering; he is the special trailblazer of the modern human and the capitalist, the individualist way of life, the sober habit of thought, the utilitarian philosophy – the first brain capable of reducing beefsteak and ideal to one common denominator.[28]

The entrepreneur mainly employs his heroic powers to overcome the kinds of difficulties that inevitably confront pioneers. Reliable information and agreed rules of engagement have been left behind at the frontier; there is no preset plan, the entrepreneur must create a new one, more error prone because it is an untested

representation of the represented ... Acting on the basis of it and conventional action are as different as *building* a path and *following* a path. And building a path is no more a heightened following than the imposition of new combina-tions is merely different in degree from repeating the conventional.[29]

The entrepreneur is not driven by hedonistic motives but by the desire for independence, for struggle and victory, for success, and finally by the joy of activity and creation.[30]

Schumpeter puts the entrepreneur in the context of a political anthropology that opposes dynamic leaders with the static led. In real people, the two properties can combine in different ways but in the economic process itself there are only innovators and imitators, either novel creation or routine, blazing a trail or following one – there is no third term. Economic develop-ment is advanced exclusively by the entrepreneurs while the others merely administer resources. The dominant semantic is that of mobilization: *plus ultra*, as Schumpeter writes, is the entrepreneur's motto – further beyond.[31]

The entrepreneur as risk bearer

Frank H. Knight defines the entrepreneurial function from the point of view of the uncertainty of human knowledge and action. He distinguishes two forms of contingency. On the one hand, there are risks, uncertainties, the probability of which can be objectively quantified. These can be absorbed by insurance or prevention and can therefore be treated as a simple cost element. On the other hand, there is 'pure uncertainty' which can't be insured for or prepared for because its frequency and parameters are entirely unknown.[32] The ability to cope with this form of uncertainty produces greater specialization of functions within a society, leading finally to the speciation of the entrepreneur. With this approach, Knight places more emphasis than Schumpeter, Mises and Kirzner on the way entrepreneurship founds and maintains institutions.

Knight's entrepreneur 'is simply a specialist in risk-taking or uncertainty bearing'.[33] This characteristic involves two aspects. First, because she produces for the market, she must make decisions based on future demand. Future consumer needs cannot be accurately foretold. Second, she has to direct the production process and the labour force, whose income uncertainty she temporarily alleviates by guaranteeing a set wage. Although she can influence workers' behaviour, she cannot control it completely, so here too the success of her efforts is uncertain. By bearing uncertainty, the entrepreneur performs the function of assuming responsibility. This function is inseparable from that of leadership. Knight writes:

> With human nature as we know it it would be impracticable or very unusual for one man to guarantee to another a definite result of the latter's actions without being given power to direct his work. And on the other hand the second party would not place himself under the direction of the first without such a guaranty ... The essence of enterprise is the specialization of the function of *responsible direction* of economic life, the neglected feature of which is the inseparability of these *two* elements: *responsibility* and *control*.[34]

This unity of responsibility and control is, for Knight, the essence of entrepreneurship. The paid manager who is not at least a partial shareholder in the company is not an entrepreneur because he directs but does not bear the economic consequences of his decisions.

Pure uncertainty is also the source of all profit. However, in Knight's conception, the amount left over for the entrepreneur after all contractual cost factors have been subtracted is not compensation for assuming the risks but rather the difference, resulting from uncertainty, between the expected and the actual value of the production factors. Profit only exists because economic activities take place in a constantly changing environment and so the results of different courses of action are unknown:

> Profit arises out of the inherent, absolute unpredictability of things, out of the sheer brute fact that the results of human activity cannot be anticipated and then only in so far as even a probability calculation in regard to them is impossible and meaningless. The receipt of profit in a particular case may be

argued to be the result of superior judgment. But it is judgment of judgment, especially one's own judgment, and in an individual case there is no way of telling good judgment from good luck, and a succession of cases sufficient to evaluate the judgment or determine its probable value transforms the profit into a wage.[35]

In other words, profit is a consequence of error. Only because a large number of people tend to misjudge the issue of uncertain actions and events can the luckier ones profit from them. By concentrating on uncertainty, Knight brings into relief the intuitive and decision-making aspects of entrepreneurial practice. Entrepreneurs are defined by their 'confidence in their judgment and disposition to "back it up" in action'.[36] They are willing to transform pure uncertainty into calculable risk where possible, while bearing in mind that success cannot be calculated with absolute accuracy. No enterprise can do without rational planning and control, but to be an entrepreneur, on Knight's definition, means hazarding uncertainty again and again.

The entrepreneur as coordinator

Entrepreneurs bear not only risks but also responsibility. They coordinate production processes and deploy workers, procure working capital and make strategic decisions. In short, entrepreneurs are to enterprises what the sovereign is to the state. The 'managerial revolution'[37] may have long since replaced the rule of the company owner, handing over organization and planning to administration employees and controlling experts. Yet, in times of crisis, it becomes apparent who is really holding the sceptre. To rephrase Carl Schmitt, the entrepreneur is he who decides when the company is in a state of exception.

The function of the entrepreneur as coordinator and decision-maker is at the heart of Mark Casson's work, who somewhat tones down the dramatics of the entrepreneurial decision by framing it as information economy. Casson's definition runs as follows: 'an entrepreneur is someone who specializes in taking judgmental decisions about the coordination of scarce resources'.[38] According to Casson, only individuals can really make decisions, whereas institutions can only do so by aggregating individual votes. Therefore, only individuals can be entrepreneurs, more specifically those individuals assuming decision-making functions within a social division of labour. Since economic decisions always relate to resource allocation, the main feature of Casson's entrepreneur is that she optimizes utility by *modifying* allocation, by the act of coordination. The entrepreneur is thus an 'agent of change'.[39] This definition of the entrepreneurial function presupposes that inefficiency is the rule and that there is always room for increasing efficiency and hence raising profits. A person just needs to know where it is. The preconditions, the main means of the entrepreneurial decision process, are therefore acquisition and processing of information. The entrepreneur is convinced she possesses more information or better combinations of information than the other economic actors and can consequently make decisions more appropriate to the situation. She believes she is right while the others are in error: 'Thus the essence of entrepreneurship is being different – being different because one has a different perception of the situation'.[40] Like Schumpeter's innovator, Casson's entrepreneur swims against the current and needs high self-confidence in order not to doubt her own estimations, which will only be taken up and imitated by others if they are successful. Of course, many people are convinced of the superiority of their decisions, but not all of them are capable of really attaining profit. The entrepreneur's decisions are wagers on the future; the referee is the market. The chances for future profit cannot be exactly predicted but uncertainty is nevertheless not incommensurable with reasonable decision making. The reasonable basis for entrepreneurial practice is based on a cybernetic model of 'contingency planning'. On the one hand, past decisions must be evaluated rigorously in order to learn from experience. On the other hand, different case scenarios need to be anticipated in order to prepare appropriate strategies to be implemented as soon as a particular case arises. The planning remains, however, incomplete and provisional. The options are revised based on new incoming information. The entrepreneur is, for Casson, an active planner – a function taken up in Hayek's version of the market as information processor. The active planner runs continuously through a cycle of decisions consisting of three stages: formulation of the decision problem; generation of the data; and execution of the decision.[41]

Gaining and retaining an information head-start incurs costs. To cover these, the entrepreneur needs information capital. Information access depends partly on social contacts, family or clubs and associations, which connect the entrepreneur to bearers of information. The entrepreneur must also take steps to protect his information from others. The law of optimal resource allocation also applies to information processing. This means that a person is acting enterprisingly when their spending harvests the highest possible return on investment, though without exceeding expectations. Because there is a market for the acquisition, processing and protection of information (as for other entrepreneurial activities), the entrepreneur can occasionally lower costs by outsourcing to specialists. Accordingly, one of the key entrepreneurial skills, in addition to foresight, imagination, negotiation and organization, is the ability to delegate tasks. Entrepreneurial coordination means, not least of all, deciding which employees and which outside providers can perform which tasks the most efficiently and inexpensively.[42]

The logic of entrepreneurial practice

The functions of the entrepreneur elaborated on in the texts referred to above cannot be sharply distinguished one from the other. Kirzner's *alertness* translates at least partially into Schumpeter's *innovation* and Casson's *utility-optimizing resource allocation*. The same applies to Schumpeter's *leadership*, Knight's *responsible leadership* and Casson's *coordination*, and to Knight's *bearer of uncertainty*, Casson's *allocation decisions* and Mises' *speculation*. The disparate definitions illuminate some of the different facets of one and the same behavioural disposition, overburdened by the authors with the status of universal traits of humanity, with the paradoxical twist of also being unequally distributed among human beings. These economists are delivering more than just a theoretical explanation for market success. By correlating economic success with specific types of behaviour, they are also prescribing the right way to lead a life. The analysis of entrepreneurial practice is inseparable from the implicit imperative directed at readers to adapt their own conduct to the model as closely as possible. Entrepreneurship is 'man's emergence from his self-incurred unproductivity', write Jan Masschelein and Maarten Simons in a new version of Kant's definition of enlightenment:

> Unproductivity is the inability to make use of one's own capital without direction from another. This unproductivity is self-incurred when its cause lies not in lack of human capital but in lack of resolution and courage to use it without direction from another. '*Have the courage to self-mobilise! Have the courage to use your own capital!*' is therefore the motto of entrepreneurship.[43]

The theories we have analysed above all distinguish the entrepreneurial function from that of the calculating, instrumentalist, rationalist manager. The economic historian Peter Temin writes: 'Entrepreneurs are the agents of change, managers of stability ... Entrepreneurs are needed to introduce new machines and engines; managers are needed to operate them. Entrepreneurs strike out into the unknown; managers implement the known'.[44] Max Weber was already thinking in terms of this dichotomy when he identified the capitalist entrepreneur as 'the only type who has been able to maintain at least relative immunity from subjection to the control of rational bureaucratic knowledge'.[45] The spirit of enterprise is not made flesh by the prudent bookkeeper weighing up debit and credit before every decision or the taylorist labour theorist seeking the *one best way*. Entrepreneurship finds its model rather in the artist genius, the resolute master strategist of war, the athlete going for gold.

Schumpeter adheres to Weber's theory of rationalization in believing that economic development will leave less and less space for entrepreneurial initiative and innovation, driving this capitalist strain of the revolutionary subject to extinction. The coming administered world neither needs nor can sustain heroes of creative destruction. As Schumpeter speculates:

> [r]ationalized and specialized office work will eventually blot out personality, the calculable result, the 'vision'. The leading man no longer has the opportunity to fling himself into the fray. He is becoming just another office worker – and one who is not always difficult to replace.[46]

Sixty years on, there are reliable indications that the reverse has occurred: the economic definitions of the entrepreneurial function have become the guiding light for private life as well as for governing, both on the micro and macro levels. Since the individual has become replaceable and indeed super-fluous, rigorously adjusting her conduct by the creative 'imposition of new combinations'[47] seems the only way to avoid being taken out of operation. The maxim of the entrepreneurial self today could read something like this: *if you are not prepared to throw yourself into the fray, you have already lost.*

Entrepreneurial initiative has come to be regarded as a universal therapy for everyone and everything and deficiency in entrepreneurial spirit as the cause of all ills. The spirit of enterprise is supposed to overcome economic stagnation and promote general prosperity, shaving away the bureaucratic crust and bursting political narrow-mindedness, pacifying society through the spirit of market exchange and leading all to final success and happiness. And what helps everyone should be available to everyone. The call to be enterprising is not limited to huge corporations and independent business-people. Even those who have nothing to bring to market but their own skin should be allowed to act enterprisingly. If only the invisible hand is allowed to guarantee the greatest happiness to the greatest number, as the proponents of market radicalism affirm, then everyone had better resign themselves to the state of general competition. To vary Kirzner's image: the 'alert' self-entrepreneur recognizes that he himself is the ten-dollar bill to be found and picked up.

Contemporary calls for the entrepreneurial self radicalize the dynamic moment elaborated on by the macroeconomists to the point where the only constant left to the individual is the necessity of constantly transform-ing herself to cope with the discontinuities and accelerating turbulence of the market. Willpower and audacity are no longer the opposite of cool calculation. The entrepreneur of her own self must combine the two. She must, above all, become alert, innovative and take on uncertainty; yet she should also possess minute self-control and clear-sighted planning, har-monizing creative non-conformity and pedantic stinginess in one person. The Australian sociologist Pat O'Malley reflects on this paradox when he construes the hybrid 'enterprising-prudent subject' as the final goal of neo-liberal social and self technologies. His conjecture is that enterprising and calculating types reinforce each other: 'Such subjects expend resources on the means of risk management from the surplus they create through the exercise of uncertainty'.[48] O'Malley's diagnosis corresponds to the conclusions being drawn in this book, though there is a difference in terminology. O'Malley equates being enterprising with acting under uncertain circumstances, thus rendering the 'new prudentialism' the necessary complement of the entrepreneurial spirit, whereas my claim is that entrepreneurial practice embraces both elements.

Common to all entrepreneurial activity is the logic of *pushing back limits* and *outdoing*. This means that entrepreneurship is determined by comparison. You only act enterprisingly when you are more innovative, alert, daring, self-responsible and more of a leader than all the others. The invocation of the entrepreneurial spirit is therefore inherently paradoxical. Everyone should become an entrepreneur; but if everyone really did, none of them would be. Individually, everyone *could* be, but not everyone together. This fact of a general possibility that can only be realized in a select few, forces the individual to self-optimize on the economic terms dictated by the entrepreneurial self, at the same time accusing those lagging behind of being personally responsible for their failure. No one is an entrepreneur all the time but everyone can and ought to work to increase their entrepreneurial virtues. Success at this can only be measured against the competition and therefore only temporarily. The fact that entrepreneurial qualities can only become manifest in comparison with others endows the practice with the character of a sporting competition. It is a contest no one is excused from, but not everyone plays in the same league. No matter how unequal the chances of climbing the ladder really are, every player can, in theory, improve her position, as long as she is more alert, innovative, self-reliant and assertive than the others. Inversely, everyone is threatened by descent, in the worst case by abyssal descent, if the competition starts overtaking. Since everyone's existence is at stake, there is not much room for playful levity and noble sportsmanship. As an ideal image everyone is supposed to model their own self on, the flipside of the entrepreneurial self is the image of fear. What everyone is supposed to become is at the same time what menaces everyone.

Notes

1. Don DeLillo (2003) *Cosmopolis*, New York: Picador, pp. 92f.
2. Ludwig von Mises (1996) *Human Action* (4th edition), San Francisco: Fox R Wilkes; Israel M. Kirzner (1973) *Competition and Entrepreneurship*, Chicago: University of Chicago Press; Israel M. Kirzner (1979) *Perception, Opportunity and Profit: Studies in the Theory of Entrepreneurship*, Chicago: University of Chicago Press; Joseph Schumpeter (1934) *The Theory of Economic Development: An Inquiry into Profits, Capital, Credit, Interest, and*

the Business Cycle, Cambridge, MA: Harvard University Press; Joseph Schumpeter (1928) Art. 'Unternehmer', in: Ludwig Elster, Adolf Weber and Friedrich Wieser (eds), *Handwörterbuch der Staatswissenschaften*, Vol. 8 (4th edition), Jena, pp. 476–487; Frank H. Knight (1921/1964) *Risk, Uncertainty, and Profit*, New York: Augustus M. Kelley; Frank H. Knight (1942) 'Profit and Entrepreneurial Functions', in: *The Journal of Economic History*, 2, pp. 126–132; Mark Casson (1982) *The Entrepreneur: An Economic Theory*, Oxford: Wiley-Blackwell; Mark Casson (2000) *Enterprise and Leadership*, Cheltenham: Edward Elgar. For a survey of the macroeconomic literature, see: Robert F. Hébert and Albert N. Link (1988) *The Entrepreneur: Mainstream Views and Radical Critiques* (2nd edition), New York: Praeger; Alberto Martinelli (1994) 'Entrepreneurship and Management', in: Neil J. Smelser/ Richard Swedberg (eds), *The Handbook of Economic Sociology*, Princeton, NJ: Princeton University Press, pp. 476–503; C. Mirjam van Praag (1999) 'Some Classic Views on Entrepreneurship', in: *De Economist*, 147, pp. 311–335.

3. For an historical-sociological approach to the figure of the entrepreneur, see: Werner Sombart (1915) *The Quintessence of Capitalism: A Study of the History and Psychology of the Modern Business Man*, New York: T. Fisher Unwin; Werner Sombart (1909) 'Der kapitalistische Unternehmer', in: *Archiv für Sozialwissenschaft und Sozialpolitik*, 29, pp. 689–758; Werner Sombart (1913) *Der Bourgeois: Zur Geistesgeschichte des modernen Wirtschaftsmenschen*, Munich/ Leipzig: Facsimile; Fritz Redlich (1949) 'The Origin of the Concepts of "Entrepreneur" and "Creative Entrepreneur"', in: *Explorations in Entrepreneurial History*, 1(2), pp. 1–7; Fritz Redlich (1949) 'The Business Leader in Theory and Reality', *American Journal of Economics and Sociology*, 8(3): 223–237; Fritz Redlich (1959) 'Entrepreneurial Typology', in: *Weltwirtschaftliches Archiv*. 82, pp. 150–168; zur Begriffsgeschichte vgl. Hans Jaeger (1990) Art. 'Unternehmer', in: Otto Brunner, Werner Conze and Reinhart Koselleck (eds), *Geschichtliche Grundbegriffe: Historisches Lexikon zur politisch-sozialen Sprache in Deutschland*, Vol. 6, Stuttgart: Klett-Cotta, pp. 707–732; Sophie Boutillier and Dimitri Uzunidis (1999) *La légende de l'entrepreneur*, Paris: Syros; Sophie Boutillier and Dimitri Uzunidis (2006) *L'aventure des entre-preneurs*, Paris: Group Studyrama.

4. On the psychology of the entrepreneur, see the already classic works by David C. McClelland (1961) *The Achieving Society*, Princeton, NJ: Van Nostrand, pp. 205–300; David C. McClelland (1972) *The Achievement Motive*, New York: John Wiley; David C. McClelland (1987) 'Characteristics of Successful Entrepreneurs', in: *Journal of Creative Behavior*, 21, pp. 219–233; Manfred F. R. Kets de Vries (1977) 'The Entrepreneurial Personality: A Person at the Crossroads', in: *The Journal of Management Studies*, 14, pp. 34–57; Elizabeth Chell, Jean Haworth and Sally Brearly (1991) *The Entrepreneurial Personality: Concepts, Cases and Categories*, London/New York: Cengage.

5. Mises (1996) *Human Action*, p. 251.

6. These distinctions have already been made by the social historian Werner Sombart, who undertakes, 'in the face of [his own] enormous opposing

doubts', 'to name several functions, which we see reappear everywhere, in larger or smaller proportions, where entrepreneurial activity occurs and to construct out of them all something like the typical entrepreneurial function as a whole'. Sombart's 'modern omni-entrepreneur' unites the 'human types' of the inventor, the discoverer, the conqueror, the organizer, the speculative calculator and the 'negotiator' ((1909) *Der kapitalistische Unternehmer*, pp. 724ff.).

7. Schumpeter (1934) *The Theory of Economic Development*, p. 111.
8. Schumpeter (1934) *The Theory of Economic Development*, p. 116.
9. Joseph Schumpeter (1949/1991) 'Economic Theory and Entrepreneurial History', in: Richard V. Clemence (ed.), *Essays on Entrepreneurs, Innovations, Business Cycles, and the Evolution of Capitalism*, New Brunswick/London: Transaction, pp. 253–271, here: p. 260.
10. Mises (1996) *Human Action*, p. 19.
11. Mises (1996) *Human Action*, p. 10.
12. Mises (1996) *Human Action*, p. 106.
13. Mises (1996) *Human Action*, p. 257.
14. Mises (1996) *Human Action*, p. 255.
15. Mises (1996) *Human Action*, p. 328.
16. Mises (1996) *Human Action*, p. 328.
17. Mises (1996) *Human Action*, p. 313.
18. Israel M. Kirzner (1978) *Perception, Opportunity and Profit: Studies in the Theory of Entrepreneurship*, Chicago: University of Chicago Press, p. 7.
19. Israel M. Kirzner (1973) *Competition and Entrepreneurship*, Chicago: University of Chicago Press, p. 48. An examination of Kirzner from a cultural-sociological perspective is undertaken by Don Lavoie (1991) 'The Discovery and Interpretation of Profit Opportunities: Culture and the Kirznerian Entrepreneur', in: Brigitte Berger (ed.), *The Culture of Entrepreneurship*, San Francisco: ICS Press, pp. 33–51.
20. Kirzner (1973) *Competition and Entrepreneurship*, p. 47.
21. Kirzner (1978) *Perception, Opportunity and Profit*, p. 148.
22. Kirzner (1978) *Perception, Opportunity and Profit*.
23. Kirzner (1978) *Perception, Opportunity and Profit*, p. 149.
24. Joseph Schumpeter (1976) *Capitalism, Socialism and Democracy*, London: Harper, p. 132.
25. See Kirzner (1973) *Competition and Entrepreneurship*, p. 79.
26. Schumpeter (1928) Art. 'Unternehmer', p. 482.
27. Schumpeter (1934) *The Theory of Economic Development*, pp. 128f.
28. Schumpeter (1934) *The Theory of Economic Development*, p. 134.
29. Schumpeter (1934) *The Theory of Economic Development*, pp. 124f.
30. Schumpeter (1934) *The Theory of Economic Development*, pp. 138f.
31. Schumpeter (1934) *The Theory of Economic Development*, p. 137.
32. See Knight (1921/1964) *Risk, Uncertainty, and Profit*, pp. 197ff. Niklas Luhmann took up Knight's distinction between risk and 'pure' uncertainty as the basis of his (1993) *Risk: A Sociological Theory*, New York: De Gruyter.

33. Knight (1942) 'Profit and Entrepreneurial Functions', p. 129.

34. Knight (1921/1964) *Risk, Uncertainty, and Profit*, pp. 270f.

35. Knight (1921/1964) *Risk, Uncertainty, and Profit*, p. 311.

36. Knight (1921/1964) *Risk, Uncertainty, and Profit*, p. 270.

37. Taken from the title of James Burnham's (1941) bestseller *The Managerial Revolution: What is Happening in the World?* New York: Penguin.

38. Casson (1982) *The Entrepreneur*, p. 23.

39. Casson (1982) *The Entrepreneur*, p. 24.

40. Casson (1982) *The Entrepreneur*, p. 14.

41. Casson (1982) *The Entrepreneur*, p. 29.

42. This was already a central thesis of Ronald H. Coase, formulated in his basic text of institutional economics: (1937) 'The Nature of the Firm', in: *Economica*, 4, pp. 386–405. See also the following chapter of the present book.

43. Jan Masschelein and Maarten Simons (2005) *Globale Immunität oder Eine kleine Kartographie des europäischen Bildungsraums*, Zurich/Berlin: Diaphanes, pp. 84f.

44. Peter Temin (1991) 'Entrepreneurs and Managers', in: Patrice Higonnet, David S. Landes and Henry Rosovsky (eds), *Favorites of Fortune: Technology, Growth, and Economic Development since the Industrial Revolution*, Cambridge, MA: Harvard University Press, pp. 339–355, here: pp. 339f.

45. Max Weber (1978) *Economy and Society*, Berkeley, CA: University of California Press, p. 225.

46. Schumpeter (1976) *Capitalism, Socialism and Democracy*, p. 133.

47. Schumpeter (1926) *Theorie der wirtschaftlichen Entwicklung*, p. 125.

48. Pat O'Malley (2000) 'Uncertain Subjects: Risks, Liberalism and Contract', in: *Economy and Society*, 29, pp. 460–484, here: p. 480.

5

THE CONTRACTUAL WORLD

Would you consider undertaking a joint venture with yourself?

A hen chicken proposes a joint venture to a pig. The pig asks the hen what they would produce together. The hen answers: ham and eggs. Impressed by the market, the pig falls into a long meditation. Then, finally, it has an important idea: but that would mean that I get slaughtered and you'd be doing better than ever. The hen answers nonplussed: what do you expect? That's the whole point of a joint venture.

You start a joint venture only if you are a hen, but if you do a joint venture with yourself then you're also the pig.[1]

There are contracts everywhere in everyday life: contracts of purchase, rent, employment, insurance, schooling, marriage, security pacts and peace treaties regulate all manner of relations among individuals and organizations. Without contracts, there would be no market economy. The modern state bases its legitimacy on the fiction of the social contract. Law, at least civil law, can be regarded as an institution for regulating and safeguarding contractual arrangements. Lastly, according to contemporary self-management literature, we would all do well to structure our relations to ourselves like contracts. Is 'society', the object of sociology, nothing more than the effect of contractual relations?

This at least was the liberal utopia of the 19th century, ranging from Herbert Spencer's 'industrial type of society' in which 'the power and range of authority decrease while uncontrolled action increases' until 'the relation of contract becomes general',[2] to the anarchist programme for liberating society from the state, a programme which opposed the principle of free association to the force of law, extolling social cohesion as the network of voluntary arrangements able to be rescinded at any time among autonomous individuals and groups. Proudhon writes: 'In place of laws, we will put contracts. No more laws voted by a majority, not even unanimously; each citizen, each town, each industrial union, makes its own laws. In place of political powers, we will put economic forces'.[3] There are many different discourses of the contract: the state as adjudicator and protector of the freedom to engage in contract, or as something that should be abolished altogether, or the unfettered 'struggle for existence' Spencer propagates, demanding that 'the superior shall have the good of his superiority; and the inferior the evil of his inferiority',[4] or the version of Kropotkin, who founds free association on the communist principle 'All belongs to all'.[5] In all these cases, the principle of contract always stood for progress, the free balance of interests, equality and self-determination. It was the positive alternative to bureaucratic regimentation, authority and force. Manchester liberals and libertarian communists alike agreed that 'the movement of the progressive societies has hitherto been a movement *from Status to Contract*'.[6] Spencer put his faith in the unstoppable tendency of society toward a 'universal relation of contract' with an emphatic affirmation of natural selection by the market. The entrepreneurial self is contained in inchoate form in Spencer's theory:

> If each as producer, distributor, manager, adviser, teacher, or aider of other kind, obtains from his fellows such payment for his service as its value, determined by the demands, warrants; then there results that correct apportioning of reward to merit which ensures the prosperity of the superior.[7]

By framing all action as market action involving contracts between market participants, the call to be entrepreneurial makes the contract appear as *the* fundamental social institution. On the same logic, the purpose of all human activity is to maximize utility, and entering into contracts in particular incurs costs, so contractual relations are the privileged purview of economic analysis. Conversely, regarding all social relations as contractual relations makes it possible to analyse them economically, which in turn has the practical, performative effect of making all contracts subject to an economic explanation. This is precisely what transaction cost economics and James M. Buchanan's theory of the social contract, which will be discussed in the following sections of this chapter, proceed to do. Before we turn to that, however, we must make several remarks on the current expansion of contractual relations.

Expansion and multiplication of the contract

The evolutionary certainties and revolutionary hopes of the 19th century have largely evaporated, but the faith in contractual reason has stayed, establishing itself as a model of social relations that has shaken off the dense aura of modernist philosophies of history and utopian hopes of redemption. The contractual arrangements between institutions were formerly held up by rigid hierarchies and regimes of discipline within the institutions themselves. Now, the current politics of the contract permeates those institutions that were once homes of hierarchical authority: the family, the school, state administration, the company.

An example of this change is the plethora of bestsellers on raising children that emerged in the 1970s, advising stressed parents not to assert authority when fighting with their progeny but instead to convene a 'family conference'[8] to negotiate cohabitation rules acceptable to all parties, thus replacing disciplinary sanctions with a contract pedagogy. This starts with the very youngest, with today's kindergarten teachers nurturing their charges' social competence. The obligatory daily sitting together on the floor session, the infant version of the round table, is dedicated to working out the social contract intended to guarantee peaceful co-existence in the playground. Older children are equipped with a 'school contract' intended to ensure a sense of community harmony and wellbeing:

> In the contract the students promise each other they will be friendly and courteous, will not commit acts of violence or scare each other. The teacher, school head and parents are co-signatories. Children who do not adhere to the terms of the contract will be reminded of their responsibility to do so by the head teacher.[9]

This educational programme could be entitled *Applied Hobbes for Children*.

Contracts regulating economic relations are nothing new. Paid work presupposes an employment contract, while an exchange of goods presupposes a contract of purchase. For a long time, however, the order of the market and the factory followed opposing rationales. On the formal model, the labour market was a place for sellers and buyers of labour to meet as free and equal contract partners. This freedom and equality ended at the factory gates. Signing a work contract meant subordinating yourself for the duration of the work day to the commands of the wage payer. Today, the spheres of production and trade are generally regarded as working in the same way. The factory is no longer 'governed' by authority and discipline, but rather by the invisible hand of the market, and this means by contracts. According to the credo of 'management by objectives', production goals are better achieved when not simply decreed by management but rather negotiated with employees. The resulting agreements lead to a more sustained sense of duty than does a regime of orders and controls. This principle of 'intrepreneuring' effectively inverts the company's external contract relations, extending them to its internal structure. Every employee is turned into an autonomous 'profit centre', entering into trade and cooperation contracts with other such centres analogous to the way the enterprise as a whole does with its customers and suppliers. Properly entrepreneurial are those employees who manage to prevail on the internal and external markets by entering into more profitable contracts than the competition. Alertness, innovation, risk-taking and the other entrepreneurial virtues are ineffectual if not given tangible form in the contract.

The extent to which contractual reason has penetrated state bureaucracy is demonstrated by a change in semantics. Citizens are no longer social welfare recipients, unemployed or tax payers; in short, applicants. Instead, they walk into service centres, agencies and government offices as customers. State agencies have adopted the trappings of the service sector, with many functions outsourced to private enterprise by the government for budget reasons. In the USA and Great Britain, prisons are run often entirely as private enterprises, receiving their customers from the courts and putting them away at a lower fee than state penal institutions. Hierarchical directives are replaced by service agreements between and within government departments and between government and NGOs or private companies. Despite the invocation of a new contract culture, arrangements between the service state and its citizen customers are asymmetrical. One contract partner decides when a contract is sealed and lays down the conditions to which the other side must adhere. The form of contractual arrangement also varies and there is a consistent tendency to objectify and quantify the terms of fulfilment. The 'customer' obtains thereby a new power. She is no longer at the mercy of the authorities, since she can assert legal rights, yet at the same time she is subject to the power of experts who define in minute detail the terms under which her claims are valid.

The extension of the contract principle to relations that were not previously regulated in this way both adds to and subtracts from the substance of the contract. A standard German encyclopaedia, the *Brockhaus*, defines the contract as 'a legal transaction between two or more parties involving proposal and acceptance'. The new development leads to a proliferation of such transactions, expanding the domain of contractual relations. The rule of law, which guarantees enforcement and resolves conflicts of interpretation, is replaced by autonomous specialist systems – what have been called 'private governance regimes' – which assume, 'in new forms and contexts, the legislative, administrative, regulatory and conflict-resolution functions formerly fulfilled by classical law'.[10] These include swap meets and branch-specific mediation centres as well as mafia-like networks with armed agents for encouraging contract acceptance. When parties fail to adequately fulfil the terms of the contract, the task of third-party enforcement is no longer assumed by the government.[11] The contract becomes a hybrid; it 'is splintered into a number of different operations in closed systems. It is transaction, production and debt relation all at once. But it is also something else, the interstices between the various systems of acts'.[12] The cohesion of these 'autonomous chains of events in the legal system, the economic system and the production system'[13] is no longer guaranteed by a sovereign power enforcing the right of law. Instead, it must be continually reinstated from scratch by a ceaseless work of translation between participating systems.

On the other hand, the new contractualism elevates a specific type of contract, the commercial contract, as the paradigm for all types of contract, indeed for all social activity, systematically excluding alternative traditions of contractual thought and practice and all dimensions irreducible to the economic function. The axiom of contractualism is that it is reasonable to make contracts because they ensure the efficient allocation of resources and keep transaction costs low. Spencer's liberal vision of a universal 'exchange of services under agreement'[14] is enjoying a renaissance, while the communist mutualism of the anarchists has been largely forgotten.

Transaction economics

Contracts organize economic transactions. Inversely, the problems of economic organization can be framed as contract problems. Such is the approach of the new institution economics,[15] in particular transaction cost theory, that it reduces the entire spectrum of economic cooperation, 'from discrete market exchange at the one extreme to centralized hierarchical organization at the other, with myriad mixed or intermediate modes filling the range between',[16] to the form of contract, evaluating each instance according to its ability to save transaction costs. Enterprises and other organizations can be taken in this way as bundles of contracts regulating internal decision making, hierarchy, rights of property, work times, work productivity and payment. In other words, the contract is the *tertium comparationis* of comparative institutional analysis.

In their article 'Production, Information Cost, and Economic Organization', a key text from institutional economics, Armen A. Alchian and Harold Demsetz subsume all formal organizations under the contractual model. On their account, in terms of the power to enforce demands, enterprise is not distinguished 'in the slightest degree from ordinary market contracting between any two people'.[17] Just as a dissatisfied customer has the power to no longer purchase a seller's goods, the entrepreneur has no other power over employees than to cancel the employment arrangement: 'Telling an employee to type this letter rather than to file that document is like my telling a grocer to sell me this brand of tuna rather than that brand of bread. I have no contract to continue to purchase from the grocer and neither the employer nor the employee is bound by any contractual obligation to continue their relationship.'[18] By framing relations of subordination and control as contractual, Alchian and Demsetz flatten the difference between hierarchic organization and free competition. They are now no longer two opposing models of social relations but rather the extreme ends of a continuum of 'organisational contracting'. A business is nothing other than a 'privately owned market',[19] not a means of production but one form of governance that must compete against others.

Economic transactions take place between the poles of public and private markets, between centralized and decentralized decision making, contracts of purchase and contracts of labour, activated and deactivated price mechanisms.

Collecting all the diverse forms of organization under the heading of contract as their constituting and sustaining principle makes it possible to describe the choice between different contractual arrangements as consisting in a cost-benefit analysis. This theoretical step entrains practical consequences. To frame hierarchies, markets and collaborations as types of trade relation means investing social institutions with the logic of competition. This implies in turn that such institutions can legitimately be subjected to permanent evaluation on economic terms. Different types of cooperation incur different transaction costs. For economists, costs are simply the opposite of preferences, because they place restrictions on the satisfaction of individual needs and desires, for which reason the aim is always to lower costs. Transaction costs are like friction in physics. They encompass all the expenses incurred by the preparation, negotiation, performance and adjustment of acts of exchange, as well as search and information costs, costs of decision making and controlling and, finally, costs of enforcing contracts, including the potential costs incurred in the case of bankruptcy of the contract partner.[20] Entrepreneurial practice is focused on negotiating more favourable contractual conditions, part of which is selecting the form of cooperation that incurs the least transaction costs. The competitive edge goes to the one who decides more skilfully than the competition which goods and services to obtain from the market and which to obtain from inside the company, and which organizational structure to impose on the company. 'Make or buy?' is the question when considering any input factor. The answer supplies the 'new categorical imperative' that extends the principle of choice to economic organization: 'act only on that maxim that at the same time reduces your transaction costs'.[21]

Transaction cost theory systematizes the diversity of exchange processes and types of contract, providing general criteria for the economic optimization of contractual arrangements. These criteria vary, among other factors, according to the specificity, the degree of uncertainty and the frequency of the agreed transactions.[22] Generally speaking, a low specificity of the exchanged goods and services indicates a market exchange, whereas a high specificity indicates a transaction within the company. When buyer and seller only meet once, they will include more provisos than would contractual partners doing business long term. The most cost-effective contractual arrangement cannot be determined in advance, if only for the reason that the transaction costs cannot be pre-calculated with exactitude. If at all, it can only be calculated after the fact why one contract was more effective than another. Like any entrepreneurial decision, the choice of a particular type of contract demands a mixture of skill and luck and its rightness is only ever measurable in comparison to the competition.

Gunther Teubner objects to the view in transaction economics that contract and organization are indistinct, asserting that they involve fundamentally diverse types of act. The contract is a case of exchange, whereas organization is a case of cooperation. The two therefore represent 'two autonomous, autopoietic social systems of a second order, that differ principally not just gradually by the intensity of the governance structures'.[23] This is certainly accurate as a definition of social phenomena. However, Teubner goes no further than the accusation of reductionism and the 'coercion of economic thinking'.[24] The demonstration that this thinking is deficient does not change the fact that it is has a powerful effect on individuals' behaviour and on social institutions. At this point, Teubner's theory of social systems and the present analysis of the rationale and practices of governing part ways. It is one thing to analyse the specific difference between the social relations 'contract' and 'organization' (networks being the reincarnation of this distinction in both markets and hierarchies), and quite another to study how the imperative to 'lower transaction costs!' obtains legitimacy and effectively transforms social relations into contracts. The 'coercion of economic thinking' that Teubner laments consists indeed in theoretically oversimplified, compulsive ideas but, above all, in thought patterns capable of exerting coercive power. It may be that the specific character of organization is missed by describing it as contract, but organizations are altered by believing this false interpretation of them.

An economic theory of the social contract

Public choice theory and *constitutional economics* also adopt the view that organizational problems are contractual problems, and contracts strictly an issue of economic efficiency. By thus deriving political institutions from economics, they reformulate the notion of the social contract. For James M. Buchanan, one of the main proponents of the school, the economy is more 'a "science of contract" than a "science of choice"'.[25] Buchanan explains the emergence of property rights, states and constitutions using the hypothetical model of a contractual agreement between rational individuals motivated by self-interest.[26] Like all social contract theorists, Buchanan is concerned to justify a certain political order, in this case constitutional democracy. In doing so, he relies not on transcendental norms such as natural justice or religion, but rather follows the premise from methodological individualism that human action is exclusively motivated by personal interest. On this view, consensus is a type of calculation, a weighing up of such personal interests, and does not depend on an antecedent commonality of interest.

In relinquishing metaphysical foundations, Buchanan is following Hobbes. However, in contrast to Hobbes, he sees the foundation of state power not in people's fear of each other's violence in the state of nature, but rather, closer to Locke: 'from the wish to secure property, avoid conflicts over ownership und guarantee unhindered economic exchange'.[27] The lines of his argument converge on the notion of the 'ordered anarchy' of the market, which in Buchanan's opinion provides the 'maximal scope for private, personal eccentricity, for individual freedom in its most elementary meaning', by ensuring that

> Individuals can deal with one another through wholly voluntary behaviour without coercion or threat. They can enter into and complete exchanges without detailed knowledge of the political persuasions, sexual attitudes, or economic statuses of their actual trading partners. The traders may be unequal in any or all of such descriptive characteristics, yet they can and do deal with one another as equals in the exchange itself. In this classic sense, economic exchange is wholly impersonal, which seems to be precisely the ideal-type interaction embodied in ordered anarchy. Each person is treated strictly as he is, and presumably as he wants to be, in such a relationship. The fruit stand operator may beat his horse, shoot dogs, and eat rats. But none of these qualities need affect my strictly economic trade with him.[28]

If individual freedom is the highest aim and the market the best means to its attainment, then the necessary preconditions for market cooperation must be created and hindrances removed. Friction-reduced exchange requires, above all, clearly defined property rights – if people want to buy and sell things they must know what belongs to whom – and political institutions to guarantee them. Without this secure right of property, there would be no exchange – just violent expropriation and the counter-violence necessary to defend against it. Buchanan bases his theory on the hypothetical assumption of such a state of affairs, characterized more by permanent conflict than by scarcity. This pre-contract state, parallel to Hobbes' war by all against all, forces people to expend great efforts to defend 'their' goods and conquer 'alien' goods. These costs lead them finally to mutual recognition of property rights. Buchanan's individualist simply can't afford to go on living in a lawless state of nature. This applies not only to the weaker. For, according to Buchanan, the rule of law is first agreed on when the stronger also accepts by dint of reason that such agreement profits him by lowering his costs of conquest and defence.[29] The social contract is thus predicated on inequality, not equality. The stronger will not voluntarily bid farewell to arms until the distribution of goods has balanced out to a 'natural distribution' in accordance with people's different relative strengths. This asymmetrical equilibrium is attained when for all parties the marginal benefit of defence drops down to the level of its marginal costs:

> Law serves here to secure the unequal distribution anchored in the natural inequality of distribution of goods and the freedom to dispose of them. The fact that law does not eliminate the inequality of distribution, but instead

transforms the naturally occurring inequality in one secured by law results from the further fact that those disadvantaged by natural distribution also profit by disarmament and the establishment of rule by law.[30]

In contrast to Hobbes, Buchanan does not see law as originating in the sovereign decision of the Leviathan equipped with a mandate from the citizens. Law derives solely from the agreement of all citizens to lay down their arms. The ensuing state of peace is admittedly unstable; the situation resembles what game theory describes as the prisoner's dilemma: 'All persons will find their utility increased if all abide by the "law" as established. But for each person, there will be an advantage in breaking the law, in failing to respect the behavioural limits laid down in the contract'.[31]

   To solve this problem, Buchanan designs a multi-stage contract: the disarmament treaty is followed by a constitutional contract laying down the rule of law, specifying individual rights (especially property rights) and establishing the state as their impartial and powerful guarantor. This is called the protective state and is followed by post-constitutional contracts, dealing partly with the exchange of private goods and partly with the supply and financing of public goods. This is the productive state and provides the required material infrastructure. Both states are however concerned with the same problem:

> Which system of rules must be established to bring about a real and generally favoured improvement of the situation of natural distribution and private consumption? How can utility be increased by means of legal security or the availability of public goods?[32]

Buchanan's version of the social contract is no more an historical reconstruction than were its Hobbesian and Rousseauian predecessors. Like them, it seeks to lay the normative foundation for the state, claiming for its legal and political order the explicit consent of its subjects. This implies the view that social institutions issue from a contractual agreement because the contract provides the type of social cohesion that takes most account of individual preferences. The test of every law and every political decision is: does it agree with citizens' utility? Citizens consent to legal restrictions on their freedom from rational self-interest, preferring this to the alternative – the absence of property rights – as too costly and risky.

   Buchanan carries over the model of free exchange from economics to politics, treating economic and political action as parallel. To be more precise, he analyses political action as economic action. The two spheres of action can be 'regarded as strictly analogous as examples of competition the rules of which determine to what degree actors can contribute to social cooperation'.[33] Buchanan's version of economic imperialism not only extends the dominion of economic rationale, it also shifts its focus from a problem of maximization to that of coordination and thus of contractual agreement. The latter nevertheless remains subordinate to the principle of utility as the main motivation for action since the contract partners enter into a collective contract for their own individual purposes. The crucial shift in perspective consists in treating not only the individual moves in the game but also the collective negotiation of the rules as economic matters. In an early article, Buchanan rejects positing Robinson Crusoe alone on his island as the primal scene of economic theory. Economic action begins when he has company:

> The uniquely symbiotic aspects of behavior, of human choice, arise only when Friday steps on the island, and Crusoe is forced into association with another human being. The fact of association requires that a wholly different, and wholly new, sort of behaviour takes place, that of 'exchange', 'trade', or 'agreement' … Crusoe, if he chooses to avoid pure conflict, and if he realizes that Friday's interests are likely to be different from his own, will recognize that mutual gains can be secured through cooperative endeavor, that is through exchange or trade. This mutuality of advantage that may be secured by different organisms as a result of cooperative arrangements, be these simple or complex, is the one important truth in our discipline.[34]

In other words, contracts are always win–win situations. It is not a requirement that everyone profits in the same measure. But no one will agree to a contract if they expect to be worse off with it than they would be without it. By explaining state constitutions and rule by law in terms of an economic version of the social contract, citizenship is made to coincide with being an economic subject. This is not to reconcile an antagonism between politics and economics but rather to subsume the political under the economic. This move in Buchanan's constitutional economics morphs the human into the figure of the entrepreneurial self. Individuals act enterprisingly when they vote, pay taxes, fulfil mandates or even engage in political dissidence. In order to better pursue their individual interests, they create and alter social institutions that end up placing restrictions on that pursuit. Which rules of play they agree upon is a matter to be negotiated, but that rules need to exist at all is dictated by economic reason.

The anthropology of homo contractualis

To summarize the foregoing: the contemporary 'régime of contract'[35] accords with a theory of the human as a rational, calculating and self-serving being that is social entirely *because* it is self-serving, that chooses between alternatives and is made capable of organizing exchange with its fellows by binding agreements. For a human, to act socially at all means to negotiate.

In his transaction economics, Oliver E. Williamson sharpens this definition of the human condition, criticizing two assumptions about human
behaviour from classical and neoclassical economics. First, he replaces the
idea of a rational economic actor with that of one striving for maximal benefit but limited in the ability to attain it.[36] All actors fundamentally intend to
behave rationally but doing so remains an unattainable ideal. Rationality is
limited for one thing because no actor has access to all the information and
even if they did they could not fully process it. This assumption has practical
consequences. If rationality is sought after but cannot be absolutely obtained,
it becomes comparative. Acting rationally means acting more rationally than
the competition, with more forethought and more institutional backing.

Williamson's second assumption about human behaviour has to do with
the intensity with which people pursue their preferences. He proposes taking
opportunistic behaviour as the default setting, by which he means

> By opportunism I mean self-interest seeking with guile. This includes but
> is scarcely limited to more blatant forms, such as lying, stealing, and cheating.
> Opportunism more often involves subtle forms of deceit. Both active and
> passive forms and both ex ante and ex post types are included. More gen-
> erally, opportunism refers to the incomplete or distorted disclosure of
> information, especially to calculated efforts to mislead, distort, disguise, obfuscate,
> or otherwise confuse.[37]

People entering into contracts will consequently adopt security measures
to prevent their partner(s) behaving opportunistically. Since the available
information is incomplete, such measures are always fallible. All contract
partners have to weigh up the prospective gain against the security costs – a
procedure of margin benefits calculation subject to Williamson's original
principle of limited rationality. A 'contractual man'[38] knows that a contract
only comes about when all participants gain or at least avoid loss, but he also
knows that he can never be entirely sure he will not be deceived by the other
signees. He trusts his contract partners (or the institutional mechanisms for
enforcement) at least to the extent of agreeing to the contract while pre-
serving enough mistrust to not relinquish control. The anthropology behind
the world of contracts withholds judgement on whether humans are good
or bad by nature, while judging them fundamentally capable of every evil
due to the fact they are driven by interest.

In both the essentialist rendition and Williamson's tempered version, the
description functions as a prescription. Humans should adapt themselves to
what the theory assumes them to be already. This entails a criterion of exclusion from humanness. If all social relations are (or should be) based on the
form of the contract, the only genuine humans are those capable of acting in
this way, those who possess *capacity*, in the legal sense of the term. Governing
by contract presupposes subjects capable of governing themselves and by

presupposing them already begins to produce them. Since contracts imply consent, an order based on the contract obliges people to grasp themselves as the kind of responsible agents capable of consenting to enter into contracts and are also called upon to demonstrate their capacity to do so:

> To be a contractual person is to be socially positioned as one who enjoys a particular standing or status as an individual who is sufficiently autonomous as to be regarded as contractually capable, that is, as one who can assume responsibility for his or her own intentions, desire, choices and acts.[39]

It follows that contract capacity is to be regarded as a human capital that must be invested in. Therefore, the subject of the contract is a mode of subjectification that must be stimulated and nurtured by appropriate social technologies and technologies of the self. The prerequisites are not innate but must be acquired through incentives, which should be provided as soon as possible. The hegemony of the new contractualism manifests itself in at least two areas: first, the competency to enter agreements and adhere to them has become a basic component of most school syllabi and teachers are trained to foster it in pupils; and second, in old age all are expected to provide for the eventuality that they will no longer be able to express their will and enter contracts by signing a patient decree.

Individuals also demonstrate legal capacity by being the reliable contract partner of their own self, reconciling their various wishes and needs, setting clear goals, submitting to obligations to themselves, instead of being driven by unstable affects and passions. Inquiring after our own wishes and abilities, committing to goals, performing regular checks to see we're on track, enforcing contract fulfilment by self-imposed sanctions; all this constitutes a form of self-governing combining self-discipline and self-mobilization, where the self signs a contract with itself having itself as its object. Self-commitment thus becomes the continuation of the stoic art of living by contractual means.

Contracts can only be signed regarding matters the signees have control of. A function of the contractualist theory of human nature is therefore the notion of the human as property owner. The human is regarded as capable of entering contracts by virtue of legally possessing material goods, knowledge, abilities, a body, organs or a lifetime.[40] She is divided up into an aggregate of disposable property or capital and a legal subject to manage it, invest it and accumulate more of it, abstracting body, gender, biography and social context into the referent for a series of calculations, choices and promises to which she has the authority to set down the legally binding signature. This split self is a *real fiction* (see Chapter 1). It is a fiction because no actual person can perform such dissection in reality, yet it is real to the extent that it is performed in every contractual act. The split is necessary if the parties are to meet as equals. The equality of terms required for contractual agreements is predicated on the eradication of difference.

The current contractualism draws no small part of its attractive power from the democratic ethos of *liberté* and *egalité*. Anna Yeatman lists three essential principles inherent in the notion: 'informed consent, negotiation by mutual adjustment and accountability'.[41] The promise of universal free association that inheres in these principles is also behind the tendency to extend contractual logic into the furthest corner of social life. Yet where the contractualist programme seizes territory, from kindergarten to the United Nations, the freedom to enter contractual agreements actually turns into an obligation to do so.[42] At the same time, the formal equality of the contract partners consolidates and legitimates their real, material inequality. Contracts are power dispositifs, as Max Weber was well aware: 'The result of contractual freedom, then, is in the first place the opening of the opportunity to use, by the clever utilization of property ownership in the market, these resources without legal restraints as a means for the achievement of power over others'.[43]

The current demand that every person acts as the entrepreneur of their own self, dramatically increases the number of such opportunities. Entrepreneurial skill is demonstrated by those capable of concluding clever contracts to the end of maximal personal aggrandisement. Whether the result is that one party gains what the other loses or that all contract partners profit, possibly by gaining an advantage over third parties, the contract is always a move in a power play that shifts power relations in one direction or another. The fact that in contractualism freedom is here not defined as the opposite of power but rather the very medium of freedom justifies the assymetrical distribution of power by making it a point of general agreement. Because the 'contractual association'[44] makes exploitation and repression conditional on the consent of the exploited and repressed, none of them has cause for complaint: *coactus voluit*, having been forced, I was willing.[45]

Beyond contractual reason?

Spencer's assumption was: the more contracts the more progress. In contrast, Emile Durkheim emphasized that contracts are not self-sufficient but must rest on foundations that are not contractual.[46] Without a minimum degree of trust and safety from violence, exchange and cooperation would collapse. Society is not held together by an invisible hand weaving together diverse individual interests. Individuals must do the weaving themselves if they are to coordinate their interests: 'For where interest is the only ruling force each individual finds himself in a state of war with every other since nothing comes to mollify the egos, and any truce in this eternal antagonism would not be of long duration'.[47]

Durkheim opposes the liberal contract with a conception of the contract as corrective to the anomic tendencies of the self-regulating market. In liberal economic theory, as whose proponent Durkheim sees Spencer, the institution of the contract is limited to the following function: 'In the context of these theoretical premises, the contract and contract law have the function of guaranteeing the legal security of the market participants and thus excluding opportunistic behaviour, deceit, and violence'.[48] The theory further states that under the assumed condition of total competition, the antagonistic interests of the economic actors would be subject to pareto optimal adjustment via market price mechanisms. According to Jens Beckert, Durkheim determined the contract as

> the institution that transforms the antagonistic nature of market exchange into a venture aimed at society's notion of justice. To achieve this result, the institution of contract must connect the actors closely enough so that exchange partners agree to prices as defined by a just social order, which means a Pareto-inferior exchange of goods for at least one of the parties involved.[49]

Opposition among contract theories, between those based on individual interests and those based on norms of solidarity, continues to the present day. The new institutional economics colonizes the principle of a shared notion of justice emphasized by Durkheim by reformulating it as economic rationale. Contrariwise, contemporary economic sociologists, among them Mark Granovetter, discuss the problem of the non-contractual preconditions of contracts under the title embeddedness. On this account, economic behaviour, like any other human behaviour, can only be adequately described by taking the agents' social relations into account:

> Actors do not behave or decide as atoms outside a social context, nor do they adhere slavishly to a script written for them by the particular intersection of social categories that they happen to occupy. Their attempts at purposive action are instead embedded in concrete, ongoing systems of social relations.[50]

Granovetter arrives at a more pluralist conception of social connection than does Durkheim, emphasizing the function of informal networks and cultural contexts in bringing about and shaping contractual arrangements. There is not only one band of common values but rather many, continually rewoven by agents in different relations, with varying reach and durability, pre-forming the contracts of economic life. Granovetter deploys empirical studies to show that economic activity is particularly dependent on personal networks, and exclusive orientation on cost-benefit analysis can hinder entrepreneurial success.[51]

Granovetter's empirical demonstration that entrepreneurial activities and the contracts which express them are always socially situated and dependent on relations that cannot be assimilated entirely to the principle of utility maximization only holds up as an objection to explicit or implicit economic imperialism if its assumptions about human nature are understood as descriptive rather than prescriptive. Durkheim is more sceptical. While economic network theories are content to weaken the implications of *homo economicus* by pointing out the persistence of other forms of behavioural models, Durkheim sees in the project of turning society into an economy the peril of society's destruction. As soon as the contract principle exhausts the cohesion it needs but cannot itself generate, it is no longer able to create any kind of order at all. On this account, a society based on contracts alone ceases to be a society at all, becoming a state of anomie.

Notes

1. Händler (2002) *Wenn* wir *sterben*, pp. 454f.
2. Herbert Spencer (1900) *Principles of Sociology*, *Vol. 2*, New York: D. Appleton & Co., p. 611.
3. Pierre-Joseph Proudhon (2004) *General Idea of the Revolution in the Nineteenth Century*, New York: University Press of the Pacific, pp. 245f.
4. Spencer (1900) *Principles of Sociology*, *Vol. 2*, p. 610
5. Peter Kropotkin (1926) *The Conquest of Bread*, New York: Vanguard Press, p. 10.
6. Henry Sumner Maine (1861) *Ancient Law: Its Connection with the Early History and its Relations to Modern Ideas*, London: John Murray, p. 170.
7. Spencer (1900) *Principles of Sociology*, *Vol. 2*, p. 611.
8. Thomas Gordon (1970) *Parent Effectiveness Training: The Proven Program for Raising Responsible Children*, New York: Three Rivers Press.
9. Kirsten Wörnle (2002) 'Unterricht mit Schulvertrag', in: *Badische Zeitung*, 2 October, p. 19.
10. Gunther Teubner (1998) 'Vertragswelten: Das Recht in der Fragmentierung von Private Governance Regimes', in: *Rechtshistorisches Journal*, 17, pp. 234–265, here: p. 242.
11. See Claude Ménard (2000) 'Enforcement Procedures and Governance Structures: What Relationship?', in: *Institutions, Contracts and Organizations: Perspectives from New Institutional Economics*, Cheltenham: Edward Elgar, pp. 234–253.
12. Gunther Teubner (1997) 'Im blinden Fleck der Systeme: Die Hybridisierung des Vertrages', in: *Soziale Systeme*, 3, pp. 313–326, here: p. 314.
13. Teubner (1997) 'Im blinden Fleck der Systeme', p. 315.
14. Spencer (1900) *Principles of Sociology*, *Vol. 2*, p. 640.
15. For an overview, see Eirik G. Furubotn and Rudolf Richter (2005) *Institutions and Economic Theory: The Contribution of the New Institutional Economics* (2nd edition), Ann Arbor, MI: University of Michigan Press.

Talcott Parsons and Neil J. Smelser already stress the contract as the foundational economic institution in the title of the relevant chapter of their seminal work on the sociology of economics: (1956) 'Contract: The Central Economic Institution', in: *Economy and Society*, London: Routledge, pp. 104–139.

16. Oliver E. Williamson (1985) *The Economic Institutions of Capitalism: Firms, Markets, Relational Contracting*, New York: Free Press, p. 16.

17. Armen A. Alchian and Harold Demsetz (1972) 'Production, Information Cost, and Economic Organization', in: *American Economic Review*, 62, pp. 777–795, here: p. 777.

18. Alchian and Demsetz (1972) 'Production, Information Cost, and Economic Organization'.

19. Alchian and Demsetz (1972) 'Production, Information Cost, and Economic Organization', p. 795.

20. The concept is drawn from Ronald H. Coase, who discusses the problem of transaction costs (he refers to 'marketing costs') in connection with the genesis of firms: '[T]he operation of a market costs something and by forming an organisation and allowing some authority (an "entrepreneur") to direct the resources, certain marketing costs are saved. The entrepreneur has to carry out his function at less cost, taking into account the fact that he may get factors of production at a lower price than the market transactions which he supersedes, because it is always possible to revert to the open market if he fails to do this' ((1937) 'The Nature of the Firm', p. 392).

21. This ironic reformulation of transaction cost economics is from: Gunther Teubner (1992) 'Die vielköpfige Hydra: Netzwerke als kollektive Akteure höherer Ordnung', in: Wolfgang Krohn and Günter Küppers (eds), *Emergenz: Die Entstehung von Ordnung, Organisation und Bedeutung*, Frankfurt: Suhrkamp, pp. 189–216, here: p. 194.

22. See Williamson (1985) *The Economic Institutions of Capitalism*, pp. 52ff.

23. Teubner (1992) 'Die vielköpfige Hydra', p. 195.

24. Teubner (1992) 'Die vielköpfige Hydra', pp. 194f.

25. James M. Buchanan (1975) 'A Contractarian Paradigm for Applying Economic Theory', in: *The American Economic Review*, LXV, pp. 225–230, here: p. 229.

26. The following account of Buchanan's thought concentrates on his (1975) study, *The Limits of Liberty: Between Anarchy and Leviathan*. Buchanan had already developed an economic theory of the constitution in 1962 in *The Calculus of Consent*, written together with Gordon Tullock.

27. Kersting (1994) *Die politische Philosophie des Gesellschaftsvertrags*, Darmstadt: Auflage, p. 327.

28. James M. Buchanan (1975) *The Limits of Liberty: Between Anarchy and Leviathan*, Chicago: University of Chicago Press, p. 18.

29. Buchanan (1975) *The Limits of Liberty*, p. 35.

30. Kersting (1994) *Die politische Philosophie des Gesellschaftsvertrags*, p. 335.

31. Buchanan (1975) *The Limits of Liberty*, p. 26.

32. Kersting (1994) *Die politische Philosophie des Gesellschaftsvertrags*, p. 338.
33. Ingo Pies (1996) 'Theoretische Grundlagen demokratischer Wirtschafts- und Gesellschaftspolitik – Der Beitrag James Buchanans', in: Ingo Pies and Martin Leschke (eds), *James Buchanans konstitutionelle Ökonomik*, pp. 1–18, here: p. 9.
34. James M. Buchanan (1963/4) 'What should Economists do?', in: *The Southern Economic Journal*, XXX(3), pp. 213–222, here: pp. 217f.
35. Spencer (1900) *Principles of Sociology, Vol. 2*, p.638
36. Williamson (1985) *The Economic Institutions of Capitalism*, p. 45f. Williamson borrows the concept of 'bounded rationality' from: Herbert A. Simon (1972) 'Theories of Bounded Rationality', in: Charles B. McGuire and Roy Radner (eds), *Decision and Organization: A Volume in Honor of Jacob Marschak*, Amsterdam: North-Holland Pub. Co., pp. 161–176.
37. Williamson (1985) *The Economic Institutions of Capitalism*, p. 47.
38. Williamson (1985) *The Economic Institutions of Capitalism*, pp. 43ff.
39. Anna Yeatman (1997) 'Contract, Status and Personhood', in: Glyn Davis, Barbara Sullivan and Anna Yeatman (eds), *The New Contractualism*, Melbourne: Palgrave MacMillan, pp. 39–56, here: p. 41; see also Barry Hindess (1997) 'A Society Governed by Contract', pp. 14–26 in the same book.
40. This is the reason why a libertarian, radical pro-market economist like Murray N. Rothbard insists on understanding human rights as property rights:' in the most profound sense there *are* no rights but property rights … There are several senses in which that is true. In the first place, each individual, as a natural fact, is the owner of *himself*, the ruler of his own person. The "human" rights of the person that are defended in the purely free-market society are, in effect, each man's *property right* in his own being, and from *this* property right stems his right to the material goods he has produced' ((1970/2004) 'Power and Market', in: *Man, Economy, and the State with Power and Market*, Auburn, AL: Van Nostrand, pp. 1047–1369, here: p. 1337).
41. Anna Yeatman (1998) 'Interpreting Contemporary Contractualism', in: Mitchell Dean and Bary Hindess (eds), *Governing Australia: Studies in Contemporary Rationalities of Government*, Cambridge: Cambridge University Press, pp. 227–41, here: p. 231.
42. The philosopher Carole Pateman has examined the ambivalent effects of framing the individual as proprietor of her own self in her critique of feminist positions that expect a weakening of patriarchal power through the expansion of contractual and therefore consensual and egalitarian rules to marriage and intimate relationships. According to Pateman, the contractualist utopia of free arrangements, when it is consistently applied to relations between the sexes, flips over into the dystopia of universal commodification: 'The most advantageous arrangement for the individual is an endless series of very short-term contracts to use another's body as and when required. Other services presently provided within marriage would also be contracted for in the market. A universal market in bodies and services would replace marriage. The logic of contract is that marriage would be supplanted by contracts for access to sexual property. Marriage would give way to universal

prostitution. Moreover, "individuals", and not "men" and "women", would enter these Contracts. Contract would then have won the final victory over status (sexual difference) … The conclusion is easy to draw that the denial of civil equality to women means that the feminist aspiration must be to win acknowledgment for women as "individuals". Such an aspiration can never be fulfilled. The "individual" is a patriarchal category' (Carole Pateman (1988) *The Sexual Contract*, Stanford, CA: Stanford University Press, p. 184).

43. Max Weber (1978) *Economy and Society*, Berkeley, CA: University of California Press, p. 730.

44. Max Weber (1978) *Economy and Society*.

45. The phrase is from the *Digest*, the 6th-century compendium of Roman law (see *Digest* 4:2:21:5).

46. Emile Durkheim (1893/1933) *The Division of Labor in Society*, New York: Free Press, Chapter 7. See also Jens Beckert's reconstruction of Durkheim's argumentation: (2002) *Beyond the Market: The Social Foundations of Economic Efficiency*, Princeton, NJ: Princeton University Press, pp. 69–132.

47. Durkheim (1893/1933) *The Division of Labor in Society*, p. 203.

48. Beckert (2002) *Beyond the Market*, p. 92.

49. Beckert (2002) *Beyond the Market*, p. 93.

50. Mark Granovetter (1985) 'Economic Action and Social Structure: The Problem of Embeddedness', in: *American Journal of Sociology*, 91, pp. 481–510, here: p. 487.

51. See Mark Granovetter (1990) 'Entrepreneurship, Development and the Emergence of Firms', in: *Wissenschaftszentrum für Sozialforschung Berlin, Forschungsschwerpunkt Arbeitsmarkt und Beschäftigung*, discussion paper FS I 90-2, April.

PART 2

Strategies and Programmes

6

CREATIVITY

Remember my mantra: distinct … or extinct.[1]

As the educational theorist Hartmut von Hentig writes, creativity is without doubt *a*, if not *the*, 'salvational word' of the present moment. In it, the age finds the 'measuring rod for the idea of the kind of life the age demands'. Even if real lives are far off making the mark, the word shows the way to fulfilment and deliverance.[2] The term creativity awakens entirely positive associations and any ill can be shown to originate in a lack of creativity and be curable by increased creative effort. Whatever the problem is, creativity is the solution. Faith in the creative potential of the individual is the secular religion of the entrepreneurial self.

Creativity is certainly a word with what can be called, as for Marx, 'theological niceties'. *Creatio ex nihilo*, creation out of nothing, is a divine act. Inserting something into nothing means generating a world in miniature. Even for secular humans, the power of creativity cannot get rid of its 'metaphysical subtleties', to quote Marx again. We can determine the conditions that favour the generation of novelty, analyse its emergence into ever smaller steps, describe the concurrent events in the brain, but there remains an inexplicable leap, or, to state it theologically, a miracle. Even if creativity is, as they say, 99 percent perspiration, one percent still remains inspiration. Similes recalling the Pentecostal advent of the Holy Spirit are reminders of this: inspiration, the flash of recognition, lights going on, and not to forget brainstorming, where, 'the wind bloweth where it listeth, and thou hearest the sound thereof, but canst not tell whence it cometh and whither it goeth' (John 3:8). Calls to creativity always have something of an invocation of the divine: *veni creator spiritus*.

Like all religions, creativity is easy to uncover as ideology – for example, as a response to the compulsion to innovate inherent in capitalist modernization or, more generally, as a reaction to economic necessities. However, the fact that creativity fulfils a function explains neither why it is so unquestionably accepted, nor how it comes about and how it can be awakened.

Like all religions, the religion of creativity consists, in addition to articles of faith, of social practices and adepts announcing its works and guiding the laity. The general call for creativity expresses not only a 'necessarily false consciousness' but also a way of exerting influence upon yourself and others. In other words, creativity is a programme of governing, a means of governing the self and others.[3]

Governing creativity

The difficulty of governing creativity is its unavoidable contingency. Creative acts either just happen or just don't happen. They can be 'enticed' by perseverance or enthusiasm but not forced. As Max Weber wrote, 'ideas occur to us when they please, not when it pleases us'.[4] Creativity's incalculability makes it ambivalent. It is both a desirable resource and a threatening potential. With the experience of contingency and moral ambiguity comes a need to direct it, to utilize its productive and limit its destructive capacity. On the one hand, creativity is meant to be mobilized and set loose; on the other hand, it is meant to be regulated and bridled, directed at specific problems and held apart from others. Its unleashing and its domestication are inseparably interwoven. The dream of total control is doomed to disappoint because creativity cannot be had without an element of anarchic freedom and desire for destruction.[5] Control regimes change, but the efforts to take control of creativity remain. Description and prescription coincide here. Creativity is, first, something everyone possesses, an anthropological constant, a human *faculty* or *power*. It is also something everyone *should* possess, a *norm*. It is, third, something one can never possess fully, an unattainable *goal*. Finally, it is something that can be increased by systematic training, a learnable *competency*.

Not only calls to creativity in public discourse, but also creativity research, and its popular version in countless training programmes, advice books and tests, follow this social-engineering impulse. What creativity means, which types of creativity are fostered and which feared, are revealed by the ways creativity is attributed, evoked and steered. There are several factors here. First, the understanding of who is called to and capable of creative activity: Is it everyone or just a select few? How do we find out who? Second, the definitions of the object: In which domains does creativity show itself? Third, the changing strategies and tactics for influencing creativity: How is creativity roused, repressed and directed? Fourth, the aims of the efforts at control: What is the aim of creative practice? Fifth and finally, the sources of legitimacy: In the name of which authority is creativity called for? We have to explore the historical semantics of creativity as well as the various technologies for forming the human capacity for exploration, shaping and making sense, the various role models of creative perfection and self-perfecting (from the genius kissed by the muse to the mind-mapping lateral thinker), the differing types of creative specialist (from artists to psychologists and managers) and finally the justifications for creative activity in different fields: didactic (personal growth), economic (competitive edge) and political (how to order a community).

The following considerations will not answer all these questions. They begin with a sketch of sociological and anthropological conceptions of creative practice that follow works by Heinrich Popitz and Hans Joas. This is followed by an overview of psychological research from the decades after World War II, in which basic elements of the creativity discourse were established, as well as a large number of instruments for advancing creative potential. Concepts in the psychology of creativity exhibit strong affinities with the economic conception of entrepreneurial practice. Several psychologists have indeed translated their theories directly into economic categories. Likewise, economic sociologists and economists have discovered creativity as a location factor important to the knowledge and information society and celebrate the rise of a creative class. After a section contouring this psychological and sociological economics of creativity, we conclude with an analysis of prominent techniques of creativity that refine the general demand into practical instruction.

Anthropology

Humans cannot create something from nothing. Their creations are always derivative, re-creations of something already there. But because humans appropriate the world by interpreting it and doing things with it, their products always go beyond what was already there. We can and must bring about new things but our inventions and innovations are never absolute. The attempt to nail down creative people, acts or products inevitably leads to an infinite regress. Something old lurks within everything novel; the new builds on the old, modifies it, distances itself from it. The closer one looks, the more familiar is what stares back. Inversely, a moment of creative variation lurks within every repetition. One does not step twice into the same river. For this reason, it can be said of just about anything that it is creative or not. The old will always be evident in the new and the new in the old. What decides is the angle of vision.

According to Popitz, there are three basic ways of generating novelty: (1) *explorative/investigative*: exploring and discovering, searching for new knowledge; (2) *shaping*: producing and forming artefacts; and (3) *sense making*: interpreting, stating reasons, justifying.[6] This classification is intended as operative since in reality the three types overlap as do their appending social functions and role models.

The root of human creativity is the ability to have mental representations of absent things (the 'power of imagination') and, building on top of that faculty, the ability to have mental representations of non-existent things ('fantasy'). These faculties are always socially embedded, since even the most fantastical ideas are related in some way to sensory experience, regardless of how far they diverge from it. The negation of the given is always a determinate negation. There can be no ideas of other worlds without experience of the present world. Imagination and fantasy therefore do not constitute an extemporal domain of pure freedom, but rather are subject to historical change and are objects of a multitude of efforts at control. As Popitz writes:

> Control of imagination is a basic building block of social control. Taboos learnt more or less well in childhood enforce themselves. That which we are forbidden to do we are also forbidden to imagine – preventative protection of standards. The removal of seductions in good time is one of the main achievements of cultural discipline. There is a Saint Anthony buried in each member of society. Taboos need to be reinforced by fantasies. You must keep fantasies busy if you want to tame them. The providers of fantasies are the producers and distributors of all myths and fables and naturally all mass communication programmes.[7]

Even the most rigid control and the most subtle suggestion are unable to determine individual imagination and fantasy. Nor are we masters of our own creative faculties: 'Our ability to imagine things beyond all our experience gives us the freedom to be creative. Yet all creativity bears a burden of imagination the self cannot control'.[8] All creative products and all efforts to influence them occur within the cleavage between these two terms.

Since the new is a relational category, being creative means creating distinctions. This can consist in the invention of previously unknown artefacts, knowledge or sense. Novelty is also the recombination or variation of already extant objects of this sort, prizing previously deplored ones or deploring previously prized ones.[9] The possibilities for the creation of novelty are unlimited. Being decisive is the element of difference.

Despite the contradictions encountered in the attempt to define creativity, we can identify a series of associative fields where various concepts coalesce. Along these lines, Hans Joas has set out to provide a 'typology that characterizes the most important forms in which the idea of creativity has surfaced and become influential', distinguishing five metaphors, to which a further will be added in the following.[10] Each corresponds to different traditions of thought in general and notions of human nature in particular. The dividing lines are blurred and there are many overlaps.

First, creativity is associated with artistic practice and with an emphasis on expression. Human beings are regarded as capable of expressing and needing expression. The model here is the artistic genius. This tradition goes back at least to Renaissance philosophy, passing by Johan Gottfried Herder and German romanticism, as well as the philosophical anthropology of Max Scheler, Helmuth Plessner and Arnold Gehlen. Second, creativity is approached as a form of *production*. The human being labours to create works, making things real or objective. The model here is the craftsperson. This notion goes back to Aristotle's distinction between praxis and poiesis. One of its most prominent formulations is found in the young Karl Marx's ontology of labour. A current version has been submitted by the Italian postoperaists with their concept of 'immaterial labour'.[11] Third, creativity is alternately understood as *problem solving*. The emphasis here is on invention and innovation. This approach's implicit anthropology states that humans are creatures that cope with things in life and can rely exclusively neither on instinct nor routine. Creativity is here always concretely situated, responding to challenges calling for new and yet situation-appropriate solutions. This aspect is exemplified by the inventor. The idea is developed into a theory of knowledge and practice in American pragmatism, as well as in Jean Piaget's theory of cognitive development. Fourth, creation is *revolution*, liberating and re-inventing society. Humans face the world as barricade-raising 'creative destroyers'. The prototype of this dimension of creativity is the rule breakers, non-conformists and dissidents of all varieties. The programmatic blueprint is to be found in the manifestos of the artistic and political avant-gardes. Fifth, creativity is associated with *life*. There are metaphors here of conception and birth as well as biological evolution. They generally invoke phenomena of emergence. Creativity is the manifestation of personal or super-personal vital energies staying their course, despite resistance but also in virtue of resistance. The focus is on human drives, on the creativity of desiring machines, but also on non-intentional processes of adapting to the world by natural selection. The relevant theories here are to be found in Nietzsche, Bergson and Freud, as well as in Darwin and his followers. Sixth, probably the most well-known conception of creativity is *play*,[12] equating creativity with non-purposive activity: 'In play, humans are creative in a non-productive way'.[13] The model for this *homo ludens* is the child. This conception can be traced back to the ideal presented in Plato's Laws of 'spend[ing] life in making our *play* as perfect as possible'.[14] Schiller's famous dictum – 'man plays only when in the full meaning of the word he is a man; and he is only completely a man when he plays'[15] – is along the same lines.

Which conceptions are invoked in which combination will depend on which creative potential is to be stimulated. The diverse aspects of creativity serve different expectations and correspond to different ways of affecting and influencing it. The leading conception of the contemporary discourse of creativity is without doubt *problem solving*, which does not so much dispose of the other concepts as subsume them. The problem to be solved is always the same: successful and innovative self-assertion in competition, acquiring buyers for oneself and one's products. Practical inventiveness is the least requirement. Also required are artistic fantasy, hard work, the desire to subvert and destroy, unbridled vitality and ludic levity.

Psychology

The word *Kreativität* was imported to Germany from the USA after World War II. Until then, the German language was familiar with *Einbildungskraft* (the power of imagination), *Schöpferkraft* (the power of creation), *produktives Denken* (productive thought) and *Genius*. The import wave to Europe in the 1950s from US Air Force psychology labs and corporation research institutes had little to do with the Old European cult of genius.[16] American creativity research developed as a reaction to the one-sidedness of traditional intelligence tests, which proved incapable of detecting the kind of budding problem-solving talent needed for science and other 'high potentials' fields.[17] The pioneers of creativity research were looking for effective methods for personality assessment and talent support, with the aim of proliferating technical advancement, product improvement, and finding new marketing techniques:

> Four main research projects have come together under the title 'creativity' since 1950: first, many researchers ... encountered problems selecting inventors and leaders, too few of whom could be singled out, while intelligence test 'geniuses' proved unsuitable for the new challenges. Second, creativity research absorbed too much material from the 'Institute of Personality Assessment and Research'. The institute was financed by private enterprise, had elected 'personal effectiveness' as its object of research and the spreading of 'mental health' as its final purpose ... Third, (applied) creativity research was run by institutions interested in providing 'new ideas' for industrial ends.[18]

Despite its logic of selection and optimization, the basic impulse of creativity psychology was and remains democratic. This distinguishes it from the romantic ideal of the genius whose heroic creative force is endowed on a select few and people either have it or don't have it. In contrast, creativity belongs to everyone but in varying degrees – some have more of it than others. Genius moved in a separate sphere beyond the normal, for which common sense placed it in immediate proximity to madness, with criminal anthropologists and psychiatrists producing genius pathologies.[19] Creativity, on the other hand, is normal and thus distributed according to normal or Gaussian distribution. It belongs to what Jürgen Link has called *flexible normalism*.[20] Geniuses achieved excellence in the arts, sciences and sometimes in war and politics to boot, whereas the attribute 'creative' ennobles even the most banal act. In a presidential address to the American Psychological Association in 1950, generally regarded as the launch of the new creativity research, Joy Paul Guilford stated:

> [c]reative acts can therefore be expected, no matter how feeble or how infrequent, of almost all individuals. The important consideration here is the concept of continuity. Whatever the nature of creative talent may be, those persons who are recognized as creative merely have more of what all of us have.[21]

By defining creativity as a resource for all and sundry, psychologists also significantly increased the number of objects they could study. Detailed case studies of individual excellent scientists and artists were supplemented by quantitative studies with masses of participants, in particular creativity tests. Older studies had followed Francis Galton[22] in seeking hereditary factors or analysed thought patterns in scientific discoveries.[23] Now, the focus was on how to foster creativity through education. This re-orientation was reinforced by the Sputnik shock in 1957 and the associated fear of Soviet technical and therefore military superiority. There was a consensus in the USA that creative potential needed to be mobilized in order to reassert its leadership in the race to be the best political system. The logic of the cold war thereby intensified the already heated up competition within creativity research and promotion and placed it once and for all under the dictate of comparison.

Guilford complained that scientific psychology had neglected creativity up to that point due to its behaviourist bent, naming a set of challenges it must confront: 'How can leaders with imagination and vision be discovered? Can such qualities be developed? If those qualities can be promoted by educational procedures, what are those procedures?'[24] Guilford's research programme is conspicuously utilitarian, as was post-World War II psychological creativity research in general, in which creativity is largely equated with problem solving. Guilford opposed the widespread conformist approach, invoking a conception of creativity that differed from the typography developed by Joas. However, the independence of spirit he was calling for was not an end in itself, but rather the necessary precondition for the higher purpose of scientific progress and increased productivity. Obedient grovellers and pedants simply didn't provide the innovative achievements needed in administration, the military, science and industry. There was agreement among cognitive psychological, psychodynamic and social psychological approaches that the faithful following of guidelines was insufficient to deal with the challenges at hand. What was needed was divergent thinking, which could only thrive where digression from norms was not negatively sanctioned.

Psychology regarded creativity as a cognitive capacity that had nothing to do with the kind of intelligence measured by IQ tests. This conception tended to polarize: on the one side are the non-conformist, instantaneous, innovative, individualist, quirky creators; on the other are the conformist, well-behaved, reliable high scorers in IQ tests.[25] This scheme is reminiscent of Schumpeter's distinction between the entrepreneurial asserter of 'new combinations' and the mere administrator of stock. The creative non-conformist is endowed with the same heroic traits as Schumpeter's entrepreneur. Despite all the democratic egalitarianism, a vestige of genius myth persists, with the twist that the ability to think differently is basically open to anyone in the right environment willing to make use of their opportunities.

Precisely this environment was the thing lacking in post-war America. That was the diagnosis arrived at by Carl R. Rogers, the founder of person-centred therapy:

> In education we tend to turn out conformists, stereotypes, individuals whose education is 'completed', rather than creative and original thinkers. In our leisure-time activities, passive entertainment and regimented group action are overwhelmingly predominant, whereas creative activities are much less in evidence. In the sciences, there is an ample supply of technicians, but the number who can creatively formulate fruitful hypotheses and theories is small indeed. In industry, creation is reserved for the few – the manager, the designer, the head of the research department – whereas for the many life is devoid of original or creative endeavour. In individual and family life the same picture holds true. In the clothes we wear, the food we eat, the books we read, and the ideas we hold, there is a strong tendency toward conformity, toward stereotypy. To be original or different is felt to be 'dangerous'.[26]

In the shadow of the bomb, Rogers asserted, this must inevitably lead to catastrophe. The stakes of creativity were nothing less than the survival of humanity:

> Unless man can make new and original adaptations to his environment as rapidly as his science can change the environment, our culture will perish. Not only individual maladjustment and group tensions but international annihilation will be the price for a lack of creativity.[27]

This truly apocalyptic scenario cried for a salvational power, and this, Rogers found, was to be expected from an exponent of humanist psychology, inside each human being. The drive to self-expression and realization was a source of creativity in each human being and the point was to tap into it:

> This tendency may be deeply buried under layer after layer of encrusted psychological defences; it may be hidden behind elaborate facades which deny its existence; it is my belief however, based on my experience, that it exists in every individual and awaits only the proper conditions to be released and expressed.[28]

Noteworthy here is not merely the chasm between global diagnosis and individual therapy, i.e. the leap in faith entailed in the idea that the solution to humanity's problems lies in the individual. What is also striking is the linkage of creativity to psychic health. There is also the linkage of creativity to psychic health. If the aim of psychotherapy is to help people attain self-actualization as the source of creativity, then personality development and the fostering of creativity are one and the same thing. Donald W. MacKinnon, a psychoanalysis-oriented researcher, who attempted to discover creative personality traits by means of elaborate tests, reformulated this connection in

Freudian terms, stating that the proponents of creativity had 'decided that where Id was ego shall be', while the least creative people 'have determined that superego shall be where ego might have been'.[29] What society at large urgently needs is identical with what individuals need: a reduction of the social to the psychological that transforms the tragic Freudian conflict between duty and desire into a win–win situation – *become what you are and you will be what we need*.

By presupposing a human need for self-actualization as the motivation for creativity, the psychology of creativity avoids the paradox of wanting to stimulate an inner drive which experts are well aware can only come from within patients themselves. Creativity cannot be conditioned by the prospect of reward or punishment, but requires what psychologists call 'intrinsic motivation'. According to one study, an intrinsically motivated person is 'caught' by a challenge and

> compelled to be immersed in it, and with achievement of a solution the creator is 'by joy possessed'. Like Harlow's monkeys, who solve problems for the 'fun' of it, the creative man may invent a new device, paint a picture, or construct a scientific theory for the sheer intrinsic pleasures involved – pleasures in the creative process, in the attaining of a solution, and often also in the aesthetic satisfactions of achieving an 'elegant' solution.[30]

The most important part of reinforcing this creative potential would be preventing loss of motivation by discouragement, mindless routine or authoritarian regulation. Being creative must be enjoyable; morose people are unlikely to be inventive. The psychologists were agreed that promoting creativity is about controlling context. Creativity is not produced, it is enabled. Rogers illustrated this with the agricultural simile of the psychologist as gardener preparing the ground, fertilizing, weeding, to let the creative seeds sprout.

> From the very nature of the inner conditions of creativity it is clear that they cannot be forced, but must be permitted to emerge. The farmer cannot make the germ develop and sprout from the seed; he can only supply the nurturing conditions which will permit the seed to develop its own potentialities. So it is with creativity.[31]

In his foundational text from 1950, Guilford compiled a register of variables of creative thinking serving as hypotheses for the development of creativity tests. According to the register, creative people are characterized by their sensitivity to problems, the fluidity of their thinking, the originality of their ideas, flexibility, the ability to think synthetically and analytically and to reorganize or redefine givens, a range of thought and finally a talent for evaluating ideas' viability. Depth and humanist psychologists elaborated on similar personality traits, albeit less narrowly focused on cognitive abilities.

They characterized creative people as emotionally stable and mature, also attributing to them a particular vitality and willpower:

> Their energy gives them the power and stamina to regard problems as solvable and take them on. They are actively engaged with their environment and attempt to adapt the environment to *their* needs ... instead of subordinating themselves to their environment and its problems and adapting themselves.[32]

They are curious, can perform controlled regression and so let their associations play more freely; they cope with conflicts and insecurity without fleeing to rigid categories and familiar solutions. They do not tend toward inflexible views of the world and stereotypes, preferring complex patterns of thought and behaviour, are independent, unconventional and self-willed in social interaction.

It is easy to see these descriptive categories as a set of prescriptions. If creativity coincides with intelligence, mental health and maturity, then we have a catalogue of virtues. It consequently becomes everyone's duty to imitate the exemplary creative types by becoming creative. Who wants to be labelled dumb, mentally unstable or immature? Basic creative qualities such as being active and flexible are goals we can set but never reach because we can continue to augment such qualities ad infinitum. This fundamental impossibility is exacerbated by the fact that creative people excel precisely because they unite opposing traits. According to Mihaly Csikszentmihalyi's systematic creativity theory, creative people possess large quantities of energy but stay calm and relaxed. They combine intellectual subtlety with naivety, can think convergently and divergently, are disciplined and playful, responsible and uncommitted, switch between fantasy and realism, are extroverted and introverted, humble and proud, ambitious and selfless, competitive and cooperative, masculine and feminine, traditional and conservative, as well as rebellious and iconoclast, passionate yet objective in assessing their own work, sensitive to the suffering of others yet capable of intense joy.[33] Nobody can be all of that and certainly not all at once. Read as prescription, Csikszentmihalyi's reconciliation of opposites must be felt as a provocation to feel permanently inadequate (or to fall prey to spectacular hybris). This is borne out by the subheading of the German edition: *How to Do the Impossible and Transcend Your Limits*. The creative subject that we should all endeavour to become is interminably at work balancing contradictory demands, worn down by swerving between them, and can never rest in the middle.

Csikszentmihalyi also draws attention to the social dimension of creativity. The 'creative moment' may strike the lonely individual in her garret, but no one is truly creative on their own. Creative people are involved with others. They are dependent on others regarding their inventions, artefacts, interpretations, and on creators truly worthy of the predicate creative. They develop ideas together with others. They are given problems to solve by others or they are dissatisfied with solutions other people have come up with. They follow others in their footsteps or leave the already trodden paths. In short, whether or not something is creative depends on the judgement of the community. Creative acts are therefore required not only to be new but to be appropriate to some need, satisfy some desire or in some way be valuable to others, and the measure of this value is the echo they receive. 'According to this view, creativity results from the interaction of a system composed of three elements: a culture that contains symbolic rules, a person who brings novelty into the symbolic domain, and a field of experts who recognize and validate the innovation. All three are necessary for a creative idea, product, or discovery to take place'.[34]

Economy

It's just a short step from Czikszentmihalyi's constructivist economy of recognition to those psychological concepts that translate creativity entirely into micro-economic categories. Robert J. Sternberg, a successor to Guilford as president of the American Psychological Association, has elaborated, together with his collaborator Todd L. Lubart, on an investment theory of creativity that compares creative achievement with economic success.[35] The creative actor is equated with a successful entrepreneur, speculating on the future and seeking his fortune off the beaten track. 'Buy low and sell high' is his maxim. He places his bets on offbeat ideas and hopes they will become classics:

> Successful investors have to be bold, willing to take risks, and ready to act contrary to the behaviour of other investors. When they buy an out-of-favour stock or other financial instrument, they may be seen as foolish. But if that financial instrument comes to be widely recognized as a good investment, its price rises rapidly, and it is no longer possible to buy it at a low and hence favourable price. The person formerly seen as foolish may now be seen as prescient. An analogous situation can be observed for creative performance ... An individual who generates and advances a new idea in science or a new style in art may originally be seen as out-of-touch or even as foolish. But if others come to recognize the value of that work, the individual will be seen as highly creative. Of course, creativity is not an all-or-nothing phenomenon. There is a continuum of creative performance, just as there is a continuum of profits across investments.[36]

Which creations yield a return is decided on the market. The rest evaporates. And only those prepared to risk failure have a chance at success. Whether or not something is creative shows up after the event, when it pleases others or appears useful to them, i.e. when it gains appreciation or at least attention. Just going a different path than the majority is useless if no one cares. The creative is the novel that wins through.

In their anthology, Sternberg and Lubart emphasize the speculative, resourceful, risk-taking seizure of the moment type of activity, while leaving entrepreneurial functions like Schumpeter's creative destruction and the ability to organize production and marketing in the background. The creative person and the clever investor exploit the available means of analysis to ground their decisions in a rational basis, carefully weighing up costs and benefits, while nevertheless taking a sort of gamble: 'To buy low one must take the risk that what one buys at a low price will not in fact later go up in price. When selling high, one also takes the risk that what one sells at a high price may increase in value still more. One can never know for sure.'[37]

This view dispenses with the understanding of creativity as a life-long possession. When competitors catch up, profits fall and the investor is threatened with 'creative bankruptcy' unless he can find new profit opportunities. The creative imperative requires permanent change. Its enemies are homogeneity, identity, norm and repetition. Since only non-conformists have a unique selling point, being creative demands constant effort. Everyone must be creative and that means being more creative than others. No particular gift or training is needed to keep afloat in this contest, just an attitude of mind that can be adopted or not: 'Buying low and selling high can be a way of life – it's an attitude toward living. Some people choose to live creatively, others don't. But it is a choice. You can choose to follow the crowd, or you can choose to go your own way'.[38] This item of good news includes some brutal small print. If everyone has the chance to sell themselves effectively, then those no one is interested in somehow deserve it. The only consoling words for bankrupt losers that Sternberg and Lubart have on offer are: try again! 'Individuals can nonetheless recover from such bankruptcies, just as they can from financial ones. Modes of recovery are variable; they may involve changing fields, reeducating oneself, or simply deciding on a fresh angle from which to approach one's work'.[39]

To help people avoid getting into this predicament in the first place, Sternberg and Lubart provide a set of resources for improving investment chances. These resources are the human capital of the creativity entrepreneur, so it's worth cultivating them: (1) the ability to leap over conventional limits on thought, see problems in a new light, recognize which ideas are worth pursuing and which should be dropped, and the ability to gain adherents for new ideas (*intelligence*); (2) creative talents familiar with the area they are investing in (*knowledge*); (3) a specific mode of mental self-government referred to as the *legislative thinking style*; (4) personal attributes like tolerance to ambiguity, self-confidence, readiness to take risks, and assertiveness; (5) the already familiar *intrinsic task-focused motivation*; and (6) an *environment* that welcomes and rewards creative ideas.[40]

The analogy between creativity and investment inevitably leads to a call to invest in creative potential. The promotion of creativity is grasped as an accumulation of individual and collective human capital. This process is subject to the same cost-benefit considerations as other enterprises. Creativity has its price: 'investments in creative potential will be encouraged by changes which lower the costs of investment or raise the expected benefit'.[41] Marginal utility is reached when the means to be expended exceed the expected returns. Regulation occurs through the market; when the demand for innovation increases, the motivation to work also goes up. When demand sinks, the creative industry can't move its goods.

Psycho- and socio-economy merge here, and these psychological theories of the creative investor are joined by studies from social science announcing the rise of the so-called creative economy.[42] Richard Florida, whose 2002 book *The Rise of the Creative Class*[43] was a bestseller in the USA, describes creativity as 'the ultimate economic resource',[44] and moreover as a potentially inexhaustible resource that can be neither horded nor bought and sold. Like freedom and security, Florida continues, creativity is a public good and producing it therefore a public task. Florida's thesis is a variation on the theme of transitioning to a knowledge society. Because the production of ideas has become more important economically than the production of material goods or services, the number and influence of idea producers have also risen. The main gist of Florida's book is that the creative class has become the socially dominant group and is about to fundamentally change the way we work, our values and our daily lives generally. The cohesion of the creative class is its economic function. It nevertheless has no class consciousness:

> The Creative Class consists of people who add economic value through their creativity. It thus includes a great many knowledge workers, symbolic analysts and professional and technical workers, but emphasizes their true role in economy ... Most members of the Creative Class do not own and control any significant property in the physical sense. Their property – which stems from their creative capacity – is an intangible because it is literally in their heads ... [T]he members of the Creative Class do not yet see themselves as a unique social grouping, they actually share many similar tastes, desires and preferences. This new class may not be as distinct in this regard as the industrial Working Class in its heyday, but it has an emerging coherence.[45]

Florida's book is not out to advance creative people's class organization in order to make of them a class 'for itself' instead of just 'in itself'. Nor is it interested in knowing which population groups creative people come from, which schools they attend or how the creative personality is fostered. The programme laid out in the book is focused on developing particular economic regions. Florida shows which factors are responsible for higher concentrations of the creative class in particular regions of the USA, correlating this concentration with greater prosperity. The 'creativity index', developed by Florida for this purpose, consists of four equally weighted factors: (1) the proportion of creatives to the total workforce; (2) innovation, based on the amount of patents pro capita; (3) the settlement of high-tech businesses; and (4) cultural diversity, based on the *gay index*: the number of gays and lesbians in the population. Florida employs additional comparative factors, such as an article by *Men's Fitness* magazine contrasting the country's 'fittest' and 'fattest'[46] areas and a 'Bohemian Index',[47] which ranks cities according to the number of artists living there. These data are crunched to prove that the ascending creative class is especially drawn to those regions where there is a predominance and general acceptance of cultural diversity. There is therefore an argument from economics rather than cultural idealism for a climate of openness and tolerance toward different lifestyles. A greater proportion of exotic types correlates with more innovation which correlates in turn with more prosperity. The gay index is a particularly good indicator because, so the claim goes, discrimination against gays is particularly slow-dying: 'To some extent, homosexuality represents the last frontier of diversity in our society, and thus a place that welcomes the gay community welcomes all kinds of people'.[48]

The creativity psychology was directed against the pressure to conform in mass society, lionizing the self-possessed lateral thinker successfully investing in his own human capital. Now, the sociology of the creative class transposes this ideal onto the social dimension. Here, the concern is less with developing the individual than with 'community building'. Florida recommends investing in social capital, albeit without the communitarian nostalgia of a Robert Putnam.[49] Creative people are individualists, and bowling is not necessarily their favourite pastime. The creative class is characterized not by a return to old ties but by the multiplication of loose ties. It has come to cultivate a lifestyle out of the New Economy pressures to be mobile and flexible. In Florida's argumentation, the creative class assumes the same function the creative genius did for creative psychology. Whether it involves programmes for personal growth or for regional development, promoting creativity means *diversity management*. To tap into creativity as a resource, spaces must be generated where it can thrive and diversify. The rest is done by competition.[50]

Technologies

Creativity is hard work and yet demands the levity of play. The demands of economic necessity can only be fulfilled in a state of freedom. Further, the general call to be creative is a call for serial singularity, ready-made difference. The appeal to be creative is no less paradoxical than the legendary appeal to be spontaneous. Creativity can neither be commanded nor squeezed into curricula or employment contracts because only something well defined can be put into a structure. At best, a list can be drawn up of the factors that increase the probability of creativity occurring. There is no shortage of programmes of 'innovation gymnastics'.[51] We have long since gone beyond the stage of mere house recipes. An army of specialists is combing the area and supplying the creatively hungry with ever new training techniques. These methods are based on an everyday way of generating new ideas, converting them into systematic, often professionally led and institutionally backed-up strategies for innovation management. Creativity training standardizes the rupture with standard solutions, makes a norm of divergence from the norm and teaches people not to rely on what they've been taught. Paths to the particular should be the same paths for all.

Contemporary programmes draw on communication science and informatics (neuro-linguistic programming) as well as cognitive science (activating the right hemisphere of the brain). They adapt formerly marginal, alternative education concepts such as open space and future workshops, therapy techniques (free association) and practices from the artistic avant-garde (automatic writing).

Since the Eureka moment cannot be technically generated, the programmes concentrate on the other phases of the creative process. Most of the process models follow Graham Wallas' study *The Art of Thought*,[52] which distinguishes four steps to thinking through problems: (1) a *preparation* phase in which the problem is considered and the available knowledge gathered but not rigidly catalogued is followed by (2) an *incubation* phase characterized by 'a problem-based but loose and thus unprejudiced playing around with information, perspectives and mental associations'.[53] This phase – often experienced as exhausting and frustrating despite its daydreaming, meandering quality – results, if all goes well, in (3) *illumination*. The originally unconnected cognitive elements suddenly join into a new 'Gestalt' – the solution to the problem; and (4) *verification* is still needed to put the idea to the test and put it to work, otherwise its initial splendour will come to naught. Ideas must be elaborated on and rendered communicable, costs and benefits must be calculated, possible ramifications must be taken into account and then the idea must be put into practice. Creative processes are complexes of many individual acts, each of which is subdivided into preparation, incubation, illumination and verification.

Most creative techniques engage the early phases prior to illumination, trying to create the conditions for the stimulation of ideas. In particular, they employ strategies of disturbing expectation and transgressing borders. For example, to upset routine ways of thinking and acting, the synectics methodology for generating ideas developed by William J. J. Gordon combines random bits of information or draws analogies between heterogeneous domains.[54] New ways of looking at old problems and arriving at unconventional solutions are stimulated by alteration ('If we used trained ants as numbers, what kind of calculator with its own energy source could we produce?') and identification ('What would it feel like to be an aluminium piston in a running diesel engine?').[55] Other concepts like Edward de Bono's lateral thinking recommend a wild logic that replaces the linear sequence of thought with discontinuous sideward leaps. The rupture with familiar models is seen to provide room for new forms. Provocation counts more than precision, 'richness' more than 'rightness'.[56]

Such strategies for 're-patterning' thinking are tightly bound up with attempts to increase the amount of ideas being produced by eliminating internal and external censorship and facilitating the free flow of thought. Brainstorming, originally developed by Alex F. Osborn for use in an advertising agency, is paradigmatic for this type of technique for the proliferation of ideas.[57] The essential point of brainstorming is the separation of idea gathering and idea evaluation. 'No criticism!' is the main rule. The more ideas are made to gush up by the process of creative upsurge, the more hits, which is why it was developed as a conference technique harnessing the synergy of the group, unleashing 'spontaneous chain reactions' and a 'mental multi-fecundation' between the participants.[58]

Methods such as mind mapping[59] and clustering[60] also operate on the assumption that hasty judgements and rigid schemes are 'creativity killers'. These methods attempt to initiate streams of association by calling on people to order their thoughts not in a linear manner but in pictorial form. As in brainstorming, as many different solutions as possible should be taken down and probed. Gabriele L. Rico provides the following instructions for clustering:

> To create a cluster, you begin with a nucleus word, circled, on a fresh page. Now you simply let go and begin to flow with any current of connections that come into your head. Write these down rapidly, each in its own circle, radiating outward from the center in any direction they want to go. Connect each new word or phrase with a line to the preceding circle. When something new and different strikes you, begin again at the central nucleus and radiate outward until those associations are exhausted.[61]

Nietzsche's 'Chain-Thinker', for whom 'every new thought that he hears or reads at once assumes the form of a chain'[62] is resuscitated here as a guide for creative writing. The chain has simply become a rhizome, true to the age of the network.

Most creativity techniques resemble psychoanalysis in attributing key significance to free association. Like the patient on the couch, the creative person should also follow whatever drops into her head spontaneously. Both perform a controlled 'regression in the service of the ego'.[63] But contrary to the Freudian talking cure, it is not about cathartic remembering, repeating and working through; it is about systematically increasing idea output. The forces of the unconscious should neither be interpreted nor civilized but rather released and at the same time made use of, not as memory traces from the individual's psychic past but rather as an inexhaustible source of cognitive innovation. Before the wheat is separated from the chaff and the ideas are made to prove their feasibility, the selection pool should be as large as possible. Even abstruse and harebrained ideas can become catalysers for something useful and there is no such thing as a stupid question. The only cause for concern is when the flow of ideas stops: 'Faltering is generally regarded as the worst enemy of creativity; the aim of every technique of creativity is to avoid the little failures in order to prevent the big failure.'[64] The common denominator of both the strategy of disorientation and that of transgressing limits is activation.

Despite its praise of creative daydreaming and free play, creativity promotion is inscribed within the ethos of productivity. It temporarily alleviates the pressure to be productive in order to arrive at utilizable products in the form of solutions to problems. Idling is encouraged, but only in order to subsequently get the idea machine churning out even more, since it needs a break now and then to recover its breath. This is a paradoxical undertaking, and it is in permanent danger of imploding. Recovering strength is only an act of creation when it does not become permanent or merely cover up work. This tension makes tangible the disciplinary function inherent in the phase models of the creative process. The phases are mutually independent but only if one runs through all of them does the creative product emerge. At the end of the day, the emphasis is on *product*, not on *creative*.

Creativity needs leisure, while the market imposes acceleration. Under the conditions of competition for ideas, time is a scarce resource. In this context, the commandment of unfettered creativity undermines its own effectiveness. The greater the pressure to innovate, the more short-lived novelty becomes and the quicker creative potential is worn out. When leisure is systematically made scarce or expropriated for innovation work, then all that remains is a simulacrum of creativity. This mere semblance of novelty will weaken market position sooner or later. This vicious circle is difficult to escape and the permanent sense of insufficiency gives rise to an unabating hunger for new creative techniques and a corresponding boom in offers. Because such offers are available to all in the codified form of the mind map, brainstorming, etc. and every innovation is rapidly imitated, they provide only a short-term advantage. The creative economy is also subject to the law of diminishing returns. The ideal of the creative adept is therefore not just an heroic figure – active, non-conformist, inquisitive, imaginative – she is also stressed out. Inside the promise of creative individuality lurks a threat, as expressed in a Me-Inc. guidebook: 'BE DISTINCT ... OR EXTINCT!'[65]

Notes

1. Tom Peters (2004) 'Brand You Survival Kit', in: *Fast Company*, 83, June, p. 95, www.fastcompany.com/48979/brand-you-survival-kit (28.12.2014).
2. Hartmut von Hentig (2000) *Kreativität: Hohe Anforderungen an einen schwachen Begriff*, Basel: Beltz, p. 9.
3. Thomas Osborne (2003) 'Against "Creativity": a Philistine Rant', in: *Economy and Society*, 32, pp. 507–525, here: p. 508.
4. Max Weber (1946) 'Science as Vocation', in: H. H. Gerth and C. Wright Mills (eds), *From Max Weber: Essays in Sociology*, New York: Routledge, p. 136.
5. See Margo Hildreth Poulsen (1975) 'Anarchy is a Learning Environment', in: *Journal of Creative Behavior*, 9, pp. 131–136.
6. See Heinrich Popitz (1997) 'Wege der Kreativität: Erkunden, Gestalten, Sinnstiften', in: *Wege der Kreativität*, Tübingen: Mohr Siebeck, pp. 80–132.
7. Popitz (1997) 'Wege der Kreativität, p. 87.
8. Popitz (1997) 'Wege der Kreativität, p. 89.
9. See Boris Groys (2014) *On the New*, New York: Verso.
10. Hans Joas (1996) *The Creativity of Action*, Chicago, IL: University of Chicago Press, p. 70.
11. See Maurizio Lazzarato (1996) 'Immaterial Labour', in: *Radical Thought in Italy: A Potential Politics*, Minneapolis: University of Minnesota Press, pp. 133–147.
12. The seminal text here remains Jakob Huizinga (1950) *Homo ludens: A Study of the Play-Element in Culture*, Boston: The Beacon Press.
13. Heinrich Popitz (1997) 'Was tun wir, wenn wir spielen', in: *Wege der Kreativität*, pp. 50–79, here: p. 79.
14. Plato (1966) *Laws* in: Edith Hamilton and Huntington Cairns (eds), *Collected Dialogues of Plato* (4th edition, trans. A. E. Taylor), Princeton: Princeton University Press (emphasis in original), VII, 803 C.
15. Friedrich Schiller (1795/1902) 'On the Aesthetic Education of Man' (letter 15), in: *Aesthetical and Philosophical Essays*, *Vol. I*, Boston: Robertson, Ashford and Bentley, p. 56.
16. See Edgar Zilsel (1926) *Die Entstehung des Geniebegriffs*, Tübingen: JCB Mohr; see also Zilsel (1918) *Die Geniereligion: Ein kritischer Versuch über das moderne Persönlichkeitsideal*, Vienna: Braumüller.
17. On the history of creativity research, see Joy Paul Guilford (1967) 'Creativity: Yesterday, Today, and Tomorrow', in: *The Journal of Creative Behavior*, 1, pp. 3–14; Irving A. Taylor (1975) 'A Retrospective View of Creativity Investigation', in: Irving A. Taylor and Jacob W. Getzels (eds), *Perspectives in Creativity*, Chicago: Transaction, pp. 1–36; Teresa Amabile (1981) *The Social Psychology of Creativity*, New York: Springer; Robert S. Albert and Mark A. Runko (1999) 'A History of Research on Creativity', in: Robert J. Sternberg (ed.), *Handbook of Creativity*, Cambridge: Cambridge University Press, pp. 16–31.
18. Gisela Ulmann (1973) 'Einleitung: Psychologische Kreativitätsforschung', in: *Kreativitätsforschung*, Cologne: Kiepenheuer and Witsch, pp. 11–22, here: p. 12.

19. See Cesare Lombroso (1891) *The Man of Genius*, London: Scott; Wilhelm Lange-Eichbaum (1931) *The Problem of Genius*, London: K. Paul, Trench, Trubner & Company.

20. See Jürgen Link (1997) *Versuch über den Normalismus: Wie Normalität produziert wird*, Opladen: Vandenhoeck & Ruprecht.

21. Joy Paul Guilford (1950) 'Creativity', in: *The American Psychologist*, 5(9), pp. 444–454, here: p. 446.

22. Francis Galton (1869) *Hereditary Genius*, New York: D. Appleton & Co.

23. See here the exemplary text from Max Wertheimer (1945) *Productive Thinking*, New York: Harper.

24. Guilford (1950) 'Creativity', p. 446.

25. Von Hentig (2000) *Kreativität*, p. 20.

26. Carl R. Rogers (1959) 'Toward a Theory of Creativity', in: Harold A. Anderson (ed.), *Creativity and its Cultivation*, New York/Evanston, IL, pp. 69–82, here: pp. 69f.

27. Rogers (1959) 'Toward a Theory of Creativity', p. 70.

28. Rogers (1959) 'Toward a Theory of Creativity', p. 72.

29. Donald W. MacKinnon (1965) 'Personality and the Realization of Creative Potential', *American Psychologist*, 20(4), pp. 273–281. Here: p. 281.

30. Richard S. Crutchfield (1962) 'Conformity and Creative Thinking', in: Howard E. Gruber, Glenn Terrel and Michael Wertheimer (eds), *Contemporary Approaches to Creative Thinking*, New York: Atherton Press, pp. 120–140, here: p. 122.

31. Rogers (1959) 'Toward a Theory of Creativity', p. 78.

32. Siegfried Preiser (1976) *Kreativitätsforschung*, Darmstadt: Wissenschaftliche Buchgesellschaft, pp. 68f.

33. Mihaly Czikszentmihalyi (1996) *Creativity: The Psychology of Discovery and Invention*, New York: Harper, pp. 51–76.

34. Mihaly Csikszentmihalyi (1996) *Creativity*, p. 6.

35. Robert J. Sternberg and Todd L. Lubart (1991) 'An Investment Theory of Creativity and its Development', in: *Human Development*, 34, p. 1–31; Robert J. Sternberg and Todd L. Lubart (1992) 'Buy Low and Sell High: An Investment Approach to Creativity', in: *Current Directions in Psychological Science*, 1, pp. 1–5; Robert J. Sternberg and Todd L. Lubart (1995) *Defying the Crowd: Cultivating Creativity in a Culture of Conformity*, New York: Free Press; Robert J. Sternberg and Todd L. Lubart (1996) 'Investing in Creativity', in: *American Psychologist*, 51, pp. 677–688.

36. Sternberg and Lubart (1991) 'An Investment Theory of Creativity and its Development', pp. 1f.

37. Sternberg and Lubart (1995) *Defying the Crowd*, p. 45.

38. Sternberg and Lubart (1995) *Defying the Crowd*, p. 76.

39. Sternberg and Lubart (1995) *Defying the Crowd*, p. 67.

40. Sternberg and Lubart (1996) 'Investing in Creativity', p. 684; Sternberg and Lubart (1995) *Defying the Crowd*, pp. 1–10.

41. Daniel L. Rubenson and Mark A. Runco (1992) 'The Psychoeconomic Approach to Creativity', in: *New Ideas in Psychology*, 10, pp. 131–147, here: p. 137.

42. John Howkins (2001) *The Creative Economy: How People Make Money from Ideas*, New York: Allen Lane.

43. Richard Florida (2004) *The Rise of the Creative Class*, New York: Basic Books (p/b; original h/b edition 2002); see also the sequels: (2005) *Cities and the Creative Class*, New York: Psychology Press; (2005) *The Flight of the Creative Class: The New Global Competition for Talent*, New York: Collins.

44. Florida (2004) *The Rise of the Creative Class*, 'Preface to the Paperback Edition', p. xiii.

45. Florida (2004) *The Rise of the Creative Class*, p. 68.

46. Florida (2004) *The Rise of the Creative Class*, pp. 178f.

47. Florida (2004) *The Rise of the Creative Class*, pp. 260f.

48. Florida (2004) *The Rise of the Creative Class*, p. 256.

49. See Robert Putnam (2000) *Bowling Alone: The Collapse and Revival of American Community*, New York: Simon & Schuster.

50. For a sociology of culture approach to the work and living situations of the 'creative industries', see Angela McRobbie (1998) *British Fashion Design: Rag Trade or Image Industry?* London: Routledge; Angela McRobbie (2001) '"Everyone is Creative": Artists as New Economy Pioneers?', in: Open Democracy, pp. 119–132, www.opendemocracy.net/node/652.

51. Von Hentig (2000) *Kreativität*, p. 60.

52. Graham Wallas (1926) *The Art of Thought*, New York: Watts.

53. Preiser (1976) *Kreativitätsforschung*, p. 45.

54. See William J. J. Gordon (1961) *Synectics: The Development of Creative Capacity*, New York: Harper & Row.

55. The examples are taken from: Heinz Hoffmann (1980) *Kreativitätstechniken für Manager*, Munich: Moderne Industrie, pp. 143, 141.

56. See Edward de Bono (1970) *Lateral Thinking: Creativity Step by Step*, New York: Harper & Row.

57. See Alex F. Osborn (1953) *Applied Imagination: Principles and Procedures of Creative Thinking*, New York: Charles Scribners and Sons.

58. Osborn (1953) *Applied Imagination*, p. 110.

59. See Tony Buzan (2002) *How to Mind Map: The Ultimate Thinking Tool That Will Change Your Life*, London: Thorsons.

60. See Gabriele L. Rico (2000) *Writing the Natural Way*, New York: Tarcher Putnam.

61. Rico (2000) *Writing the Natural Way*, p. 35 (15th anniversary expanded edition, p. 23).

62. Friedrich Nietzsche (2013) *Human, All Too Human: A Book for Free Spirits*, Auckland: Create Space, p. 272.

63. See Ernst Kris (1952) *Psychoanalytic Explorations in Art*, New York: IUP.

64. Manuela Branz (2005) 'Gelungenes Scheitern: Scheitern in der Postmoderne', in: *Kunstforum International*, 174, Jan.–Mar., pp. 262–267, here: p. 265.

65. Tom Peters (1999) *The Brand You 50: Fifty Ways to Transform Yourself from an 'Employee' into a Brand That Shouts Distinction, Commitment, and Passion!*, New York: Knopf Doubleday, p. viii.

7

EMPOWERMENT

You are not responsible for being down, but you are responsible for getting up.[1]

In 1985, the community psychologist Julian Rappaport wrote that the notion of empowerment has one thing in common with the notion of obscenity: 'You have trouble defining it but you know it when you see it'.[2] A sifting of the literature confirms the difficulty of finding a precise definition. Empowerment is written about from both descriptive and prescriptive perspectives. It is at once a means and an end, a continual process as well as the end result of both personal and social change.[3] The term denotes a basic value on which individuals and groups orient practice, as well as a theoretical model for describing transformation on individual, organizational and social levels.[4] The term is used both in the reflexive and the transitive to mean the professional support of self-reliant everyday management as well as the 'self-empowerment' and 'self-appropriation of life forces'.[5] Its proponents announce empowerment variously as a 'world view theory',[6] a 'new way of thinking',[7] an 'attitude'[8], a 'social technology'[9] and as a 'metaphor and symbol for the goals of helping'.[10] Rappaport, who contributed significantly to propagating and codifying the concept, makes its contradictions into a programme, entitling a 1981 article that launched it in social welfare and health politics 'In Praise of Paradox'. His own definition is conspicuously broad brushed: 'By empowerment I mean that our aim should be to enhance the possibilities for people to control their own lives'.[11] Elsewhere, Rappaport explains that this can mean different things to different people: 'Empowerment for a poor, uneducated Black woman can look very different than for a middle-class college student or a 39-year-old businessman, a white urban housewife, or an elderly person resisting placement in a nursing home'.[12]

The term's polyvalence accords with the diversity of contexts in which it is used variously as a value measurement, a guide for action or a category of analysis. Citizen initiatives and grassroots movements[13] appeal to it, together with neoconservative political advisors,[14] new age adepts[15] and proclaimers of class struggle.[16] The concept features in feminist discourse[17] and in diverse types of social work.[18] It is firmly established in health research, community psychology and community psychiatry[19] and even in the penal system.[20] It occurs in education, both inside and outside of the school system,[21] it is employed in development aid programmes from the UN and the World Bank,[22] as well as by NGOs,[23] and it is invoked by psychotherapists,[24] human resource managers and management consultants.[25] Finally, a US tea-party lobby group calling itself 'Empower America' has been agitating for 'growth, economic well-being, freedom and individual responsibility' and, since 11 September, 2001, for the war on terror.[26] Empowerment is interpreted and put into practice in manifold ways. Empowerment textbooks propose didactic models, advice books provide exercises for self-empowerment and workshops provide exemplary experiences. Empowerment practitioners produce strategies, build support networks, mobilize resources and organize self-help groups.

The proliferation of the concept suggests that empowerment operates as a catchphrase for a range of disparate meanings. It is in any case popular: a 'strategy with near universal appeal',[27] a 'construct of high social desirability'.[28] It is regarded as a 'panacea for social ills'[29] and claims credibility across the board of political factions, social strata and academic disciplines. This is precisely a result of its receptivity to different meanings. The differentiation between empowering and disempowering has become a moral guideline for judging individual, professional and political action, administrative decisions, organizational structures and institutions.

The discourse of empowerment first became a prominent component of contemporary governmentality when the aim, theory and technology of leadership coalesced into that of self-leadership. In addition to the maxim that any action should promote the empowerment of the people affected by it, empowerment is predicated on a bundle of anthropological, psychological and sociological assumptions connected to power relations, and comes with a set of strategies and tactics for modifying these relations to increase self-determination. Systematic efforts to promote the empowerment of self and others and the accompanying discourse together constitute a form of government defined by the exercise of power over people aimed at increasing their ability to exercise power themselves and over themselves, i.e. to self-govern. Like other dispositifs of governing, the ethos, teachings and practice of empowerment appropriate everyday forms of communication and action and transform them into a scientific, methodical, professionalized concept. The three pillars of empowerment – 'self-determination, distributive justice, and collaborative and democratic participation'[30] – are time-honoured values, as are the principles of helping people to help themselves and of helping each other. The novel thing is putting them to work systematically, united under one heading.

Genealogy

The discourse of empowerment began to proliferate in the USA in the 1970s.[31] The term first occurred in a book title in Bryant S. Solomon's *Black Empowerment: Social Work in Oppressed Communities*, in the context of civil rights and black power.[32] A year later, Peter L. Berger's and John Neuhaus' manifesto *To Empower People* appeared, making a conservative-communitarian argument for the strengthening of neighbourhoods, family and other intermediary community levels between individuals and the 'mega-structures' of the overburdened welfare state.

The diversity of political aspirations that motivated the empowerment discourse is apparent in the early literature:

> To contemporary champions of laissez-faire economics and minimal government, empowerment means handing off to people in local areas the responsibility for making their everyday lives better. To present-day advocates of an activist democracy – a polity that embraces the vigorous pursuit of a socially secure condition for all citizens by all of those citizens and their government and their corporate leaders – empowerment invokes the principle of subsidiarity, by which 'larger and more powerful political and economic institutions sustain smaller communities instead of dominating them' and encourage 'a new experiment in participatory democracy in the American workplace and polity'.[33]

In other words, 'the left uses empowerment to generate political resistance; the right, to produce rational economic and entrepreneurial actors'.[34]

The sometimes latent, sometimes manifest intellectual currents that flow into the concept of empowerment are also characterized by political ambiguity. One of them is the protestant dissenter tradition of unmediated access to the divine and the ideal of an egalitarian community based on mutual support. Others are Thomas Jefferson's democratic optimism schooled in Rousseau and Locke with his trust in ordinary people's ability to govern themselves rationally; and Ralph Waldo Emerson's Transcendentalism with its ethical, religious programme of individual self-realization grounded in the conviction that all people can improve their personal and social condition if they follow their inner voice.[35] Other earlier currents include the utopian settlement experiments in the early North American settler period, the communitarian and mutualist currents in anarchism, the union movement and the emancipation movements of women and Afro-Americans.

The pioneer spirit of participatory social reform informed professional social work in its beginnings in the USA, from the establishment of individual case work by Mary Richmond and Jane Addams' settlement movement in the early 20th century to the conflict-oriented work begun by Saul D. Alinsky in the 1940s. Alinsky's much-discussed *Rules for Radicals* appealed for an empowerment strategy in the form of community organization. In his view, the most important function of community organization is waking people out of their lethargy and giving them the sense that they can change something if they set themselves goals and work together. The point of departure was a general sense of powerlessness and lack of orientation:

> The simple fact is that in any community, regardless of how poor, people may have serious problems – but they do not have issues, they have a bad scene. An issue is something you can do something about, but as long as you feel powerless and unable to do anything about it, all you have is a bad scene. The people resign themselves to a rationalization: it's that kind of world, it's a crumby world, we didn't ask to come into it but we are stuck with it and all we can do is hope that something happens somewhere, somehow, sometime … [Enter the community organizer:] Through action, persuasion, and communication the organizer makes it clear that organization will give them the power, the ability, the strength, the force to be able to do something about these particular problems. It is then that a bad scene begins to break up into specific issues, because now the people can do something about it. What the organizer does is convert the plight into a problem. The question is whether they do it this way or that way or whether they do all of it or part of it. But now you have issues.[36]

The community organizer is like an athletics coach and must have the same degree of sensitivity:

> It is almost like taking a prize-fighter up the road to the championship – you have to very carefully and selectively pick his opponents, knowing full well that certain defeats would be demoralizing and end his career. Sometimes the organizer may find such despair among the people that he has to put on a cinch fight.[37]

Whereas Alinsky was concerned with mobilizing power from below, the Johnson administration's Equal Opportunity Act of 1964 aimed at combating poverty by empowering the economically disadvantaged from above. According to a government guideline:

> The long range objective of every community action program is to effect a permanent increase in the capacity of individuals, groups, and communities afflicted by poverty to deal effectively with their own problems so that they need no further assistance. Poverty is a condition of need, helplessness and hopelessness.[38]

Under the heading 'maximum feasible participation', local planning, infrastructure measures and service programmes were subjected to formal civic participation procedures and a number of model projects were initiated. All these programmes issued from the conviction that the war on poverty could only be won if the poor overcame their 'apathy' and got engaged to improve their situation. It was seen as more important to motivate people to action than to provide material support through welfare measures:

> New jobs can be provided but some people are unwilling or afraid to apply for them. New housing projects can be built but some tenants will turn them into slums. New community centers can be opened but only a few people may choose to use them. Exciting educational programmes can be conceived but the people can let them die for lack of participation. Therefore, attention must be paid to the underlying motivations, attitudes, and values of the people of the city.[39]

The honeymoon period of this community action programme was rather short. After the troubles in many US cities in the late 1960s, government support was stopped. Under the Nixon administration, which came to power in 1968, the zeal for social reform began to die down and with the 1973 recession public spending on poverty was drastically cut.

The government's anti-poverty campaign can be interpreted as a way of responding to the social movements of the 1950s and 1960s by appropriating their demands for participation and translating them into state policies. The civil rights movement was particularly important in the development of the idea of empowerment. Martin Luther King estimated that the biggest success of civil disobedience activities had been in generating 'a new sense of somebodyness'.[40] His emphasis on developing a sense of self independent of white cultural dominance intersected with the otherwise divergent, more militant and separatist segments of the black power movement. Further impulses were provided by feminism, the gay and lesbian movement, new left groups and a variety of self-help initiatives. All these movements were based on volunteer work and were fighting against discrimination and state oppression. They all experimented with forms of grassroots democracy within their own organizations and built up people's self-esteem while strengthening community self-organization.

The notion of empowerment involved vestiges of Kant's definition of enlightenment as a person's emergence from their self-imposed tutelage. Empowerment proponents shared an enlightenment faith in the liberating power of education and drafted concepts of how to harness it. Paulo Freire, with his literacy campaigns in Brazil and China and his concept of critical pedagogy, was perhaps the most important methodological reference for empowerment theories and is cited in almost all of them. His *Pedagogy of the Oppressed*, drawing on such diverse traditions as Marxist dialectic, Husserlian phenomenology, Sartrian existentialism and Buber's philosophy of dialogue, criticizes the traditional '"banking" concept of education', which practises subjugation while propagating emancipation. The method treats education as a kind of depositing, in which the students are the depositories and the teacher is the depositor. Instead of communicating, the teacher issues communiqués and makes deposits which the students patiently receive, memorize, and repeat ... The more students work at storing the deposits entrusted to them, the less they develop the critical consciousness which would result from their inter-vention in the world as transformers of that world. The more completely they accept the passive role imposed on them, the more they tend simply to adapt to the world as it is and to the fragmented view of reality deposited in them.[41]

Freire opposes this with his notion of education as consciousness raising (*conscientização*), replacing the vertical relation between teacher and stu-dent with a process by which knowledge is acquired mutually in dialogue: 'Authentic liberation – the process of humanization – is not another deposit to be made in men. Liberation is a praxis: the action and reflection of men and women upon their world in order to transform it'.[42] In the course of rais-ing consciousness, the teacher and the student gain a deeper understanding of their social reality and explore ways of changing it:

Whereas the banking method directly or indirectly reinforces men's fatalistic perception of their situation, the problem-posing method presents this very situation to them as a problem ... A deepened consciousness of their situation leads people to apprehend that situation as an historical reality susceptible to transformation. Resignation gives way to the drive for transformation and inquiry, over which men feel themselves to be in control.[43]

Freire accuses the paternalistic 'assistentialism' of degrading people to the status of passive receivers of aid. He also attacks the Leninist model of revo-lution, on the terms of which humans are instruments of the world spirit as decreed by party leadership.[44] The professional educator does not disappear in Freire's theory, but her role is fundamentally altered. Teachers become learners, 'teacher-students', in creating, together with the 'student-teachers', the conditions 'under which knowledge at the level of the *doxa* is super-seded by true knowledge, at the level of *logos*'.[45]

In addition to his critique of expertocracy and his advocacy for democratic participation and self-emancipation, Freire influenced the development of the empowerment concept with his practical work. With his literacy pro-gramme, he elaborated his philosophy of education into a complex system, thereby demonstrating that empowering the powerless and leading people need not be mutually exclusive (remember that the *Pedagogy of the Oppressed* is first and foremost a pedagogy (paidagōgía, with an emphasis on the Greek root agein, to lead). However, the methods he developed for Latin American farmers and slum dwellers could not be applied directly to other groups and societies. As a result, it was mainly Freire's call for dialogic between teacher-pupils and pupil-teachers and his insistence on the unity of action and reflection that entered empowerment discourse.

Theory of power

The empowerment concept varies across different programmes. They nevertheless all share a basic common denominator: a special theory of power. On this view, power is a social resource available in principle to all but in reality unequally distributed. These theories leave undetermined whether power is to be regarded as something people have, i.e. a property, or rather an external relation of force between people. In any case, the uneven distribution of power is not viewed as something obtaining once and for all, but is instead a continuous bone of contention. The authors are less interested in what causes this inequality, whether it is economic exploitation, political repression, institutional hierarchy, a lack of access to education and health care or discrimination on the basis of gender, skin colour or creed. Whatever the causes, the concern is with the psychological and social effects. It is not the power relations themselves that are the issue but the sense of powerlessness felt by those who do not have power: 'an attitude of self-blame, a sense of generalized distrust, a feeling of alienation from resources for social influence, an experience of disenfranchisement and economic vulnerability, and a sense of hopelessness in socio-political struggle'.[46] This sense of powerlessness reinforces and magnifies the power gap by causing the potential for autonomy and participation to lie fallow. Fatalist feelings of being the author of one's own failure, general mistrust and 'learned helplessness'[47] are the inner responses to this persistent experience of heteronomy, deprivation and lack of recognition. The loss of self-determination is only perpetuated when the disempowered are beleaguered by professional helpers incrementally cementing their own authority and the dependency of their clients.

This focus on self-attribution and on the dichotomy between the powerful and the powerless has two effects on empowerment strategies. First, it becomes possible to embrace diverse problems within a common definition. Whatever restricts people's conduct of their lives can be referred back to a lack of power. By means of this concept, large numbers of individuals with different experiences and ways of interpreting them can be made into a homogeneous group characterized by what they all lack: power. The unifying diagnosis is followed by a uniform, universal therapy: empowerment. On the empowerment model, all interventions in the political realm should be calculated to augment the power of those who have been designated as powerless. The more powerful they feel, the fewer problems they will have – and the fewer problems they will create.

This theory of power omits from its view the fact that it is itself an exercise of power, not a form of repression as such but something that nevertheless radically changes the situation. By attributing to specific groups of people a feeling of powerlessness and making them the subject of empowerment measures, the theory produces a definition of the problem and the victims. As Barbara Cruikshank points out in her analysis of community action programmes, 'the "powerless" do not exist as such prior to the application of technologies of citizenship; the "powerless" are the object and the outcome of the will to empower'.[48] In order to shake the powerless out of their lethargy, they need to be construed as a group by empowerment programmes, they need to be explained by sociology, guided by pedagogy and supported by psychology. This calls for experts, who, however, define their function differently to earlier researchers and helpers. They make no injunctions, degrade no one to the status of passive receiver of aid, but they do decide who should be a recipient of empowering activation. The power of these experts is first of all the power to define: 'deciding who should be empowered is a sign of power'.[49]

Empowerment measures consequent on this act of definition are also determined by the narrow theoretic focus on the ways people cope with power inequality. Empowerment is only secondarily concerned with redistributing real power. The main aim is to overcome the debilitating sense of powerlessness. It is not to solve problems but to cultivate the skills required to do so. Subjective and objective factors are considered dialectically. Becoming conscious of your own strengths and the changeability of power relations is the precondition for actually changing those power relations. On the other hand, nothing is so effective at promoting the consciousness of your own strength as successfully exercising it. In practice, however, this dialectic falls apart. The concept of empowerment presupposes learning by experience ('Empowerment is not a commodity to be acquired, but a transforming process constructed through action'[50]), but precisely because it does so it starts with the subjects, the people themselves. The disempowered are supposed to change the way they see themselves and the political situation in order to be able to overcome the objective 'power blocks'. A study of 'citizen empowerment', that observed grassroots activists from neighbourhood groups, environmental initiatives and migrant organizations over long periods, concluded that:

> the participants in this study ... did not view themselves as 'having more power' but rather as 'feeling more powerful'. They had not gained significant social influence or political control, but they did see themselves becoming more efficacious participants in the political process and local decision making. While they did not assess themselves as having acquired more absolute power to dictate the shape of their environments, they did believe they were growing better able to engage effectively in the dynamics of social and political exchange.[51]

While empowerment theory largely defines power as the sense of possessing power or as an inner force, power can also be understood as an expanding resource. Occasionally, one group of people gains power without others losing it. According to the concept of power explicated in many pro-grammatic theories of empowerment, it need not be a zero-sum game; it can be a win-win situation. This attitude dispenses with the antagonism between the powerful and the powerless, substituting for it a synergetic model that promises both reconciliation and redress: 'Paradoxically the more the resource is utilized, the more there is to be utilized'.[52] The harmonious, conflict-free utopia depicted here is only the first con-sequence. It is more important perhaps that the shift from *power over something* to *power to something* makes empowerment a never-ending project. This version of empowerment is governed by the law of accu-mulation instead of the law of conflict, with the consequence that no one can ever be empowered enough.

Anthropology

The liberal model of society – according to which an invisible hand guides the economy of power as well as the economy itself, thereby serving the mutual advantage of all citizens – corresponds to an anthropology according to which the basic human need is control over one's own life. In an article deploying the empowerment concept for management theory, the authors write: 'We assume that everyone has an internal need for self-determination and a need to control and cope with environmental demands'.[53] Another article devoted to realigning social work on a philosophy of human strengths is less sober:

> All people possess a wide range of talents, abilities, capacities, skills, resources, and aspirations. No matter how little or how much may be expressed at one time, a belief in human potential is tied to the notion that people have untapped, undetermined reservoirs of mental, physical, emotional, social, and spiritual abilities that can be expressed … Those who hold a strengths per-spective assume that this inner wisdom can be brought into more conscious use by helping people recognize this capacity and the positive power it can have in their lives.[54]

Here again, a specific definition of what it is to be a human being becomes the guideline for social practice, for what people should be made into and make themselves into. It may be speculative to posit such a hard-wired need for autonomy and vital energies, but as an ethical maxim it has effects. The golden rule of empowerment theory can be stated with a reformulation of Kant's categorical imperative: act only by that maxim which you give yourself, instead of receiving it from others or just subsiding into passivity.

This commandment should apply especially to those who are accustomed to the opposite:

> The subject model in the concept of empowerment ... is subtended by the
> belief in the ability of individuals to gain more autonomy, self-realization and
> self-determination by their own efforts, and this should also be possible for
> the addressees of welfare aid whose life management is buried under a layer
> of dependency, resignation and impotent opposition.[55]

The notion here is that empowerment merely uncovers the basic human
equipment that has sadly been kept hidden and dormant by adverse circumstances. On this view, there are no weaknesses, just suppressed or
undeveloped strengths waiting to be made conscious and brought to bear
on reality. In addition to constructing powerless people as a homogeneous
group, empowerment theory postulates that this group only feels powerless
because its members have not yet recognized their own power and experienced it in action.

In order for empowerment specialists to promote people's potential to
self-govern, they must first frame their problems as essentially caused by
a lack of self-government. This certainly involves individualizing if not
the causes of the problem then the solution. If empowerment consists
exclusively in strengthening people's faith in their own abilities instead of
strengthening the abilities themselves, then disappointment and therefore
further disempowerment are inevitable. The power of faith alone has not
been known to move mountains.

This criticism has also come from the proponents of empowerment
themselves. Many among them have complained of the theoretical reductionism and accompanying depoliticizing of the concept and demanded an
evaluation of the success empowerment work has had not only on people's
sense of control but on the real control they exercise.[56] Criticism has also
been levelled at the programmes for being biased, tailored to the standard
of the autonomous subject, thereby undermining the ethos of mutual aid,
another important tenet of empowerment. The empowerment of specific
individuals and marginalized groups can endanger greater social cohesion,
unleashing anomic forces:

> Does empowerment of disenfranchised people and groups simultaneously
> bring about a greater sense of community and strengthen the ties that hold
> our society together, or does it promote certain individuals or groups at the
> expense of others, increasing competitiveness and lack of cohesion? ... Group
> or community development inevitably will clash, at some point with that of
> the individual, and the empowerment of one person or group will conflict
> with that of another.[57]

Since this tension between social cohesion and individual and group
empowerment is regarded as incapable of resolution, the response has been
to concentrate on the need to find a balance.

The communitarian objection to the individualist use of the empowerment concept makes it clear that the opposition is not between political and apolitical readings of empowerment but rather between two different political models. Like other contemporary social and self technologies, empowerment mobilizes two contrary positions at the same time. A community of autonomous self-governing subjects, on the one hand, and community solidarity, on the other, would seem to be mutually exclusive ideas and yet they can be made to run in parallel.

Levels and processes

The empowerment literature both confronts and conceals this contradiction by treating it as a question of different levels of reference. Personal, organizational and community empowerment each have their own methods, but they are supposed by the literature to build on one another, supplement each other and develop synergistic effects:

> Empowerment processes cannot be reduced to the level of developmental psychology or organizational sociology. On the contrary, the force of such processes lies in the reciprocal dependency and integration of *change on the individual, group and structural levels.* Empowerment processes do not run along one of these levels independently, but rather *reinforce one another mutually by their interaction.*[58]

This harmony between the individual pursuit of happiness, group cohesion and social integration is not prestabilized; it must first be brought about by empowerment. Self-responsible and self-confident individuals, organizing in groups and actively participating to shape institutions, are precisely the autonomous citizens needed by a society founded on civil engagement. On all levels, the focus therefore needs to be on the strengths instead of the weaknesses, reinforcing people's confidence in their own power and promoting autonomy and democratic participation.

The same call to action is made to individuals, to various groups and institutions and to society as a whole: the call to self-actualize is a process of continuous empowerment and self-empowerment. As Charles Kieffer writes in his seminal article 'Citizen Empowerment', this process is modelled on the development of the child into a responsible adult. He elaborates further on the steps of this process of maturation: '[T]he transition from powerlessness to participatory competence can best be characterized as a dynamic of long-term development from socio-political illiteracy or "infancy" to socio-political "adulthood".'[59] The empowerment process often begins thus:

crucial and painful experiences (falling seriously ill or having relations fall ill) or ruptures in everyday life (unemployment, the loss or threat of loss of a natural environment) are often the first trigger to begin actively resisting a seemingly inevitable 'fate'.[60]

Kieffer compares this 'era of entry' to birth, characterized by uncertainty and initial tentative exploration of our own possibilities. This is followed by an era of advancement in which first progress is visible but the development process still needs support from without. In this second phase, corresponding to the developmental stage of childhood, it is important to have the support of experienced mentors as well as membership of a group of people in the same situation or with the same sensibility. Social back-up as well as the experiences and unavoidable disappointments of first attempts at action lead to a more realistic view of the political balance of power and its mechanisms. The tasks of the third phase, the era of incorporation, correspond to those of adolescence:

> In this phase the persons/groups must cope with the fact they have changed and moved on, 'grown up' socio-politically ... They must learn to deal with their new role as an important factor for society – with all the accompanying role conflicts within the group (leadership claims etc.) but also within the context of the previous social network.[61]

In the fourth phase, the era of commitment, the maturation process issues finally into adulthood. Participative skills are integrated into behaviour and self-identity, the conviction that we can contribute to shaping the world around us persists despite disappointments and setbacks, and this 'burning patience'[62] encourages younger people and groups beginning to form.

Empowerment is pictured here as a kind of *Bildungsroman*, whose characters become the authors of their own story. But the story must not only be lived, it must also be told. Only narration can endow the individual, group or society with the sense of coherence necessary for belief in their own capacities. Empowerment needs empowerment stories:

> The processes of self-reflection and self-mythologizing that occur by storytelling are important for propelling empowerment. They make change possible, and generate unity, identity and strength. It is the stories, not the results, which constitute the call to action, to begin telling one's own story and continue retelling it.[63]

This kind of learning from stories of the past is not done in order to critique the present but to provide affirmation and provoke imitation. Recalling the past is done in order to cope with the future.

Psychology

The reference to different temporal registers indicates the importance within the empowerment concept of compensation by helping and of coping with problems. A frequently cited 1982 article by a US psychologist collective distinguishes four basic forms of help and self-help by cross-tabulating the parameters: 'Attribution to self of responsibility for a problem high/low and attribution to self of responsibility for a solution high/low'.[64] While the *medical* (people are not responsible for problems or solutions), the *moral* (people are responsible for problems and solutions) and the *enlightenment* (people are not responsible for solutions but are responsible for problems)[65] models tend either to release people from responsibility for their lives or burden them with guilt, the *compensatory model* (people are not responsible for problems but are responsible for solutions) combines self-responsibility with not blaming the victim. On this model, self-orientation and other problem coping is supposed to encourage people without degrading them, mobilize without debilitating, and thereby resolve the practical contradiction inherent to traditional calls for more responsibility. Seen through the compensatory lens, everyone is responsible for their own fortune, yet without being responsible for their misfortune. The psychologists quote Jesse Jackson: '[b]oth tears and sweat are salty, but they render a different result. Tears will get you sympathy; sweat will get you change'.[66]

In the age of classical liberalism, the invocation of the autonomous subject followed the moralist model that made individuals responsible for their own successes and failures. The model was content to presuppose a natural free will while not further concerning itself with the nature of this faculty, providing for aid only in the form of discipline and paternalist charity.[67] In contrast, on the neo-liberal model, the entrepreneurial self requires continuous stimulation of its potential for self-determined action. Consequently, help must always consist in helping people to help themselves and should avoid instilling feelings of guilt. If the aim is to reinforce people's strengths, neither a bad conscience nor an interminable analysis of their weaknesses will prove helpful. Compensatory relief, however, does not involve deferring blame to others, such as society, capitalism, parents or genes. In fact, the question of root causes recedes into the background altogether. All the energy is focused on the solution. The rationale of empowerment states that uncovering sources of power is more effective than searching for the sources of powerlessness.

Translated into medical or psychological terminology, this involves a shift in focus from *pathogenesis* to *salutogenesis*, from risk factors to protective factors. The question is then not what made someone sick or threatens to make them sick, but rather what keeps them healthy. This is more than just a variant of positive thinking. The Israeli stress researcher Aaron Antonovsky, who coined the term salutogenesis,[68] treats sickness and health not as mutually exclusive but rather as two ends of the one continuum. On this view, sickness is a low level of health: 'We are all terminal cases. But as long as we have a breath of life in us we are all, to a certain extent, healthy'.[69] Antonovsky's notion of health parallels empowerment theory's interpretation of power as a quantifiable resource. A person's position on the health–sickness scale is a function of the relation between the stressors they are exposed to and the protective resistance resources they can mobilize: 'Stressors or resistance deficits lead to entropy, whereas resistance resources introduce negative entropy into the human system'.[70]

According to Antonovsky, the most positive influence on health, the one which 'orchestrates this battleground of forces'[71] and concentrates resources of resistance, is a basic cognitive, emotional and motivational attitude he refers to as a 'sense of coherence' and for which he has developed a standardized scale:

> [It is a] global orientation that expresses the extent to which someone possesses a thorough, enduring and yet dynamic feeling of trust. This feeling, first, structures the demands from the inner or outer experiential world in the course of life, making them predictable and explicable, and, second, makes available the resources required to meet the demands. Third, these demands must be challenges that deserve investment and engagement.[72]

Antonovsky also presupposes that this basic feeling is a relatively stable magnitude which is largely fully developed by adulthood. The sense of coherence thus greatly enhances the consciousness of one's own strength aspired to by the empowerment programmes. Together with related concepts from educational psychology such as *self-efficacy*,[73] *locus of control*[74] and *hardiness*,[75] the salutogenetic model delivers a meta-theory of the efficacy of the psychological and social protection factors that can be strengthened by empowering interventions.

The empirical description thereby becomes a social norm, whose claim to validity is irrefutable because it is supported entirely by empirical research. The 'productive personality traits' identified by stress researchers and health psychologists as 'antecedents of successfully coping with life' function as markers everyone should orient themselves on if they want to increase their potential. This list of health protection factors translates effortlessly into a set of demands for the entrepreneurial self: a firm belief in your own goals, the malleability of the world around you and your own skills for coping with it, active engagement with problems and the ability to integrate unpredictable changes into your life plan ('change as challenge'). Anyone seeking to prevail on the marketplaces of work, relationships and attention needs to accumulate this 'personality capital'.[76] Healthy, resilient, reliable, flexible and active people not only feel good physically but are a role model for others.

Yet absolute health is as impossible to attain as absolute power or economic success. Consequently, the mobilizing of resistance resources is an unending task; success can only ever be temporary.

Despite the analogy between salutogenesis and empowerment, there are clear differences. The German theorist of social work Norbert Herriger criticizes salutogenesis for its implicit 'assumption of a fixed, personal set of protective factors (mainly genetically predetermined temperamental traits)'. This leads, according to Herriger, 'to a resigning, fatalist view', responded to with 'conventional psychological competency programmes', whose sole aim is to 'psychically equip the person with a cushion against the danger of new experiences of helplessness'. Against such 'doubtful individualization of empowerment thinking', Herriger proposes 'solidarity networking and self-organization in social action' to generate 'the power of the plural'.[77]

This psychological and sociological critique of reductionist personality psychology once again manifests in the opposition between individualist and communitarian concepts of empowerment. However, instead of hardening into irreconcilable antagonism or resolving themselves at a higher dialectical level, the opposing terms co-mingle in the pluralist insight that different life situations demand different approaches.

Strategies

Whether the energy is to come from within the individual or from the group, empowerment is in psychological terms a motivation programme:

> To empower means to give power to. Power, however, has several meanings. In a legal sense, power means authority, so that empowerment can mean authorization. Power may also be used to describe capacity ... However, power also means energy. Thus, to empower can also mean to energize. This latter meaning best captures the present motivational usage of the term.[78]

The strategies employed by empowerment are mainly directed at injecting energy and encouraging participation as a means of amplifying freedom of choice and action and thus strengthening initiative and personal responsibility.

In this spirit, a sourcebook on development policy published by the World Bank with the title *Empowerment and Poverty Reduction* identifies four principles of empowerment intervention. For people to make use of their rights, use public services, negotiate their needs and seize opportunities, they require: (1) *access to information*: without education and media, no one can take steps to improve their situation; (2) *inclusion and participation*: this requires dismantling mechanisms of exclusion to involve marginalized groups in the reform process and presupposes democratic decision making and that everyone can exert an influence; this in turn presupposes:

(3) *accountability*: this refers to clearly assigned responsibilities and the power to make institutions and enterprises answerable for their policies and actions; corruption and abuse of power must be prosecuted and there must be secure rule of law for development programmes to be effective; (4) *local organizational capacity*: this is the ability of people to work together, organize themselves and mobilize resources to solve problems of common interest. Local associations and networks are not only a laboratory for democratic self-organization, but also the most important connection between state and international organizations on the one side and aid recipients on the other.[79]

Empowerment is here construed as the basis for 'good governance'. It should provide 'social cohesion and trust', 'quality of life and human dignity', 'pro-poor growth' and 'project effectiveness and improved service delivery'. It is at once an end in itself and also the means to other ends, since 'reducing the human degradation of powerlessness and releasing the energies of people to contribute to their societies through empowerment are two sides of the same coin'.[80] It is good governance, both morally and functionally, that promotes people's ability to govern themselves. To ensure this active democratic participation, standard procedures have been developed, together with process monitoring and quality management. Cooperation partners in receiver countries often have to implement a programme in order to be granted aid.[81] These 'technologies of citizenship'[82] constitute a control regime that calls for responsible political subjects who display solidarity, and ties this interpellation both to a promise and a demand for transparent operating procedures, self-empowerment and societal participation.

While these programmes differ from the development concepts from the 1960s and 1970s they are still locked into the political logic of modernization. Empowering and disciplining go hand in hand in a development process on the Western model:

> what people are 'empowered to do' is to take part in the modern sector of 'developing' societies ... as citizens of the institutions of the modern state; as consumers in the increasingly global market; as responsible patients in the health system; as rational farmers increasing GNP; as participants in the labour market, and so on. Empowerment in this sense is not just a matter of 'giving power' to formerly disempowered people. The currency in which this power is given is that of the project of modernity.[83]

Empowerment is here largely co-extensive with participation and is depicted not only as benefiting everyone – the participants as well as those letting them participate – but also as a system that can be applied elsewhere. It is in particular this marriage of ethics and efficiency that helped empowerment to become a key concept in development work.

Corporate management strategies using the empowerment label work on similar lines, basing leadership models on 'commitment' rather than on authority, 'initiative' rather than control. Empowerment in corporations is human resource management by another name. The calls to empower are delivered mostly to the upper and middle echelons, who are supposed to recognize the 'slumbering potentials' in subordinate employees, awakening those potentials and putting them to work in the interests of the company. A German management handbook states that empowerment makes employees 'capable of creating on their own the conditions they need to produce the necessary results. The enterprise trusts in its employees' ability to do this and supports them with all its force'.[84] The recommendation is not to abnegate leadership, but to replace it with a more efficient programme of self-leadership. The self in the self-empowerment of the powerless recedes from view and is overshadowed by the directive to the powerful to delegate their decision-making authority in the interests of the corporation: 'empowerment is something that is done to you by others, or that you do to others who thus become empowered by your actions not their own'.[85]

In another handbook, the mobilization rhetoric invoking empowerment while making utterances the performative force of which implicitly repudiates it, a list of abilities is given which make up the 'leadership attitude', which in turn characterizes the 'leader of potential': first, the ability to shape a 'vision' for the corporation and 'instil employees with a living image of it and inspire them to take part'; second, an 'everything will work out fine' attitude, 'the strength to decide on a course of action and then unremittingly stay on course'; third, 'mobilise employees, generating a 'magnetic field' and unleashing zeal'; fourth, 'supply a road map', entailing 1. 'Coordinating the individual factors into a web of causal connections' and 2. 'Breaking down such abstract concepts into precise instructions for putting them into practice'; and finally, fifth, 'making others capable of performing good work'. This is not restricted to communicating knowledge but involves also nurturing capacities on the motivational level.[86]

In comparison with these injunctions, other models of leadership, such as trusteeship and service, are gentle. In *The Empowered Manager*, Peter Block argues for a strategy based on personnel autonomy and social responsibility. This approach will achieve the realization democratic principles, spiritual harmony and customer satisfaction: 'The concept of stewardship rests ... on the sense of responsibility of each individual, but concentrates on service for the general good instead of on control. That is why it is a vehicle for influencing the extent of participation and responsibility that each individual develops toward the success of the organization, the society and their own lives'.[87] Even here, however, the imperative mood is not entirely lacking. In the invocation of the 'unbound employee' there is a threatening undertone:

> Indifference or authoritarian thinking is a form of passive aggression, a latent dismissal. Employees who hang their ability to think and act for themselves on the coat rack and perform their work as zombies will end up driving us into the grave. The difficulty is that we are especially dependent on our employees' commitment at a point in time where we are unable to offer workplace security in return ... we must create a work environment that boosts individual employees' efforts but is not built on false promises ... We must instil in every employee the firm conviction that they are performing an active function in the organisation.[88]

In plain language: employees who fail to let themselves be empowered will be fired and the rest can be glad they still have their jobs, for the time being that is.

There is a long road from Freire's *Pedagogy of the Oppressed* and Solomon's *Social Work in Oppressed Communities* to the training programmes for assisting managers 'get the best out of their employees'.[89] However, instilling enthusiasm is only one side of this latter day version of empowerment. Committed employees need more than charismatic leaders sweeping them up into general euphoria. Above all, they need an organization that strengthens self-responsibility and initiative while ensuring these autonomous agents cooperate effectively towards a collective goal. It is to this end that the management literature has appropriated emancipative concepts of empowerment.

Freire's 'teacher-student' and Alinsky's community organizer return *mutatis mutandis* in the idea of the 'leader personality' as a 'development worker' helping her team to 'develop a culture of learning':

> The task of managers (especially in middle management) has long since ceased to be surveillance of employees. Managers are called on to foster their employees, motivating their personal growth, career development and openness for change. They must develop a team to cooperate in the best way possible instead of merely supervising the individual performances of a group of employees.[90]

Even the social reformist, if not revolutionary, demand to 'change the system' has been adopted by management literature. In contrast to liberation pedagogy and radical community organizing, the permanent revolution of the corporation will not be negotiated democratically because it has already been agreed upon. When phrases like 'corporate empowerment' and 'liberation management'[91] are deployed to propagate a fundamentally new approach to work and to the company on the part of employees and a new quality of cooperation, the aim remains the same as before: market success. The power of the empowered ends when they are unable to fulfil this market imperative. The idea is to overturn the organizational structure of the corporation, not the corporation itself as an economic and legal structure.[92]

This is certainly an instrumentalist reduction of the maturity postulate, but the punchline to the empowerment discourse is that it presupposes absolute identity between the interests of the employees and the interests of the company, between personal growth and developing corporate competitiveness. The struggle for individual autonomy becomes identical with the struggle against bankruptcy. Finally, individual employees should even profit from the demands made upon them when the business liquidates their jobs:

> First of all, the employee today is encouraged to get actively and creatively involved in pursuing company goals. This new work style produces more personal satisfaction and motivation. The individual can learn to exceed his own limits and recognize the results of his efforts. Second, the sense of dependency grows less to the extent that someone assumes responsibility for his own career future. The more the individual employee develops his personal abilities, the more he recognizes that it is useful to possess and train various abilities and the more he develops a type of inner trust in his ability to take care of his own professional future, especially when the enterprise he is currently part of can make no clear statement to him regarding it.[93]

As constituent elements of corporate empowerment, the instructional literature recommends the same kind of strategies as the World Bank aid programmes: *transparency, recognition, participation*. Comprehensive information serves as an important motivator. Institutional hierarchies should disappear and with them secret management knowledge, making way for a feeling of collective endeavour: 'People need information to know how they and the company are doing, and if their actions are making a difference ... By opening the books to all employees, management begins to let them know that "we are in this thing together"'.[94] It is equally important to give employees a sense of being valued by both acknowledging and demanding achievement and initiative. One part of this is being flexible toward individual needs, such as working hours and further training. Since traditional incentives such as job security, remuneration and promotion opportunities are gradually diminishing, the empowerment experts focus increasingly on immaterial factors, justifying them as more motivational: 'New insights about the true needs of today's employees give cause for relief' declares one seminal advice book: 'Everyone wants to be treated as a VIP'.[95] Motivation through participation necessitates abandoning the old pyramidal organization and replacing it with networks of teams with individual responsibility: 'Your co-workers want to decide for themselves how to attain a specific aim and in which way they want to fulfil a specific task. "New" managers do not give work instructions. Instead, they request their co-workers to select together with them the best way of going forward'.[96] Freedom from disciplinary authority is granted to employees in exchange for a commitment to constant self-optimization. Employees are empowered by compelling them to exercise a specific power over themselves. This bending back of the subject on itself is thought to be more productive than the application of external authoritarian pressure.

We have seen that the social work and community psychology origins of the empowerment discourse present no obstacle to its deployment as a management strategy. On the contrary, when resource and competency-oriented approaches can help people suffering from marginalization, health deficiencies or other disadvantages, enabling them to better cope with their everyday lives and actively participate in the world around them, then such approaches will be all the more effective at strengthening those not confronted by such obstacles and already competing successfully. Empowerment strategies are practically universal in application, since they treat power as potentially available to everyone, as something everyone needs and something no one can ever have enough of. Who wouldn't want to learn to master their lives better?

Paradoxes of empowerment

The fact that empowerment is called for everywhere implies that it is everywhere lacking. By presupposing a feeling of powerlessness, the empowerment discourse confirms it, thus rubbing salt into the wound it is intended to heal.

This is certainly not the only paradox inherent in this form of governing. The project of freeing people from heteronomy by social technologies leads inevitably to an internal contradiction: 'the very institutional structure that puts one group in a position to empower others also works to undermine the act of empowerment'.[97] This contradiction persists even where the empowered and the empowering are one and the same group of people. The self-empowering subject is split into someone who needs more control over her life and someone who must make exertions to procure that control. Such subjects work concertedly to change their own conduct, to heighten their self-esteem and self-confidence; they recognize and utilize their resources and combat their own lethargy and feelings of resignation. In the process, they are forced to rely on the models society has on offer: pedagogical concepts, political role models, media icons, advice literature. People can assume or repudiate them; either way the models receive confirmation as the a priori of the work on the self that all subjects are beholden to undertake.

Like empowering others, self-empowerment follows the democratic ideal of the mature citizen who assumes responsibility for herself and is actively involved in building her community. As much as we may value this ideal, as much as we may hold it indispensible, even as counterfactual or at least counter-intuitive, we must accept that self-government remains a programme of government, and that empowerment therefore remains, even as a technique I apply to myself, a social technology, a 'technology of citizenship', as Barbara Cruikshank has called it:

> Democratic modes of governance are not necessarily more or less dangerous, free or idealistic than any other. Even democratic self-government is still a mode of exercising power – in this case, over oneself. Like government more generally, self-government can swing between the poles of tyranny and absolute liberty. One can govern one's own or others' lives well or badly.[98]

Promising to give everyone unlimited power does not eliminate the pitfalls of power. Strengthening someone also means straightening them, corseting them.

Notes

1. Jesse Jackson, cited in Philip Brickman, Vita Carulli Rabinowitz, Jurgis Karuza Jr, Dan Coates, Ellen Cohn and Louise Kidder (1982) 'Models of Helping and Coping', in: *American Psychologist*, 37(4), Apr., pp. 368–384, here: p. 372.
2. Julian Rappaport (1985/86) 'The Power of Empowerment Language', in: *Social Policy*, 16(2), pp. 15–21, here: p. 17.
3. Isaac Prilleltensky (1994) 'Empowerment in Mainstream Psychology: Legitimacy, Obstacles, and Possibilities', in: *Canadian Psychology/Psychologie canadienne*, 35(4), pp. 358–375, here: pp. 359f.; Carolyn Swift and Gloria Levin (1987) 'Empowerment: An Emerging Mental Health Technology', in: *Journal of Primary Prevention*, 8(1/2), pp. 71–94, here: p. 73; Ruth J. Parsons (1991) 'Empowerment: Purpose and Practice Principle in Social Work', in: *Social Work with Groups*, 14(2), pp. 7–21, here: p. 10.
4. Marc A. Zimmerman (2000) 'Empowerment Theory: Psychological, Organizational and Community Levels of Analysis', in: Julian Rappaport and Edward Seidman (eds), *Handbook of Community Psychology*, New York: Springer, pp. 43–63, here: p. 43.
5. Norbert Herriger (1997) *Empowerment in der Sozialen Arbeit: Eine Einführung*, Stuttgart: W. Kohlhammer, pp. 14ff.
6. Julian Rappaport (1987) 'Terms of Empowerment/Exemplars of Prevention: Toward a Theory for Community Psychology', in: *American Journal of Community Psychology*, 15, pp. 121–148, here: p. 140.
7. Wolfgang Stark (1996) *Empowerment: Neue Handlungskompetenzen in der psychosozialen Praxis*, Freiburg: Lambertus, p. 16.
8. Sabine Pankofer (2000) 'Empowerment – eine Einführung', in: Tilly Miller and Sabine Pankofer (eds), *Empowerment konkret: Handlungsentwürfe und Reflexionen aus der psychosozialen Praxis*, Stuttgart: Lucius & Lucius, pp. 7–22, here: p. 13.
9. Stephen B. Fawcett, Tom Seekins, Paula L. Whang, Charles Muiu and Yolanda Suarez de Balcazar (1984) 'Creating and Using Social Technologies

for Community Empowerment', in: *Prevention in Human Services*, 3(2/3), Special Issue: Studies in Empowerment, pp. 145–171.

10. Rappaport (1985/86) 'The Power of Empowerment Language', p. 15.
11. Julian Rappaport (1981) 'In Praise of Paradox: A Social Policy of Empowerment over Prevention', in: *American Journal of Community Psychology*, 9, pp. 1–25, here: p.15.
12. Rappaport (1985/86) 'The Power of Empowerment Language', pp. 17f.
13. See Si Kahn (1982) *Organizing: A Guide to Grassroots Leaders*, New York: McGraw-Hill.
14. See Peter L. Berger and Richard John Neuhaus (1977) *To Empower People: The Role of Mediating Structures in Public Policy*, Washington, DC: American Enterprise Institute for Public Policy Research.
15. See Lynn Atkinson (1988) *Power and Empowerment: The Power Principle*, Las Vegas: New Falcon.
16. See Peter Bachrach and Aryeh Botwinick (1992) *Power and Empowerment: A Radical Theory of Participatory Democracy*, Philadelphia: Temple University Press.
17. See Ann Bookman and Sandra Morgan (eds) (1988) *Women and the Politics of Empowerment*, Philadelphia: Temple University Press; Christine Heward and Sheila Bunwaree (eds) (1998) *Gender, Education, and Development: Beyond Access to Empowerment*, London/New York: Zed Books; Patricia Hill Collins (2000) *Black Feminist Thought: Knowledge, Consciousness, and the Politics of Empowerment*, New York: Psychology Press.
18. See Robert Adams (1996) *Social Work and Empowerment*, Houndmills: Palgrave Macmillan.
19. See Zimmerman (2000) 'Empowerment Theory'. A critical investigation of the application of the concept in this field of work is provided by Elizabeth Townsend (1998) *Good Intentions Overruled: A Critique of Empowerment in the Routine Organization of Mental Health Services*, Toronto: University of Toronto Press.
20. See Kelly Hannah-Moffat (2000) 'Prisons that Empower: Neo-liberal Governance in Canadian Women's Prisons', in: *British Journal of Criminology*, 40, pp. 510–531.
21. See Robert Adams (1991) *Protests by Pupils: Empowerment, Schooling and the State*, Basingstoke: Falmer.
22. See Deepa Narayan (ed.) (2002) *Empowerment and Poverty Reduction: A Sourcebook*, Washington, DC: World Bank Publications.
23. John Friedmann (1992) *Empowerment: The Politics of Alternative Development*, Cambridge, MA: Blackwell.
24. Judith Worell and Pam Remer (1992) *Feminist Perspectives in Therapy: An Empowerment Model for Women*, Chichester: John Wiley & Sons.
25. From the many how-to books, see e.g. Peter Block (1987) *The Empowered Manager: Positive Political Skills at Work*, San Francisco: Jossey-Bass; Kenneth H. Blanchard, John P. Carlos and W. Alan Randolph (1999) *The 3 Keys to Empowerment: Release the Power within People for Astonishing Results*,

Oakland, CA: Berrett-Koehler; Ken Blanchard, John P. Carlos and Alan Randolph (2001) *Empowerment Takes More than a Minute*, Oakland, CA: Berrett-Koehler. For a critical analysis of empowerment as a management concept, see Louise McArdle et al. (1995) 'Total Quality Management and Participation: Employee Empowerment, or the Enhancement of Exploitation', in: Adrian Wilkinson and Hugh Willmott (eds), *Making Quality Critical: New Perspectives on Organizational Change*, London: Routledge, pp. 156–172.

26. The group was renamed 'FreedomWorks' in 2004. See: www.freedom works.org/campaign/empower [18.01.2014].

27. Barbara Cruikshank (1999) *The Will to Empower: Democratic Citizens and Other Subjects*, Ithaca, NY: Cornell University Press, p. 43.

28. John F. Smith, Stephen B. Fawcett and Fabricio E. Balcazar (1991) 'Behaviour Analysis of Social Action Constructs: The Case of Empowerment', in: *Behaviour Change*, 8, pp. 4–9, here: p. 7.

29. Srilatha Batliwala (1994) 'The Meaning of Women's Empowerment: New Concepts from Action', in: Gita Sen et al. (eds), *Population Policies Reconsidered: Health, Empowerment, and Rights*, Boston: Harvard Center for Population and Development Studies, p. 127.

30. See Prilleltensky (1994) 'Empowerment in Mainstream Psychology', pp. 359f.

31. For a comprehensive study, see Barbara Levy Simon (1994) *The Empowerment Tradition in American Social Work: A History*, New York: Columbia University Press; a short summary is given in Herriger (1997) *Empowerment in der Sozialen Arbeit*, pp. 18–36.

32. Barbara Bryant Solomon (1976) *Black Empowerment: Social Work in Oppressed Communities*, New York: Columbia University Press.

33. Simon (1994) *The Empowerment Tradition in American Social Work*, p. xiii; the author cites Robert N. Bellah et al. (1991) *The Good Society*, New York: Vintage, p. 282.

34. Cruikshank (1999) *The Will to Empower*, p. 68.

35. Emerson formulates this very same programme in compact form in his essay: (1841/1983) 'Self-Reliance', in: *Essays and Lectures*, New York: Library of America, pp. 257–282.

36. Saul D. Alinsky (1971) *Rules for Radicals: A Practical Primer for Realistic Radicals*, New York: Vintage, p. 125.

37. Alinsky (1971) *Rules for Radicals*, p. 120.

38. Office of Economic Opportunity (1965) *Community Action Program Guide*, *Vol. 1*, Washington, DC, p. 7, cited in Cruikshank (1999) *The Will to Empower*, p. 73. For a thorough account of the history of the community action programmes, see Peter Marris and Martin Rein (1967) *Dilemmas of Social Reform: Poverty and Community Action in the United States*, Chicago: Transaction.

39. From a brochure on financing community action programmes cited in Cruikshank (1999) *The Will to Empower*, p. 74.

40. Cited in Simon (1994) *The Empowerment Tradition in American Social Work*, p. 142.

41. Paulo Freire (2005) *Pedagogy of the Oppressed*, London, pp. 72f.
42. Freire (2005) *Pedagogy of the Oppressed*, p. 79.
43. Freire (2005) *Pedagogy of the Oppressed*, p. 83.
44. Paulo Freire (2013) *Education for Critical Consciousness*, London: A&C Black, p. 138.
45. Freire (2005) *Pedagogy of the Oppressed*, p. 81.
46. Charles H. Kieffer (1984) 'Citizen Empowerment: A Developmental Perspective', in: *Prevention in Human Services*, 3(2/3), Special Issue: Studies in Empowerment, p. 16.
47. The term comes from Martin E. P. Seligman's eponymous (1975) *Learned Helplessness: On Depression, Development and Death*, San Francisco: W. H. Freeman.
48. Cruikshank (1999) *The Will to Empower*, pp. 71f.
49. Karen Baistow (1995) 'Liberation and Regulation? Some Paradoxes of Empowerment', in: *Critical Social Policy*, 15(42), pp. 34–46, here: p. 41.
50. Kieffer (1984) *Citizen Empowerment*, p. 27.
51. Kieffer (1984) *Citizen Empowerment*, p. 32.
52. Richard Katz (1984) 'Empowerment and Synergy: Expanding the Community's Healing Resources', in: *Prevention in Human Services*, 3(2/3), Special Issue: Studies in Empowerment, pp. 201–226, here: p. 202.
53. Jay A. Conger and Rabindrah N. Kanungo (1988) 'The Empowerment Process: Integrating Theory and Practice', in: *Academy of Management Review*, 13, pp. 471–482, here: p. 474.
54. Ann Weick, Charles A. Rapp, W. Patrick Sullivan and Walter Kisthardt (1989) 'A Strengths Perspective for Social Work Practice', in: *Social Work*, 34(4), pp. 350–354, here: pp. 352f.
55. Herriger (1997) *Empowerment in der Sozialen Arbeit*, pp. 74f.
56. See e.g. Stephanie Riger (1993) 'What's Wrong with Empowerment?', in: *American Journal of Community Psychology*, 21, pp. 279–292.
57. Riger (1993) 'What's Wrong with Empowerment?', p. 290.
58. Stark (1996) *Empowerment*, p. 129.
59. Kieffer (1984) 'Citizen Empowerment', p. 18. The influence of Erikson's psychology of maturity is evident here, with its ideal of successful integration between subject and society. See e.g. Erik H. Erikson (1980) *Identity and the Life Cycle*, New York: Norton.
60. Stark (1996) *Empowerment*, p. 121. Stark interprets here Kieffer's study.
61. Stark (1996) *Empowerment*, p. 124.
62. Stark (1996) *Empowerment*, p. 41.
63. Stark (1996) *Empowerment*, p. 49.
64. Brickman et al. (1982) 'Models of Helping and Coping', p. 370.
65. As an example of this model, the authors cite groups like Alcoholics Anonymous, which requires its members to assume total responsibility for their drinking problem instead of assigning it to inheritance, relationships or other external factors. At the same time, they must profess at every sitting that they cannot escape their alcoholism on their own and for that reason need the help of the Deity and the group.

66. Brickman et al. (1982) 'Models of Helping and Coping', p. 372.
67. See François Ewald (1986) *L'Etat-Providence*, Paris, Part 1.
68. Aaron Antonovsky (1987) *Unraveling the Mystery of Health: How People Manage Stress and Stay Well*, San Francisco: Jossey-Bass.
69. Aaron Antonovsky (1989) 'Die salutogenetische Perspektive: Zu einer neuen Sicht von Gesundheit und Krankheit', in: *Meducs*, 2, pp. 51–57, here: p. 53.
70. Jürgen Bengel, Regine Strittmatter and Hildegard Willmann (1998) *Was erhält Menschen gesund? Antonovskys Modell der Salutogenese: Diskussionsstand und Stellenwert*, Cologne: BZgA, p. 34.
71. Aaron Antonovsky (1987) *Unraveling the Mystery of Health. How People Manage Stress and Stay Well*, San Francisco: Jossey-Bass Publishers, p. 164.
72. Aaron Antonovsky (1993) 'Gesundheitsforschung versus Krankheitsforschung', in: Alexa Franke and Michael Broda (eds), *Psychosomatische Gesundheit: Versuch einer Abkehr vom Pathogenese-Konzept*, Tübingen: DGVT, pp. 3–14, here: p. 12.
73. Albert Bandura (1977) 'Self Efficacy: Toward a Unifying Theory of Behavioral Change', in: *Psychological Review*, 84, pp. 191–215; Albert Bandura (1997) *Self Efficacy: The Exercise of Control*, New York: Worth.
74. Julian B. Rotter (1966) 'General Expectancies for Internal versus External Control of Reinforcement', in: *Psychological Monographs*, 80, No. 609.
75. Suzanne C. Kobasa (1979) 'Stressful Life Events, Personality and Health: An Inquiry into Hardiness', in: *Journal of Personality and Social Psychology*, 37, s. 1–11; Suzanne C. Kobasa (1982) 'The Hardy Personality: Toward a Social Psychology of Stress and Health', in: Glenn S. Sanders and Jerry Suls (eds), *Social Psychology of Health and Illness*, Hillsdale, NJ: Lawrence Erlbaum, pp. 3–32.
76. Herriger (1997) *Empowerment in der Sozialen Arbeit*, p. 178.
77. Herriger (1997) *Empowerment in der Sozialen Arbeit*, pp. 178, 186.
78. Kenneth W. Thomas and Betty A. Velthouse (1990) 'Cognitive Elements of Empowerment: An "Interpretative" Model of Intrinsic Task Motivation', in: *Academy of Management Review*, 15, pp. 666–681, here: p. 667.
79. Narayan (2002) *Empowerment and Poverty Reduction*, pp. ix-xx.
80. Narayan (2002) *Empowerment and Poverty Reduction*, pp. 4, 8.
81. See Michael Schönhuth and Uwe Kievelitz (1994) *Participatory Learning Approaches: Rapid Rural Appraisal and Participatory Appraisal – An Introductory Guide*, Rossdorf: TZ-Verlag; United Nations Development Programme, *Empowering People*. For a critical appraisal, see: Frances Cleaver (1999) 'Paradoxes of Participation: Questioning Participatory Approaches to Development', in: *Journal of International Development*, 11, p. 597–612; Bill Cooke and Uma Kothari (eds) (2001) *Participation: the New Tyranny?* London/New York: Zed Books; Kerlijn Quaghebeur (2006) 'Pathways of Participation: A critical exploration of participation as a dominant learning perspective in the world of development cooperation', dissertation, Katholieke Universiteit, Leuven.
82. Cruikshank (1999) *The Will to Empower*, p. 67ff.

83. Heiko Henkel and Roderick Stirrat (eds) (2001) 'Participation as Spiritual Duty; Empowerment as Secular Subjection', in: Bill Cooke and Uma Kothari (eds), *Participation: The New Tyranny?*, pp. 168–184, here: p. 182.

84. Heiner Koppermann (1996) 'Empowerment: Schlummernde Potentiale wecken', in: Dietrich Buchner and Wolf W. Lasko, *Vorsprung im Wettbewerb: Ganzheitliche Veränderungen, Netzwerke, Synergie, Empowerment, Coaching – Das Veränderungshandbuch von Winner's Edge*, Wiesbaden: Gabler, pp. 291–306, here: p. 292.

85. Baistow (1995) 'Liberation and Regulation?', p. 37.

86. Bernd Wildenmann (2000) *Professionell führen: Empowerment für Manager, die mit weniger Mitarbeitern mehr leisten müssen* (5th edition), Neuwied/Kriftel: Luchterhand, pp. 33–37.

87. Peter Block (1997) *Entfesselte Mitarbeiter: Demokratische Prinzipien für die radikale Neugestaltung der Unternehmensführung*, Stuttgart: Schäffer-Poeschel, p. 19.

88. Block (1997) *Entfesselte Mitarbeiter*, pp. 21–22.

89. Cynthia D. Scott and Dennis T. Jaffe (1995) *Empowerment – mehr Kompetenzen den Mitarbeitern: So steigern Sie Motivation, Effizienz und Ergebnisse*, Vienna: Ueberreuter, p. 95.

90. Scott and Jaffe (1995) *Empowerment*, pp. 97–98. For a critical view, see Thomas A. Potterfield (1999) *The Business of Employee Empowerment: Democracy and Ideology in the Workplace*, Westport, CT: Greenwood.

91. This oxymoronic phrase is the title of a book by Tom Peters: (1992) *Liberation Management: Necessary Disorganization for the Nanosecond Nineties*, New York: A.A. Knopf.

92. Dirk Baecker (1999) *Die Form des Unternehmens*, Frankfurt: Suhrkamp, p. 9.

93. Scott and Jaffe (1995) *Empowerment*, pp. 72f.

94. W. Alan Randolph (1994/95) 'Navigating the Journey to Empowerment', in: *Organizational Dynamics*, 23(4), pp. 19–31, here: p. 22.

95. Scott and Jaffe (1995) *Empowerment*, p. 65.

96. Scott and Jaffe (1995) *Empowerment*, p. 122.

97. Judith Gruber and Edison J. Trickett (1987) 'Can We Empower Others? The Paradox of Empowerment in the Governing of an Alternative Public School', in: *American Journal of Community Psychology*, 15, pp. 353–371, here: p. 370.

98. Cruikshank (1999) *The Will to Empower*, p. 2.

8

QUALITY

In God we trust – all others have to prove their quality.[1]

The term quality tends to have two meanings: how something is, and how good it is. The first meaning is descriptive; something or someone possesses this or that attribute. The second meaning is a value judgement; the attribute makes the thing or the person good or valuable. Quality is therefore at once objective and subjective. Attributes can be defined and tested, whereas value judgements involve preference. In both cases though, quality is a marker of difference. Attributes or properties differentiate things, people acts and institutions from other things, people, acts and institutions respectively. The collective preferences are as diverse as the individual ones. What is important to one individual or group may be worthless to another. The term quality melds together facts of the matter and matters of concern; the way things are and the way they should be. All things inherently have qualities in the first sense, yet quality in the second sense is something we are constantly striving to attain. Qualities in the sense of attributes can be found all over. Quality as value bestows privilege.

In the context of economics, quality is also what distinguishes goods from one another. The 'immense accumulation of commodities', as Marx referred to the wealth of societies,[2] is so immense because the capitalist mode of production is constantly generating new commodities with new inherent properties, i.e. new qualities in the sense of attributes. In the same place, Marx defines the commodity as 'that which through its qualities satisfies human needs of whatever kind'. Only those commodities regarded as valuable on the marketplace, i.e. accorded quality in the second sense, find a buyer. In order to succeed then, the producer of commodities is obliged to continually improve the quality of her commodities above that of her competitors. It will have the same effect as an improvement in quality when she produces the same product at a lower cost or in a shorter space of time. The only valid criterion of value here is customer preference, meaning that quality as a distinction of privilege is bestowed by the market. The rarest of objects is worthless if no buyer is prepared to pay the price demanded, while trash products possess quality if people will pay for them.

The upshot of all this is that performing on the marketplace is centrally about being concerned with the market's attributions of quality. By extension, entrepreneurial practice consists in quality management. What is the nature of quality? Like the nature of entrepreneurial innovation (Schumpeter), or of optimal reallocation of resources (Casson) (see Chapter 2), the nature of quality can only be determined case by case. Quality can consist in a multitude of factors: structural quality, process quality, outcome quality,[3] an ideal conception, the physical properties of a product, its relation to real or imagined consumer needs, or the relation between margin costs and margin utility.[4] The entity subtending them all is the pressure to optimize: 'In the broadest sense, quality is something that can be improved'.[5] The function of quality management is precisely to find this room for improvement and since entrepreneurship is quality management it is the very activity that makes the entrepreneur an entrepreneur.

There is a wealth of quality management techniques on offer to today's entrepreneurs. Two examples of concepts transmitting the quality imperative in condensed and paradigmatic form will be analysed in what follows. The first to be studied is *total quality management* (TQM). A large number of practice-oriented handbooks have addressed this topic. The TQM programme promises improved efficiency and market success for businesses and other institutions by committing all of its members to entrepreneurial behaviour. TQM systematizes tools from other management concepts. At the same time, almost all quality assurance and development programmes assimilate elements from TQM. The second example is *360-degree feedback*, incorporating a set of procedures from human resource management that immerse employees in a regime of quality improvement through permanent evaluation by themselves and others.

Total quality management

According to the international standard definition of ISO 8402, Total Quality Management (TQM) is

> a management method of an organization to which quality is of central importance, which is based on the cooperation of all its members and which aims at long-term success by satisfying its receivers and by being useful to the members of the organisation and society.

Older concepts of quality assurance were based on control and evaluation of the production process and only indicated technical, functional product quality. TQM extends quality control to all corporate activities, with especial focus on customer relations, 'from advertising to sales negotiation, product delivery and billing and, if necessary, repair'.[6] This is combined with a preventative approach – mistakes should be avoided in the first place not just corrected later. This is achieved by zero-error programmes consisting of early warning systems and weak point elimination. Prevention expands to the size of a universal paradigm: 'not wasting energies and resources but deploying them purposefully and effectively – this applies to the value chain, to ecological considerations, to the political and social environment and last but not least to relations between people'.[7] The responsibility for product quality is no longer carried by a separate division for quality control. Each employee is charged with the tasks of error avoidance and quality improvement for their work area. Monitoring quality becomes a chief concern for higher employees and management, whose function is increasingly the development, implementation and permanent upgrading of quality management systems as well as training and advising employees in their use. These new quality specialists no longer monitor product quality; they monitor the monitoring.

The only unit of measurement for quality is customer satisfaction, and customers make ever new and ever higher demands. Moreover, since every product or service could always be faster, cheaper and more user-friendly, it is not enough to just maintain standards. Quality acquires a 'proactive or offensive character'; it is 'not a final purpose but rather a process that is never over, not a result but rather a parameter of action'.[8] The requisite circumspect care in handling all possible customer needs, including those they are still unaware of, transcends objective measurement and indeed there is no such measurement when the word *enough* has no meaning. As well as systematically gathering information on customer wishes, enterprises need a hermeneutic of desire that anticipates customers' thoughts before they are formed, thereby bringing forth the deprivation the products promise to alleviate. The customer-focused qualities required by the individual employee have been condensed into a set of rules of conduct in an easy-to-learn acronym form:

> **C**are about customers as individuals; **U**nderstand their point of view; **S**erve their human and business needs; **T**hank them for their business; **O**ffer to go the extra mile; **M**anage their moments of truth; **E**mpathize and listen to their concerns; **R**esolve problems for them; **S**ee customers as the reason for your job.[9]

Such maxims are hung in offices and factory floors over the ordinances from the old era of discipline. The imperative tone is still there, but order, hard work and punctuality have been replaced by customer service as the highest virtue, and it is according to this virtue that worker subjectivity is now shaped. The old discourse of discipline moulded the worker into a fixed form. Now, the TQM discourse operates by generating a magnetic pull, drawing the individual on, habituating her to follow and anticipate the movements of the customer.

As the proponents of quality management insistently reiterate with a dramatic and vaguely menacing undertone, the urgency of the programme arises from the intensification of competition. Since in almost all Western economies supply exceeds demand and markets are subject to accelerated change, 'customer demands must be anticipated by products developed in increasingly shorter time frames at increasingly lower cost; products whose quality inspires her'. This accelerating closure of the cleft makes quality a question of survival, with providers rushing 'uncompromisingly toward constant improvement in all areas in the struggle to become market leader'.[10] TQM goes beyond optimizing operation details to include a rigorous quality policy that in turn requires a reorganizing of the whole enterprise. It is not enough to be 'doing things right'; the company must be constantly checking 'if they are being done right'.[11] The commandment 'quality first!' is to be taken literally, with TQM experts extolling quality over cost reduction. Quality alone sets off the vast chain reaction that fizzes along from product improvement to cost and price reduction, bigger market share and job security before finally exploding in overall company success.

From the premise that cleaving strictly to customer expectations is the only road to success, it follows that optimization is best achieved by adapting all internal operations to the customer-provider model. In other words, the enterprise survives on the market by internalizing market mechanisms. Every department, every employee, is a customer in the one phase and supplier in the next phase of the value creation chain. As internal customers, they have the right (and the duty) to demand maximum quality fulfilment from their suppliers. As internal suppliers, they must tailor the goods and services they provide to the exact needs of their receivers. Obviously, there are natural limits on transferring the customer-is-king model to the internal workings of the business itself, since the model assumes that providers and receivers are really related to one another as sellers and buyers, whereas real sellers are forced to compete with other outside sellers. Internal receivers can in some cases simulate market competition by resorting to outsourcing and profit centre models but this is usually decided on at a higher management level and not by the individual divisions themselves. The provider-customer model's real function is to establish a new culture within the enterprise by committing all employees at all levels to engage in entrepreneurial activity. The message of TQM is that enterprises increase quality and therefore success by transforming themselves into manifold 'enterprises within the enterprise'. Wage earners become intrapreneurs, assuming responsibility, showing commitment and optimizing internal and external customer satisfaction on their own steam. On the Marxian explanation, capitalist organization of labour was characterized by an antagonistic logic referred to as 'anarchy in the social division of labour and despotism in that of the workshop'.[12] Now, production and circulation are each supposed to function on the same principle.

The factory is no longer governed by authority and discipline but rather by the self-regulating market.

The TQM programme is held to be nothing less than a 'holistic corporate philosophy',[13] if not a 'total philosophy',[14] which can only be put into practice in a so-called top-down process. Management assumes the role of Philosopher King, defining quality policies and formulating an enterprise vision before conjoining the two to create a 'company philosophy'. This philosophy must be pronounced using concise, snappy phrases 'that every-one can identify with, and that excite a certain athletic ambition and an "us" feeling'.[15] From these 'basic quality principles of the corporation', manage-ment then deduces 'long term and short term aims, developing the short term aims cascade-like across all levels of hierarchy, and obtaining thereby for all levels the identification with the policies formulated'.[16] The maxim reserved for management and other higher employees is 'not *right behind you* but rather *leading the way forward*'. Quality demands that 'the respon-sible supervisor testifies everyday in her own work that continual quality improvement and customer focus are not mere slogans for her but rather deeply inscribed in her work'.[17]

Despite the emphasis on the key role of top-level management as initia-tors and role models, TQM cannot only be decreed from above. There occur admittedly 'always moments where assertiveness, rapid-fire decision-making and an authoritarian manner are important'. Nevertheless, the overriding principle of TQM is its somewhat oxymoronic 'participative leadership style',[18] that views employees as agents not as cost factors, encouraging them to act on their own initiative and involving them in setting goals. In this context, leading does not mean commanding; it means mobilizing. The ideal boss is the 'active team captain' who achieves top-rate performances in her own right, stays in close touch with her teammates and sweeps them up in her enthusiasm. It is not enough to 'just sit on the edge of the field and scream and occasionally substitute a player when things are going wrong'.[19]

Total mobilization in the name of quality demands a high degree of motivation. TQM implies that people are only motivated who can derive satisfaction from exerting effort. Just as products and services answer to the demands of external purchasers, so too must working conditions answer to the needs of employees. Joseph M. Juran, one of the founding fathers of quality management, constructed a Maslow-like hierarchy of such needs for quality motivation. Maslow's needs (physiological needs, safety, love/belonging, esteem, self-actualization)[20] now become: higher earning opportunities through the reward of quality, job security (maintaining the competitive edge through qual-ity improvement), cooperative group work, recognition by award of distinctions for quality work and provision of opportunities for participation.[21]

This anthropological account of the employee-customer as a creature with a hierarchy of needs, ascending from basic up to secondary and higher level, is a variant of the pastoral model of human government.[22] The quality manager is a good shepherd, on intimate terms with the needs of the sheep entrusted to her, concerned for their welfare and that none be lost. Through this concern for the individual sheep as well as for the herd as a whole, the shepherd secures their loyalty, increases their output and can lead the whole business to greener pastures. The catch of course is that needs can only be temporarily or partially fulfilled, making the pastoral project a Sisyphean task.

The original feature of this leadership model is not that it privileges empowerment over authority but rather the way it justifies this revaluation. The justification involves blurring the distinction between internal and external company relations. Quality equals customer satisfaction and within the company everyone is everyone else's customer. Concern for employees and concern for customers are therefore two sides of the one coin. The basic rule of conduct following from this is that management should do unto employees as it would have them do unto external customers. Management should deploy the same powers of persuasion and seduction it applies to potential customers on acquiring potential employees for the company. Tom J. Peters and Robert H. Waterman – the most commonly read (or at least purchased) management gurus – stipulate as the defining mark of 'excellent companies' the same credo as TQM:

> By offering meaning as well as money, they give their employees a mission as well as a sense of feeling great. Every man becomes a pioneer, an experimenter, a leader. The institution provides guiding belief and creates a sense of excitement, a sense of being a part of the best, a sense of producing something of quality that is generally valued.[23]

The older concept of 'management by objectives',[24] reactived by TQM, works with the semantics of the internal customer, albeit with the roles reversed, framing the relation between management and employees as a contract of purchase. This implies both parties facing each other on an equal footing and agreeing freely on terms of delivery. This discursive mutation, transforming leaders and subordinates into internal customers and providers, appears to replace asymmetrical in-company power relations with a win–win situation, rendering the rhetoric of class struggle even more obsolete than it already was.

An essential element of the strategies of motivation is a radical revaluation of the subjectivity of the worker. The worker is no longer seen, as she was in Taylorism, 'as a disruptive factor requiring operations to be rigidly controlled on the basis of scientific knowledge'. Instead, the worker's own sense of herself and what she wants to become are activated and put to use to optimize work processes. In traditional unionist or left-wing discourses, subjectivity was both the point of departure and point of resistance against working conditions seen as alienating. Now, management concepts like TQM turn subjectivity into a socio-technological resource to be tapped into:

The social and communicative dimension of work is made an explicit part of the new definition of its function. Self-guided group work makes engagement and participation a duty. Radically altered norms of self-representation are imposed on workers, who can no longer legitimately present themselves as the plaything of higher powers, as passive victims. If they want to stay out of the loser corner they must present themselves as autonomous subjects.[25]

In the 1960s and 1970s, *worker autonomy* was a class struggle catchcry for factory occupiers and strike committees. Now this notion of autonomy has forfeited its subversive aura and mutated into a tool of rationalization. The notion of self-determination has been recast in the mould of those market mechanisms it was once fighting against.

Entrepreneurship as a fundamental value and a principle of organization requires that employees assume more responsibility. How much room an employee has to make her own decisions will depend on the specific job. An assembler will have less than a technician working on product development; a checkout worker less than a customer adviser. The proclamation of freedom and responsibility does not mark the end of in-house discipline. As a technology of governing, TQM has shifted the focus from limiting contingency to raising contingency and making positive use of it, subject to the categorical imperative of market success. The traditional mechanisms of survey and punish can be dispensed with to the extent that this 'moral law' of success, to put it in Kantian terms, can be nurtured within each individual. The efforts TQM undertakes to integrate employees are a means to an end; the immediate end being to increase quality, the final purpose of which is to increase profit, and employee wellbeing is explicitly of concern as far as it contributes to this end. Employees are supposed to self-actualize but by taking on board the imperative of quality improvement: 'TQM requires employees to be responsible for managing the "quality" of their individual contributions; and, relatedly, to accept and internalize forms of surveillance and control that monitor their activity and commitment'.[26]

For employees to be entrepreneurial, creative and innovative, the company needs a climate favourable to challenging old ways. A BMW management guide includes the maxim, 'it is everyone's duty to become an *initiative taker*'.[27] When total flexibility is required, then the expert-governed regimentation of the old Taylorism inevitably looks counter-productive. A company run on TQM lines will still need a large number of standardized procedures which will determine the way workers act. But the aim is no longer to adapt behaviour to a fixed production quota that is regularly raised, but rather to ceaselessly cultivate the ability to improvise in order to reach a preset goal. In other words, TQM replaces continually raised quota fulfilment with the norm of continual improvement.

A buzzword for this phenomenon is kaizen, a Japanese word meaning literally *good change*, i.e. improvement. Self-praised in its title as '[*t*]*he key to Japan's competitive success'*, kaizen recycles earlier concepts such as the employee suggestion box and the quality circle, combining them into a strategic system. In the current literature, kaizen is treated occasionally as an element of TQM, occasionally as a management model in its own right. These texts lay the emphasis on optimizing operations not on results. Kaizen differs from the Western approach, where innovation is understood as radical, usually technologically supported change introduced by a small taskforce and generally involving a big outlay. Kaizen is performed by everyone all the time, consisting in incremental steps rather than big leaps made by employees who are conditioned by the system to seek improvement opportunities. This approach entails an altered attitude toward errors. Efficient error prevention is not the juridical affair of finding and punishing the guilty, nor the three Christian phases of confession, contrition and absolution. Continual improvement calls for an open diagnostic practice free of moralizing. Employees must be allowed to reveal mistakes without fear of punishment in order to be able to investigate and remove their root causes. Every deficit is an occasion for deterring future ones. With this functionalist approach to error, together with the fostering of work in small groups, praised as the 'democratization of the grass roots',[28] kaizen unfolds a pacifying force. 'Enemies' become 'allies',[29] more than happy to yield to the non-coercive coercion of quality improvement:

> When management wants to increase company productivity the work council will ask 'why should we? That just means that we have to work harder. What do we get out of it?' But no one can have anything against quality, not even the work council. Quality is the only way to maintain competitiveness and attain customer satisfaction. Efforts to improve quality lead on their own to improved productivity.[30]

To this end, kaizen provides a whole set of simple-to-use and handy, easy-to-master tools for statistic error analysis and visualizing cause-and-effect relations.[31] With their aid, autonomous work groups, improvement teams, can identify and eliminate weaknesses. The results 'are indeed generally barely visible at first, undramatic and often small, but in the end the results are significant and spectacular'.[32]

Quality management is not limited to motivational talks about customer focus, to all-round contentment and continual improvement. As stated above, mobilization of the entrepreneurial self through the rhetoric of empowerment is all too often accompanied by bourgeoning workloads. It is also accompanied by the effort to make the self calculable. Involvement is made co-extensive with accountability. TQM becomes a master key when it is joined to standardized procedures for planning, controlling and monitoring quality such as ISO 9000–9004.[33] This canonical text, which has been adopted by manufacturers, service companies, state administration and NGOs, provides a one-size-fits-all set of rules on how to set up and carry out quality assurance measures. The implementation of these measures is regularly evaluated by outside auditors, who award organizations a certificate for success. The biggest tool in the kit is a handbook detailing the principles and aims of quality management, prescribing organizational structure and responsibilities and specifying quality assurance procedures. The ISO 9001 handbook provides a general scheme in the form of 20 quality criteria applicable to organizations of all sizes, beginning with '(1) responsibility of upper management' and ending with '(20) statistic methods'. The system is predicated on traceability: to be able to identify errors and avoid them in the future, the complete chain of operations needs continuous documentation. As a core component, the handbook contains sets of form sheets in numbers proportionate to the size of the organization. Members of the organization are assigned to fill in specific forms, others to evaluate them, and others again to compile and archive them. The book also stipulates periodic internal audits preceding the external ones.

The certificates, which in some businesses have started to replace diplomas as decoration, are no longer just an auxiliary marketing tool. In many areas, they have become obligatory. For reasons of legal liability for product standards, many enterprises will only do business with providers who can produce certificates. Further, products requiring licenses, such as medical equipment, can only be sold when the manufacturers have introduced a certified quality management system. Standardized quality policies have worked their way into other areas as well. Hospitals, rehab centres and mobile nursing services, for example, can only bill costs to insurance agencies if they produce standardized 'product descriptions' and document their quality assurance measures. The same applies to social institutions applying for public funding. A whole certifying industry has grown up, with quality auditors rising to social power as an unchallenged monitoring force that few enterprises, government agencies and NGOs can place themselves outside of.[34] With its all-encompassing documentation requirements and ritual tests, the ISO 9000 ff. introduces a panoptic control system. This system is capable of subsuming the most diverse aspects of a company's operations into a single transparent structure. It does this by restricting itself to second-order observations. This means that quality assurance does not address itself directly to the activities of production; instead, what actually get tested are the in-house quality test procedures themselves. In a further abstraction, the quality assurance standards themselves are standardized. The research lab for this standardized and standardizing practice was an institution that had already played a star role in the classical disciplinary technologies: the military. The first quality assurance norms were laid down by the American and British armed forces as requirements for arms manufacturers.

The military striving for uniformity and control naturally does not correspond point for point to quality politics. ISO 9000 ff. is often understood as a component of quality management, and yet in important regards it follows a different logic. The extensive bureaucratic operations involved in certification tend to go against the anti-bureaucratic inclination in TQM, where the idea is to replace regulations with market self-regulation. More important still is the fact that a successful audit in no way guarantees that products and services fulfil customer needs because it only tests the correct application of standards and these may or may not correspond to customer needs. An educational institution, for example, 'will receive its much-desired certificate if it regularly and reliably monitors to ensure that it is holding up the same bad service standards it originally set down'.[35] From the perspective of TQM, an ISO 9000 ff. quality assurance is not good enough, but in a customer-focused culture defensively securing the status quo can serve to lay the foundations for more offensive quality strategies. Furthermore, ISO 9000 ff. and TQM converge in their preventative orientation and make use of the same instruments. In addition to certification, a basic tool of all quality management is the failure mode and effect analysis, a formal method 'for systematically and comprehensively detecting and representing possible risks, problems and mistakes in products as well as production and administration processes'.[36]

Although analysis transposes the test to the level of processes, the ISO 9000 ff. standard remains a static corpus and its measurements are reduced to the pass/fail distinction. A company is either awarded the certificate or it isn't. A more flexible and also dynamic form of quality measurement is the comparison between other enterprises or between different departments and employees of the one enterprise such as is performed in TQM as benchmarking[37] and by awarding prizes for quality. The standard used is neither a fixed measurement nor a statistical average; the standard is being the best, which endows the test with the character of a major sporting jamboree with all participants competing for new records. The aim of benchmarking is:

> to establish the best performance among the competitors, describe it, quantify it and ascertain what made it the best ... For the other companies this best-profile is a marker to be strived for and if possible superseded. Superseding is necessary because the other competitors are constantly working on improving their strengths and eliminating their weaknesses.[38]

Using fixed indicators to measure itself against the 'best of the best' makes it possible for an organization to clearly and distinctly identify the causes of its success. This is intended not only to awaken employees' ambitions but also to show them the concrete steps they can take to self-improve toward peak capacity and possible market leadership. Of course, not every local team can play in the champion's league, so it is better to match yourself against the leader in your own league. On the other hand, in benchmarking humility is not esteemed as a virtue but rather regarded as capitulating to the competition. The winner-takes-all economy has no room for complacent isolationism nor is modest local success good enough: 'In the short term, it may be enough for an enterprise to be better than its competitors. In the middle or long term however only a world class enterprise can be the standard'.[39] To rank quality means to quantify it and compare it to others, thereby sustaining a permanent pressure on all below first position to raise their performance and on the holders of first position to do everything in their capacity to stay there.

Benchmarking functions by imitating successful patterns of behaviour on the principle that individuals and organizations should copy the recipes of the most successful players in order to attain success for themselves. The difficulty is that if all competitors are using the same recipes, the distance between them will tend to diminish and with it the degree of measurable success. The paradox of benchmarking is that its efficacy declines in proportion to the number of people or companies using the concept. Imitators always learn the wrong stuff because yesterday's optimal procedure is already today's obsolete old standard solution that no longer provides that vital competitive edge. For the advocates of benchmarking, however, this is no objection, since it implies merely that the system of performance comparison must reign permanently: 'Successful benchmarking is not performed once and for all. Benchmarking can only exert its full effect through repeated application'.[40]

Benchmarking fosters classical Olympian virtues, which is proved by the fact that the European Foundation for Quality Management (EFQM) and its US equivalent, the Malcolm Baldridge National Quality Award, award companies with real medallions. Firms competing for these prizes are chosen by an independent jury based on criteria indicative of the quality specialists' priorities. The EFQM Excellence Award measures the following factors: leadership: 10%, people management: 9%, policy and strategy: 8%, resources: 9%, processes: 14%, people satisfaction: 9%, customer satisfaction: 20%, impact on society: 6%, business results: 15%. The finalists have then to demonstrate their strengths at a company inspection before the jury makes its final decision. The best company receives the EFQM Excellence Award as the most successful representative of total quality in Western Europe. This appropriation of rituals from competitive sports ('The trophy is engraved with the winner's name and can be retained by them for one year'[41]) is obviously not devoid of comic value; the award procedure is akin to the in-company Guinness books of records and the crowning of 'employee of the month',[42] and at the same time such market economy hall-of-fame spectacles also bear an uncanny resemblance to earlier practices in communist countries. However, the award culture also indicates that symbolic incentives are expedient to help people withstand the permanent pressure of competition. The initiators of the quality prizes provide a catalogue of criteria to 'serve companies as the foundation for analysis of their current status and for the development of concerted measures for improvement', which can be used by companies implementing TQM to improve their TQM programme without competing for the much sought-after medallions.

Benchmarking and quality contests can be seen as mere extensions of the basic TQM principle that continual quality improvement depends on continual monitoring and measurement of performance. The foundation is 'to treat every task as a process'.[43] Companies and their consultancy firms expend considerable effort gathering data on error rates, cycle times, costs and quantities, as well as customer and employee satisfaction, generating performance profiles, quantifying data, collating them into rankings, comparing it with the data of other companies and employees and deriving differentiated optimization measures. The underlying assumption is that all company activities can be precisely determined, if monitored with sufficient frequency, by quantifying them as inputs and outputs. This monitoring of operations, together with customer and personnel surveys and other statistical measurements, creates feedback loops by generating information for reinsertion into operations to improve their efficiency. As a result, the data rapidly become obsolete, so feedback must be organized as a continual process. Customer surveys must be calibrated to strike a balance between obtaining sufficient relevant data and avoiding excessively annoying respondents with long questionnaires and time-consuming telephone interviews. This makes random sampling and abbreviated questionnaires preferable to blanket coverage: 'With 10 to 17 questions and scaled answers the essential aspects of customer relations can be almost always totally illuminated.'[44]

The untiring will to knowledge occasionally causes curious excrescences. The authors of a US bestseller with the title *Reinventing Government: How the Entrepreneurial Spirit is Transforming the Public Sector* praise the police department in Madison, Wisconsin for successfully employing the 'total quality method'. Over the last five years, the department has sent a questionnaire to every 50th person who has had dealings with the police:

> whether a victim of crime, a witness, a complainant or a criminal (it is now up to every 35th person). Every month, more than 200 people receive the survey, which comes with a postage-paid, self-addressed return envelope. It asks them to rate the officers they encountered on seven factors: concern; helpfulness; knowledge; quality of service; professional conduct; how well they solved the problem; and whether they put the person at ease. They can rate an officer 'excellent,' 'good,' 'fair,' 'poor,' or 'very poor.' An open-ended question asks: 'How can we improve the quality of our service in the future?'[45]

The customer-is-king principle takes on a wondrous new meaning when a drug dealer or burglar is requested to meditate on whether police conduct was 'fair' or 'poor' and notes that he would have liked to have been offered coffee and cigarettes at his interrogation.

This curious example shows that measuring customer satisfaction entails quantifying the service quality provided by the personnel. Inversely, only happy personnel make for happy customers, so an internal as well as external satisfaction barometer is needed. By the same token, since the needs of the customer are the measuring rod for the quality of provider performance, an evaluation of customer satisfaction will also imply a potential judgement of personnel. In turn, surveys of personnel, by gathering data on the general work climate and employee contentment, also provide an indication of the leadership quality of the management, who is frequently subjected to manager audits combining self-judgement with outside judgements:'First, management and employees are informed, then all receive a questionnaire on management style to be filled out by the directors as well as the other employees.' The evaluation is followed by a feedback talk and, if required, professional supervision for the management:

> In some companies the decision is made by the managers and it is up to them whether they take part or not. In other cases participation is obligatory and the results are submitted to the next superior and also registered in the personal file of the 'evaluee'.[46]

360-degree feedback: the democratic panopticon

The system of all-round evaluation reaches its furthest extreme in an instrument from personnel management: *360-degree feedback*.[47] The method combines traditional personnel and customer surveys with management audits and self-appraisal to create a comprehensive evaluation system. Usually practised to ascertain and optimize management performance, it can in principle be applied to members of an organization at any level. A large number of providers and variants are currently competing for market share, but the basic elements are the same: by means of a questionnaire, employees' professional performance is evaluated by colleagues, supervisors, subordinates and themselves. Additional feedback can be provided by customers, providers and external supervisors. Parameters to be tested include 'business and individual skills' ('recognizes problems', 'adds value to the business', 'visualizes the future'), 'customer service' ('listens actively', 'balances requests with business needs', 'treats customers as business partners'), 'teamwork' ('seeks involvement', 'builds consensus', 'puts team interest first'), 'professional and technical knowledge' ('improves existing processes', 'organizes work', 'actively increases skills') and 'manages resources' ('takes initiative', 'takes informed risks', 'anticipates change').[48] For each of these items, the respondents are usually to agree or disagree on a scale of one to five or one to ten. They are frequently requested to supply ideal values as comparison to the real values and to assess the importance of each criterion. The analysis of the results is usually done externally to preserve anonymity. The whole analysis procedure is often performed on electronic data networks. The subjects receive the result in the form of a personal performance profile. Alone or in cooperation with professional consultants, they use the profile to put together a plan of action, which will be subject to follow-up checks. In the literature and in the companies themselves, there is disagreement as to who should have access to the results apart from the subjects themselves, for example supervisors, and whether they should be used exclusively for individual coaching or also for making decisions about subjects' wages and whether or not to fire them.

A genealogy of the method uncovers roots in humanist psychology, especially in group dynamics;[49] 360-degree feedback borrows the 'hot chair' exercise from sensitivity and communication training and renders it virtual and anonymous. All participants are forced to make confessions about themselves and others, which function to trigger self-experience and improve social competency. These training groups go back further to Puritan communities, whose members would meet regularly to confess both their lapses and their good works and exhort one another. Max Weber's analysis of these types of meetings can be applied to the case in question: 'Sociologically important is the fact that the community functions as a selection apparatus for separating the qualified from the unqualified'.[50] There are also obvious affinities between all-round evaluation and rituals of critique and self-critique in communist party organizations whose claim was to obtain a perfected 'new human'. Here, the criterion for mutual evaluation was not individual performance in terms of customer needs but the authoritarian party-decreed truth to which the individual had to conform without regard to personal wishes. Finally, the procedure also adopts elements from opinion polls with which enterprises and political parties gather data for developing marketing and election campaigns. In 360-degree feedback, this kind of information is supplied to all manner of employees who are expected to use it to regard themselves as a kind of political personality or market product.

We can see that 360-degree feedback already begins to exercise control with the awareness that evaluations are going on. Those being evaluated are under surveillance from all sides, but they are also evaluating the people evaluating them. This creates a democratic panopticon. Instead of a hidden, all-seeing observer on one side and an observed subject who cannot observe back on the other side (as in Bentham's panopticon), 360-degree feedback is a non-hierarchical structure of reciprocal visibility. Everyone observes everyone and is observed by everyone. Of course, relations of power are not levelled by adding bottom-up evaluation to top-down evaluation.

Nevertheless, people in authority must at least give account of themselves if they are being judged on the same criteria as their subordinates. Everyone is equal to the extent that everyone is held up to the same standard.

This system of control is not only equally distributed, it is also generalized to include all aspects of behaviour. Earlier tests were restricted to their own internal content. In 360-degree feedback, anything the assessed person is doing or failing to do while performing the test can register in the evaluation. This adds a general exhibitionism to the general voyeurism: 'Because everyone is seen by everyone and seen constantly, everyone must present themselves in a favourable way. The consequences are impression management, aesthetification, identity work'.[51]

Being observed by others forces people to observe themselves, which is supposed to lead them to improve their self-control. This presupposes also that the results of the evaluation be taken down and communicated. The regime of seeing and being seen is supplemented by one of writing down and reading out. When the assessments have been communicated, the subjects can start modifying their behaviour: eliminating weaknesses, reinforcing strengths. In the institutions of disciplinary power, people were conditioned in mainly one direction. As the name already suggests, the feedback version of post-disciplinary control is closely linked to cybernetics. In cybernetics, the individual is a system for processing information, fluidly adapting her behaviour to the expectations of her environment that are indicated by regular inputs of bits of feedback. Regulating her behaviour directly from outside would be enormously costly and would contradict the economic imperatives of flexibility, initiative and efficiency. Feedback loops tell her when she is diverging from the norm while leaving it up to her to develop appropriate adaptive strategies. This self-control by feedback is a species of the 'conduct of conduct', identified by Foucault as an elementary formula of the exercise of power:

> [T]o 'conduct' is at the same time to 'lead' others (according to mechanisms of coercion which are, to varying degree, strict) and a way of behaving within a more or less open field of possibilities. The exercise of power consists in guiding the possibility of conduct and putting in order the possible outcome.[52] Basically power is less a confrontation between two adversaries or the linking of one to the other than a question of government. This word must be allowed the very broad meaning which it had in the sixteenth century. 'Government' did not refer only to political structures or to the management of states; rather it designated the way in which the conduct of individuals or of groups might be directed: the government of children, of souls, of communities, of families, of the sick.[53]

Feedback differs from traditional discipline apparatuses in that its norm is determined as a set of relations, which is open at the top. Instead of imposing fixed quotas on people, control sets an interminable process of self-optimization in motion. In this regime of 'flexible normality',[54] producing evaluative quantification equates with generating truth. The observations, statistically averaged and visualized, usually in the form of bar charts, are intended to liberate knowledge of self from subjective distortions and blind spots. The mirror held up to the subject is assumed to obtain objectivity by synthesizing a variety of mirror images layered one over the other to produce an average image.

In his analyses of the institutions of discipline, Foucault warns against losing sight of the productive effects of power – the way it generates new entities – by concentrating only on its repressive functions. It would be a mistake to understand 360-degree feedback as an instrument of repression that is especially perfidious because it uses self-control. Its appeal is its combination of promise and threat. On the one hand, using the feedback results to undertake a methodical work-over of self promises individuals the opportunity to develop their personal potential while at the same time contributing to the success of the company. On the other hand, under the feedback regime, everyone is in danger of sliding into the red area at the next feedback session and losing ground in the in-company contest.

Like Bentham's control architecture, 360-degree feedback, on the one hand, seeks to increase 'an "aptitude", a "capacity"', while on the other, 'it turns it into a relation of strict subjection'.[55] But in contrast to older disciplinary institutions, feedback does not systematically curtail people's autonomy and deprive them of free space in which to act. Instead, it opens this space up even more and utilizes it as a resource. It thereby substitutes contingency management for contingency elimination. Another power effect of 360-degree feedback is just as important as self-control. Before employees can use the feedback to improve their performance, they are inserted into an analytic grid or pattern that defines which aspects of their conduct are relevant for the evaluation, thus tending to pre-structure the way participants see themselves and each other. Whatever the answers turn out to be, the questions have already been decided. The activity makes everyone comparable to everyone else by supplying everyone with the same measuring instruments. The assessment results provide each subject with a profile, an individual bar chart, distinguishing them from others, thus making each individual a differential function of the fixed parameters, mapped onto the same basic diagram that is applied to all. Power is being exercised here in the way the test defines what is a desirable performance, in the choice of parameters, which pre-frame the results. These parameters are in turn determined with a view to advancing the interests of the organization, i.e. improving its market success. Standard practice is to assemble the planning group from all levels of the organization, including 'at least one in-company sceptic'. Questions are then selected according to a single criterion, which makes it clear that making people assessable is co-extensive with making them useful to the company: 'What are the critical competencies our organization will need in the future to sustain our competitive advantage in the market?'[56] What does not conform to this goal will not be assessed.

The power exercised by evaluation is justified by its objectivity. It does not arbitrarily *impose* a ranking. Instead, it provides uniform, mechanical standards for producing one statistically. This has contradictory effects. First, employees' positions in the ranking have far-reaching ramifications, so they will tend to adjust their conduct prospectively, focusing on tested factors and neglecting what falls between the grates. The feedback thus already starts to produce in advance the conditions it is meant to test, creating a general state of busy conformity, instead of the innovative capacities it advertises. Since 360-degree feedback is obliged to determine its standards before it starts measuring, it cannot take in anything new after that point. It must award the mark of excellence to the most mainstream swimmers. Comparing performance will tend rather to hamper innovation and creativity because these traits presuppose divergence from the norm and thus resist by definition standardized evaluation.

The commandment to 'know thyself' (as others see you) and the project of compelling members of organizations to self-optimize (according to the way others see them) manifest the subjectifying power of all-round evaluation. The prescribed self-exploration and the subsequent work of self-perfection lead to a regime of subjectivity that promotes individuals' autonomy while in equal measure binding them to the judgement of others: *I am what the results say I am and what I make of myself by acting according to them.*

In the introduction to the second volume of *The History of Sexuality*, Michel Foucault distinguishes four dimensions of self-constitution that lay down the foundation for his study of classical guides to the good life. This list of categories can be fruitfully mapped onto contemporary subjectification programmes like 360-degree feedback. What Foucault calls 'moral conduct', 'the manner in which one ought to "conduct oneself"', can be differentiated along four lines: (1) which aspect of the person is the object of work on self – 'determination of the ethical substance'; (2) what way people are made to recognize the obligation to conduct themselves in a certain manner – 'mode of subjection' *(mode d'assujettissement)* or the 'deontology'; (3) which techniques it uses to do so – 'forms of elaboration, of ethical work (travail éthique)' or 'ascetics'; and (4) what purpose it should serve – the 'telos'.[57] In what ways do these levels of self-relation come to the fore in 360-degree feedback?

Ethical substance: a glance at the questionnaires quickly reveals what the feedback is evaluating and consequently which aspects of themselves the participants have to work at optimizing. The questionnaires repeat in different combinations the same catalogue of key qualifications also tested in assessment centres and trained in typical personality seminars. These various hard and soft skills are measured on the basis of observable behaviour, not hidden wishes and inhibitions. Beliefs and values are relevant only to the extent that they are expressed in action. This implicit behaviourist psychology frames the subject as a collection of different skills with an almost infinite capacity for acquiring new ones. The conduct being evaluated is located in the past but the purpose of the retrospection is to prevent future failings. This generates life history as the account of what to do better in the future. The tendency is toward a subjectification of the surface. It does not need to drill deep because it takes understanding the self as a function of changing it.

Mode of subjection: self-improvement is not extolled in the name of a secularized protestant work ethic exhorting the individual to pursue economic success or the good life. The framework for this personalized mobilization is the reformation of all social relations, including the relation to self, on the economic model. The subtext of 360-degree feedback, its descriptive-prescriptive utterance, is the following: competition is everywhere, so everyone must deliver what the customer wants and do it better, faster and cheaper than the competition. This dictate of comparison applies to employees in the same way as to enterprises, because they are competing against other employees, which means they must act in every way as the entrepreneur of their own selves. All-round assessment provides them with the personalized market data they need to locate their current position in the race and know what they must do to make ground. It is left up to them what they do with this knowledge. But by the same token they must cope with the consequences on their own. At the permanent tribunal of the market there is no court of appeal.

Forms of elaboration: this subjectification programme localizes work on the self in visible behaviour. Its method of subjugation consists in compelling subjects to conduct their lives on the economic model. Instead of tightening the corset, it releases the individual's inner forces and massages them into supple flexibility. The feedback loops of reciprocal evaluation assist by producing performance profiles. The performance profiles assume the appearance of objectivity by being composed of a plurality of perspectives. The results translate into a concrete personalized training programme, with or without a coach. The subject now has to work on the qualifications the evaluation tells her she is lacking. This can be an impossible challenge: if she has a high score on 'develops and realizes an aggressive approach when pursing company goals', she will hardly have done well on 'carefully considers the overall consequences of every decision, is interested on her own initiative in overall knowledge, approaches everyone with dignity, respect and trust'.[58] The questionnaires generate a paradoxical ideal model of contemporary subjectivity. As Manfred Moldaschl and Dieter Sauer have nicely put it, the ideal people being demanded here are 'the assertive team player or the team minded loner, the customer-focused smoothy with rough edges ... they must be both modest *and* gifted self-marketers, sensitive moderators with a hunter's instinct for profit opportunities, rational profit-optimizers with a sense for holistic well-being'.[59] The inherent contradictions are of the essence. The demand is so excessive that the individual is kept constantly open to criticism. She can never rest, because improvements in one direction mean losses in another. Subjectification means here an art of maintaining balance, but a curious balance consisting in the co-presence of mutually exclusive extremes.

Telos: the final aim of self-shaping is not a stable state of personal happiness nor is it economic success. Nor do transcendental goals like living in a way pleasing to the deity or conforming to a moral law have any significance for the contemporary entrepreneurial self. The project of entrepreneurial subjectification dwells in the immanence of worldly balance charts and is as interminable as the struggle for market dominance. The development of human capital is a continuation of the law of accumulation. For the company 'Me Incorporated', growth is not merely the means to an end, but the end itself. Those who strive for this end will never arrive, but stay in perpetual motion.

In his account of Bentham's surveillance apparatus, Foucault in no way claims that people in the 19th century were governed everywhere and all the time through such mechanisms. The panopticon was 'an event of thought ... which made something new possible in the domain of government'.[60] And 360-degree feedback is another such innovation. What makes this method paradigmatic is not the growing number of providers and users but rather the fact that it makes visible, as does Bentham's design, a 'diagram of a mechanism of power reduced to its ideal form ... a figure of political technology that may and must be detached from any specific use'.[61]

Few prisons, factories, barracks, clinics and schools correspond fully to the panopticon model. Likewise, not all feedback systems attain total reciprocity where the assessors are also being assessed. Yet few people evade entirely the evaluations, quality audits, citizen, employee and customer questionnaires currently seeping into all areas of life. The panopticon concentrated the principles by which the society of discipline functioned. There are many indications that all-round evaluation may be assuming a similar role in the emerging post-disciplinary order. It crystallizes the strategies of entrepreneurial 'conduct of conduct' that are everywhere present in fragments into one unified procedure. Like the regime of surveillance and punishment, the 'micropolitics of comparison'[62] has no single centre. The various technologies of assessment that converge in 360-degree feedback are designed and refined in different institutions, operating in part independently of one another, in part copying and modifying each other. They continue to proliferate as market relations become more and more the prototype of social interaction. What Bentham said of his invention also applies to the system of mutual evaluation: '[I]ts great excellence consists in the great strength it is capable of giving to *any* institution it may be thought proper to apply it to'.[63]

This strength consists in the way all-round evaluation promises at the same time to throw open the boundaries that otherwise limit the individual's performance and to orient that performance on market needs – optimizing the individual is of course not enough. The system offers to rationalize the way people are governed, reining in divergent individual interests and pointing everyone in the one direction. The generalization of competition this unity implies promises at the same time a utopia of reconciliation. The apostles of 360-degree feedback are convinced that it not only pushes aside power hierarchies but also renders obsolete current forms of worker participation. The manager of the German internet provider Cisco gives the following reasons for why the company has no works council:

> At Cisco we make no distinction between employee interests and company interests. When we choose employees for whatever task it is very important to us that they possess entrepreneurship. We have introduced the 360-degree feedback system. That means there is no hierarchic cascade of judgement from the top down.[64]

When everyone has become an entrepreneur, there are no masters or servants anymore, no employers and employees. In the world of self-determination, there is no longer any domination, and exploitation is swept aside by a tide of win–win–situations and synergistic effects. If the prophets of the entrepreneurial spirit speak true, the democratic panopticon is, like its predecessor, 'a case of "it's easy once you've thought of it" in the political sphere'.[65]

Notes

1. This is the former motto of the evaluation agency *Evaluationsagentur Baden-Württemberg* (Evalag). The current motto: 'The purpose of evaluation is not to prove, but to improve' (Egon Guba), www.evalag.de/dedievl/projekt01/index.php?idcatside=83 [17.01.2015].
2. Karl Marx (1996) *Capital, Vol. 1*, Washington, DC, p. 1.
3. This seminal distinction within quality management was made by Avedis Donabedian. See Avedis Donabedian (1980) *The Definition of Quality and Approaches to its Assessment*, Ann Arbor, MI: Health Administration Press. *Structural quality* refers to the quality of the productive factors used as well as to development and the organization of procedures; *process quality* refers to the properties of the activities that contribute to a particular aim; *outcome quality* refers to the product or the intended state.
4. These five distinct definitions of quality – (1) transcendent, (2) product-based, (3) user-based, (4) manufacturing-based, (5) value-based – are from David A. Garvin (1984) 'What does "Product Quality" Really Mean?', in: *Sloan Management Review*, 26, pp. 25–43.

5. Masaaki Imai (1992) *Kaizen*, Munich, p. 31.
6. Armin Töpfer and Achim Mehdorn (1995) *Total Quality Management* (4th edition), Neuwied: Luchterhand, p. 10. On the history of corporate quality management, see Alan Tuckman (1995) 'Ideology, Quality and TQM', in: Adrian Wilkinson and Hugh Willmott (eds), *Making Quality Critical: New Perspectives on Organizational Change*, London: Routledge, pp. 54–81.
7. Regina von Diemer (1994) 'Motivation', in: Walter Masing (ed.), *Handbuch Qualitätsmanagement* (3rd edition), Munich/Vienna: Hanser, pp. 1061–1074, here: p. 1063.
8. Attila Oess (1994) 'Total Quality Management (TQM): Eine ganzheitliche Unternehmensphilosophie', in: Bernd Stauss (ed.), *Qualitätsmanagement und Zertifizierung*, Wiesbaden: Gabler, pp. 199–222, here: p. 201.
9. Cited in Barbara Townley (1995) '"Know Thyself": Self-awareness, Self-formation and Managing', in: *Organization*, 2, pp. 271–289, here: p. 283.
10. Rudolf Neumeier (1997) 'Qualitätsmanagement für Dienstleister', unpublished seminar document from the TÜV Akademie Hessen.
11. Töpfer and Mehdorn (1995) *Total Quality Management*, pp. 10f.
12. Marx (1996) *Capital, Vol. 1*, p. 228.
13. Oess (1994) 'Total Quality Management', p. 199.
14. See Barbara Townley (1998) 'Beyond Good and Evil: Depth and Division in the Management of Human Resources', in: Alan McKinlay and Ken Starkey (eds), *Foucault, Management and Organization Theory*, London: Sage, pp. 191–210, here: p. 197.
15. Hans-Ulrich Frehr (1993) *Total Quality Management*, Munich: Hanser, p. 69.
16. Oess (1994) 'Total Quality Management', p. 214.
17. Frehr (1993) *Total Quality Management*, pp. 27, 25.
18. Diemer (1994) 'Motivation', p. 1070.
19. Herbert Henzler, Chairman of the McKinsey Corp., as cited in: Frehr (1993) *Total Quality Management*, p. 32.
20. Abraham H. Maslow (1970) 'A Theory of Human Motivation', in: *Motivation and Personality* (2nd edition), New York: Harper & Row, Chapter 4, pp. 35–58.
21. Cited in Rolf Schildknecht (1992) *Total Quality Management*, Frankfurt: Campus, p. 156.
22. Michel Foucault (1981) 'Omnes et Singulatim: Towards a Criticism of "Political Reason"', in: Sterling M. McMurrin (ed.), *The Tanner Lectures on Human Values II*, Salt Lake City: University of Utah Press/Cambridge University Press, pp. 225–254.
23. Peters and Waterman (1982) *In Search of Excellence*, pp. 322f.
24. George S. Odiorne (1965) *Management by Objectives: A System of Managerial Leadership*, New York: Pitman.
25. Hermann Kocyba (1999) 'Das aktivierte Subjekt: Mit post-tayloristischen Formen der Arbeit ändert sich auch die moderne Berufsidee', in: *Frankfurter Rundschau*, 28 September.
26. Adrian Wilkinson and Hugh Wilmott (1995) 'Introduction', in: *Making Quality Critical: New Perspectives on Organizational Change*, London: Routledge, pp. 1–32, here: p. 9.

27. Cited in Rolf von Bühner (1993) *Der Mitarbeiter im Total Quality Management*, Düsseldorf: VDI-Verlag, p. 136.
28. Bühner (1993) *Der Mitarbeiter im Total Quality Management*, p. 214.
29. Imai (1992) *Kaizen*, p. 209: 'Employers and Employees – Enemies or Allies?' is the rhetorical question heading one of the chapters in Imai's book.
30. Imai (1992) *Kaizen*, p. 130.
31. On the 'Seven Statistical Tools' and the 'New Seven', see Imai (1992) *Kaizen*, pp. 281ff.
32. Oess (1994) 'Total Quality Management', p. 208.
33. See: Robert W. Peach (1995) *The ISO 9000 Handbook*, Scarborough, ON: CEEM Information Services; Frank Voehl, Peter Jackson and David Ashton (1994) *ISO 9000: An Implementation Guide for Small to Mid-sized Businesses*, Boca Raton, FL: St Lucie Press. On the spread of the notion, see Isin Guler, Mauro F. Guillén and John Muir Macpherson (2002) 'Global Competition, Institutions, and the Diffusion of Organizational Practices: The International Spread of ISO 9000 Quality Certificates', in: *Administrative Science Quarterly*, 47(2), pp. 207–232.
34. Michael Power (1994) *The Audit Explosion*, London: Demos; Michael Power (1994) 'The Audit Society', in: Anthony G. Hopwood and Peter Miller (eds), *Accounting as Social and Institutional Practice*, Cambridge: Cambridge University Press, pp. 299–316; Michael Power (1997) *The Audit Society: Rituals of Verification*, Oxford: Oxford University Press.
35. Maja Heiner (1996) 'Evaluation zwischen Qualifizierung, Qualitätsentwicklung und Qualitätssicherung', in: *Qualitätsentwicklung durch Evaluation*, Freiburg: Lambertus, pp. 20–47, here: p. 26.
36. Sondermann, 'Instrumente', in: Stauss (1994) *Qualitätsmanagement und Zertifizierung*, Wiesbaden: Gabler p. 244.
37. For an introduction, see Robert C. Camp (1989) *Benchmarking: The Search for Industry Best Practices that Lead to Superior Performance*, Milwaukee: Quality Press.
38. Frehr (1993) *Total Quality Management*, p. 205.
39. Werner Kreuz (1994) 'Benchmarking: Voraussetzung für den Erfolg von TQM', in: Achim Töpfer and Armin Mehdorn (eds), *Besser – Schneller – Schlanker: TQM-Konzepte in der Unternehmenspraxis*, Neuwied: Luchterhand, p. 83–108, here: p. 86.
40. Bengt Karlöf and Svante Östblom (1994) *Das Benchmarking Konzept: Wegweiser zur Spitzenleistung in Qualität und Produktivität*, Munich: Vahlen, p. 192.
41. S. Wongrassamee, J. E. L. Simmons and P. D. Gardiner (2003) 'Performance Measurement Tools: The Balanced Scorecard and the EFQM Excellence Model', in: *Measuring Business Excellence*, 7(1), pp. 14–29, here: p. 16.
42. See Imai (1992) *Kaizen*, p. 212.
43. Townley (1998) 'Between Good and Evil', p. 197.
44. Fritz Brandes (1998) 'Profitabler werden mit zufriedenen Kunden', in: *Frankfurter Allgemeine Zeitung*, Blick durch die Wirtschaft, 6 May.

45. David Osborne and Ted Gaebler (1992) *Reinventing Government: How the Entrepreneurial Spirit is Transforming the Public Sector*, Reading, MA: Prentice Hall, p. 173.

46. Johannes Thönneßen (1999) 'Mitarbeiter beurteilen ihre Chefs – das Beispiel Bayer', in: *Harvard Businessmanager*, 5, pp. 99–106, here: pp. 100f.

47. A systematic overview of the method is provided by Mark R. Edwards and Ann J. Ewen (1996) *360° Feedback: The Powerful New Model for Employee Assessment and Performance Improvement*, New York: AMACOM.

48. Edwards and Ewen (1996) *360° Feedback*, p. 86.

49. See my reconstruction of the genealogical line connecting cybernetics and group dynamics in: (2006) 'Und ... wie war ich? Über Feedback' ['So ... how was I? On feedback'], in: *Mittelweg 36*, 15(2) (Apr./May), pp. 27–44.

50. Max Weber (1978) *Economy and Society*, Berkeley, CA: University of California Press, p. 1204.

51. Oswald Neuberger (2000) *Das 360°-Feedback: Alle fragen? Alles sehen? Alles sagen?*, Munich: Rainer Hampp, p. 73.

52. 'The exercise of power consists in "conducting conducts"' is a literal translation for 'L'exercice du pouvoir consiste à "conduire des conduits et à aménager la probabilité"' (Michel Foucault (1994) 'Le sujet et le pouvoir', in: *Dits et Ecrits*, *Vol. IV*, Paris: Gallimard, pp. 222–234, here: p. 237).

53. Foucault (1983) 'Subject and Power', pp. 220f.

54. See Link (1997) *Versuch über den Normalismus*.

55. Foucault (1977) *Discipline and Punish*, p. 138.

56. Edwards and Ewen (1996) *360° Feedback*, p. 81.

57. Michel Foucault (1990) *The Use of Pleasure*, New York: Vintage Books, pp. 26–28. See also Michel Foucault (1983) 'On the Genealogy of Ethics: An Overview of Work in Progress', in: Dreyfus and Rabinow, *Michel Foucault*, pp. 229–253, here: pp. 238ff; and Ian Hacking (1986) 'Self-Improvement', in: David Couzens Hoy (ed.), *Foucault: A Critical Reader*, Oxford/New York: Wiley, pp. 235–240.

58. Cited in Neuberger (2000) *Das 360°-Feedback*, pp. 91f.

59. Manfred Moldaschl and Dieter Sauer (2000) 'Internalisierung des Marktes: Zur neuen Dialektik von Kooperation und Herrschaft', in: Heiner Minssen (ed.), *Begrenzte Entgrenzungen: Wandlungen von Organisation und Arbeit*, Berlin: Edition Sigma, pp. 205–224, here: p. 221.

60. Osborne (2001) 'Techniken und Subjekte', p. 14.

61. Foucault (1977) *Discipline and Punish*, p. 205.

62. Neuberger (2000) *Das 360°-Feedback*, p. 56.

63. Cited in Foucault (1977) *Discipline and Punish*, p. 206.

64. ULA (2000) 'Fünf Fragen an Josef Rentmeister, Mitglied der Geschäftsführung, Cisco Systems Deutschland GmbH', in: *ULA Nachrichten: Zeitschrift für Führungskräfte der Deutschen Wirtschaft*, Nr. 5/6, June, p. 2.

65. Foucault (1977) *Discipline and Punish*, p. 206.

9

PROJECTS

The sense for projects, which could be called fragments from the future, differs from the sense for fragments from the past only in terms of direction; the sense for projects is progressive, the sense for the past is regressive. The essential thing is the ability to immediately idealize, realize and embellish objects all at the same time while also partially executing them in oneself.[1]

The word project can mean different things. Even the German Institute for Standardization (DIN), whose whole raison d'être is to provide precise definitions, manages to be somewhat vague on the topic. DIN-Norm 69901 defines a project as an 'undertaking characterized essentially by the uniqueness of the conditions as a whole, e.g. by the specific aim, by limits of timeframe or personnel, by distinction from other undertakings and by a project-specific type of organisation'.[2] In ordinary usage, the contours become even more blurred. The meaning of the term encompasses the undertaking itself, the people planning it, the plan or design itself and the individual steps involved in carrying it out, i.e. the end and the means. It is a form of social cooperation as well as an individual venture. Projects are inherently bound up with the possibility that they may not work out. They are a middle-order kind of thing somewhere between a single task and a permanent activity, momentary cooperation and more complex organization, between an idea and its realization, always in a state of becoming. They incline toward fulfilment but perpetuate their own lives only so long as they remain unrealized.

The term's low resolution makes it easy to elevate almost anything anyone is undertaking to the status of a project: a relationship, a military campaign, some scrap of research work, stray leisure time, staging a play, building a power station, the citizens' initiative trying to stop the power station, or the act of launching a brand new detergent onto the market. The post-modernist media philosopher Vilém Flusser re-reads Heidegger to argue that the human who reverses her thrownness or ejection into the world by projecting herself mutates 'from subject to project', thereby becoming authentically human.[3] Jürgen Habermas has reproached such 'postmodernist' positions for seeking to jettison the modernist project.[4] Niklas Luhmann, on the other hand, is inconsistent on this issue, writing in 1990, seemingly in a state of annoyance: 'With the best will in the world, theory of society cannot be regarded as a project', only to confess a few years later, not without irony, that it was his own project: 'On my appointment to the Department of Sociology established at the University of Bielefeld in 1969, I was asked what research projects I had running. My project was, and ever since has been, the theory of society'.[5]

The academy provides a wealth of material for studying the world of projects. In 1988, the German sociologist Joachim Matthes had already lamented the result:

> What is distressing is not the fact that research can, in some circumstances should or even must, be performed in the shape of projects but rather that the principle of project-shaped research has so much insinuated itself that any idea for research is immediately caught in its gravitational pull, no future prospects for it can be imagined, even in its earliest stages of development, but as issuing in a project.[6]

The need to legitimate research work as project work and to continually acquire new projects produces its own semantics, its own social types and types of event all just waiting to be given a sociological description. Research projects give rise to artificial text genres such as 'application prose': the art of squeezing any theme into the structure of a funding application, carefully wording it to create the knowledge gaps the proposed project promises to fill. Research projects engender a new species of academic creature: the research veteran – hardened in post-graduate research groups, an old hand at crawling from one temporary contract to the next, versed in the routines and tricks of funding acquisition and reporting, looked down on by the tenured with a mixture of pity and contempt. As Joachim Matthes has written:

> For those teachers in higher education authorized to undertake projects the opportunity alters surreptitiously or openly into a welfare benefit. 'Fast breeder reactors' are set up to this purpose, often with support by research associations associated with the grant recipients. In the procession from one project to the next many a fresh academic career and many a young talent go gradually to seed.[7]

Finally, research projects also bear the main responsibility for the viral spread of academic conferences. Budget contingents are set aside funds for conferences, staff must have some activities to show for it in order to get renewal, academic communities are dependent on the networking done at gatherings, so academic personnel tour from workshop to symposium to conference churning out anthologies. All this activity is only accidentally related to the effective production and communication of knowledge, while it is essentially related to the way scholarship is forced to present itself.

Almost anything can be made into a project, but not all projects can be undertaken at the same time. Fixing on one project entails excluding others, and where several are run in parallel they need to be clearly distinguished. Projects are determined by their outer contours, especially in time. They constitute 'temporally limited structures';[8] they have a beginning and an end and they structure individual action and social processes into sequences of discrete units. This makes projects dependent on value criteria for assessing ex ante their prospects and ex post their success or failure as well as for assuring some underlying continuity between the units. As such, projects are always subtended by some larger regime. A company may introduce project-based organization but this will not affect its larger legal and economic framework. Likewise, project-based instruction occurs within the framework of the institution's *school* and remains oriented on a curriculum. Even in management guru Tom Peters' mantra 'I am my projects',[9] from his tersely titled *The Brand You 50, Or: Fifty Ways to Transform Yourself from an 'Employee' into a Brand That Shouts Distinction, Commitment, and Passion!*, all those projects cannot cohere together without the underlying *I*.

Names do not leave their objects untouched. Calling something a project means assigning it the character of a design or intent and evaluating it according to specific criteria. Among other things, this involves excluding everything 'which cannot, without contrivance, be installed between beginning and end'.[10] Calling something a 'project' is a way of organizing reality, a rational scheme, a technology, a type of relation to the self. Nothing anyone is doing is a project per se, but most things people are doing can be poured into this mould. The fact that talk about doing things has come to be so often couched in project talk says a lot about how people understand and organize themselves, their actions and their relations to others. The 'project' turns out to be a basic element of contemporary governmentality. Governing becomes project management in two ways: the governing of projects and governing by projects.

From the projector to the alternative project

The project has long seeped into diverse areas but its semantic roots are economic.[11] Since Daniel Defoe's 1697 *Essay upon Projects*, the 'projector' has been the exemplar of the adventure capitalist, with corresponding moral doubts attached. Defoe writes:

> A mere Projector, then, is a Contemptible thing, driven by his own desperate Fortune to such a Streight, that he must be deliver'd by a Miracle, or Starve; and when he has beat his Brains for some such Miracle in vain, he finds no remedy but to paint up some Bauble or other, *as Players make Puppets talk big*, to show like a strange thing, and then cry it up for a New Invention, gets

a Patent for it, divides it into Shares, and *they must be sold*. Ways and means are not wanting to Swell the new Whim to a vast Magnitude; Thousands and Hundreds of thousands are the least of his discourse, and sometimes Millions, till the Ambition of some honest Coxcomb is wheedled to part with his Money for it, and then (nascitur ridiculus mus) the Adventurer is left to carry on the project, and the Projector laughs at him.[12]

Defoe, himself an enterprising sort though not particularly successful at it, points out that the horde of deceivers should not make us forget that there did exist right-doing specimens: 'the Honest Projector is he who, having by fair and plain principles of Sense, Honesty, and Ingenuity brought any Contrivance to a suitable Perfection, makes out what he pretends to, picks nobody's pocket, puts his Project in execution, and contents himself with the real Produce as the profit of his invention.'[13]

As 'an early form of the entrepreneur',[14] Defoe's projector combines features of the inventor with Schumpeter's innovator (see Chapter 2), the speculator and the business consultant. He sells ideas rather than finished products, advertising his pie-in-the-sky schemes to regents and private investors alike and 'seeks his advantage in providing advantages to others'.[15] He is most likely to emerge at times of crisis or transition, especially at 'moments of political and economical convulsion ... he is at first the prototypical symptom of an approaching "new economy", then he is their procurator and their symbol-charged poster child and finally their administrator'.[16] Defoe at first defines 'project' pessimistically as 'a vast Undertaking, too big to be manag'd, and therefore likely enough to come to nothing'.[17] Yet he views projecting as a whole as of great social benefit, inasmuch as it 'fires the enjoyment of risk, the readiness to take initiative, combines invention and business in ever new and progressively improved ways, thus functioning as a motor for capital accumulation'.[18]

Sixty years after Defoe's depiction of the projector as a well-defined actor, with himself as the very model, Johann Heinrich Gottlob von Justi, himself an entrepreneur and self-styled 'police scientist', made the figure into an anthropological generalization. In his 1761 *Meditations on Projects and Project Makers*, Justi writes:

All humans are project makers ... In my view, we understand a project as the comprehensive design for a certain undertaking whereby our own or other people's earthly happiness should be promoted; to which end, furthermore, all measures to be taken and rules to be obeyed, in addition to the difficulties that can be reasonably expected and the obstacles and how they are to be overcome, are to be clearly presented in such a design.[19]

Justi's point of departure is that humans are obliged to take care of themselves and therefore must hatch plans, set targets and work out strategies. In other words, they must conduct their lives as projects.

Justi creates nothing less than that same figure of the entrepreneur who will return two centuries later in the higher echelons as the Nobel prize-winning human capital theory and in the lowlands of popular advice literature. While the main requirement of today's entrepreneurial self is the flexibility to throw itself into ever new projects for ever shorter periods, the police scientist Justi is focused on long-term planning. He writes:

> It is of crucial importance to make a comprehensive projection of the way of going about the business of life we want to choose right at the beginning. In this projection we must first of all take exact stock of our skills or in other words the property we already possess, which will have to be the base and beginning of all our acquisition and our greatest earthly happiness, in the course of which we have to rein in the inveigling imagination of our self-love as far as possible to prevent it taking over the pen in the drafting of our design. In this inventory, the final purpose and intent of that future course of life, which we may have reason to believe within our possibilities, must be firmly set down.[20]

Defoe was concerned with defending the benefits of projection (his own included) against the charlatans muddying its reputation. In Justi's apologue, the disreputable odour is still in the air but his considerations are cast deeper, into the essentials. His worry is not about the confidence-trickstering of a few 'avanturiers' but about erratic and ill-considered behaviour. Projection is, above all, a question of planning skill and staying power and this is what he saw most of his contemporaries as sadly lacking: 'Few and far between are those who make such a well-considered project of their lives, and the few of those who sometime do it, affrighted by the difficulties they meet on their way, leave the path they have taken and choose another'.[21]

Justi's planning pitch and accompanying optimism are of course not addressed to 'private persons' but to the 'governments of states'. Justi equates the self-government of the individual with the administration of a polity, framing both as types of enterprise. Like the work of advancing personal 'beatitude', it takes careful consideration to steer the commonwealth and 'for this reason not only the regent but also the highest servants of the state should be project makers'.[22] The model Justi demands is based on the police scientist's own self-appraisal and leans heavily on his claim of absolute certainty for his science of government. Whoever 'wants to fabricate a useful project for the advancement of the true wellbeing' must 'possess superior qualities and abilities'. He must first of all 'be in most perfect possession ... of good principles of government', i.e. of the precepts of Justi's police science. Second, he needs practical experience 'in the affairs of state and the appending businesses as well as in world trade'. Third, he must 'possess a knowledge' of the polity for which he designs his project, 'its conditions and composition as well as the moral and legal sensibilities of its people'. Yet, knowledge and experience are not enough for 'finding useful recommendations'; there must also be personal talents such as 'sound reason and power of mental representation' as well as a profound 'power of imagination and the resulting power of invention'.[23]

Justi adds two safety mechanisms to his list of virtues to make it possible to distinguish serious projectors from frivolous 'state adventurers' and prevent the ensuing economic and political damage. The first is the principle of literacy: 'When our gentleman Project Maker is not a dreaming fool who belongs in the madhouse he must surely be able at least to express in writing the final purpose and utility of his project'. The second safety mechanism is the personal unity of idea and execution:

> The person who has invented a thing and contemplated it from so many sides is the best able to provide means and procedures for dealing with whatever difficulties may come up, and the pursuit of his own benefit, which is the overriding aim, will move him more than it would others to be industrious and zealous.[24]

These mechanisms still mark project organization today. Projects need applications, synopses and presentations. They need detailed and precise plans in order for us to judge their viability. With their focus on temporary teamwork, projects also diverge from the regime of the division of labour and specialization. Project workers are at any one time specialists for a particular project, within which they are all-rounders, of a sort.

We have come to take project-based work for granted, but the gentlemen projectors in the meantime have fallen off the radar. They were already being bustled off in the 19th century by another role model, who represented 'the combination of progressive work and scientific method, economic interest and technological development': the engineer.[25] When this figure was briefly in crisis around 1900, the projector briefly re-emerged. The start-up entrepreneur from the new economy can also be seen as a latter-day throwback, but the concept of the project has changed colours. The basic concept now, already foreshadowed in Justi's version, is that of a temporary task performed by a single person or small group acting on their own authority. Projects have now come to provide more autonomy, have been loosened out of institutional hierarchies, include more consultation and promise a more holistic, harmonic blending of work and life, economic success and personal development.

This semantic shift was ushered in by the counterculture of the 1970s. Organizing projects was a way to get away from established institutions; it was a critical practice of exiting the capitalist mega-machine. The countless living, work and social projects were regarded by their practitioners as alternatives to the factory, the nuclear family and the university. They were also felt to be an alternative to other notions radiating out of 1968 which seemed to have failed, such as the long march through the institutions, armed struggle and organization on communist party lines. The German political scientist Wolfgang Kraushaar took stock of this situation in 1978:

> With the development of alternative project models (bookshops, presses, workshops, farming communes etc.), self-organization of daily life, the development of a counter-economy, and 'first-person-politics', the problems of resistance, struggle and anticipation no longer present themselves under the conditions of class society but rather above all in the form of subjective experience and concrete everyday practice. Instead of a targeted attack on the capitalist system, the development of an alternative economic system shifts the emphasis to the subjects who can start unfolding their personalities straight away. The criterion of success is no longer the social effectiveness of a given notion of class struggle but rather the degree of development of positive life concepts and the possibilities for self-emancipation they contain.[26]

The general heading 'project' emphasized the experimental side of founding communities and other types of association. But these were social projects, not the sort of business and technical undertakings launched by Defoe's and Justi's projectors; collectives experimenting together and on themselves without the guiding hand of a ruler or social engineer trained in 'police science'. The countercultural projects understood themselves as laboratories for experimenting with self-organization. This entailed grassroots democratic decision making, equality of earnings, collective ownership of the means of production and a closing of the cleft between manual work and intellectual work, work and leisure, private and political. They were also experimenting with self-motivation. Other incentives had to replace money, prestige and the force of authority. The collective aim of changing themselves and society by the project and in the project, together with identification with the group and with counterculture in general, and, most importantly, the lack of formal authority were supposed to liberate the required combination of blind enthusiasm and strict realism. This somewhat paradoxical task is described by two members of a German rural commune in the following terms:

> Things really only get done when someone commits themselves and takes care of them and gets others involved. The general plan is realized from two sides: the absolute necessity, for example, of chopping wood when it starts running out and it's getting cold, and the personal priorities set by individuals or several group members … [A]ll of the group has to learn to motivate themselves and others in such a way that everyone assumes responsibility without feeling like responsibility is being forced on them by the others. If that succeeds then it differs from capitalist value creation in that the work process is no less important than the result. And the group will have a good basis for a peaceful life together.[27]

Such counterculture projects did not fulfil the original hopes for a social revolution and today their manifestos sound antiquated. Yet looking back a quarter of a century later, it also becomes apparent that, in a different respect, they were ahead of their time. The alternative art of self-governing sought to strike a balance between individual needs, political aims and economic necessity, a balance that was continually being readjusted by trial and error. In so doing, it anticipated the programmes for autonomy, responsibility and sustainability that have been emerging in all manner of areas within society since the 1990s. In other words, such anti-capitalist social experiments involuntarily provided learning material for the entrepreneurial spirit. Their endless consultations and debates, their experiments with rotating task allocation, all the while riding on the edge of financial collapse – this all makes business start-up seminars look amateur and derivative. Operating under such precarious, under-capitalized, self-exploitative conditions, these alternative projects had to either turn professional, stay marginal or give up. Many self-organized groups mutated into innovative enterprises, which were all the more successful for their long years of practice in communication, harnessing collective energies and self-motivation. Joseph Huber, one of the theorists of the German alternative economy, succeeded in reconciling this somewhat conformist achievement with aspirations of political resistance. The ideas he sought to impress upon the alternative movement in 1980 foreshadow the neoliberal imperative of universal intrapreneurship:

> Self-organization means among other things eliminating the contradiction between the entrepreneur (capital) and the workforce. A self-organized collective whose members are wage earners is doomed to fail. Everyone has to learn to think and act *enterprisingly*, though of course in collective fashion. One of the many things this entrains is that principles of a collective management are affirmed that involve formal rules ... every part of the operation is its own department for planning and cost calculation within the whole framework.[28]

It is apparent here how a movement opposed to capitalism was gradually transduced into the imperative for every actor and every group to regard themselves as capitalists on their own behalf. As in the protestant sects analysed by Max Weber, the alternative ideals fell away, leaving the forms of organization that gave rise to a 'new spirit of capitalism'.

The 'projective city' and 'the new spirit of capitalism'

In their comprehensive study of this 'new spirit',[29] Luc Boltanski and Ève Chiapello emphasize the importance of the 'projective city'. The structure of this polis shows the extent to which people today regard themselves, their social relations and their world in terms of the project model. According to the authors, capitalism, in all its historical variants, requires ideologies to justify commitment to it and neutralize critique of it. These justifications rest on general notions of justice and common good, while laying down values and principles of equivalence by which to judge actions, things and people. The term 'city' is used to refer to the totality of these shifting orders of legitimation which come from beyond capitalism itself:

> To maintain its powers of attraction, capitalism therefore has to draw upon resources external to it, beliefs which, at a given moment in time, possess considerable powers of persuasion, striking ideologies, even when they are hostile to it, inscribed in the cultural context in which it is developing. The spirit sustaining the accumulation process at a given point in history is thus imbued with cultural products that are contemporaneous with it and which, for the most part, have been generated to quite different ends than justifying capitalism.[30]

In the 'commercial city', that person is regarded as a 'great man' who success-fully tenders coveted goods on a competitive market. Then, in the 'industrial city', human worth is measured on efficiency. The authors' comparison of management literature from the 1960s and the 1990s indicates that in the 'projective city' activity is the measure.[31] In contrast to the industrial city, where activity is equated with paid work, the projective city contains a set of activities that blur the distinction between work, leisure, wage earning, housework and volunteer work:

> Activity aims to generate projects, or to achieve integration into projects initiated by others. But the project does not exist outside of the encounter (not being integrated once and for all into an institution or environment, it presents itself as an action to be performed, not as something that is already there).

The particular kind of undertaking is of secondary importance only: 'What matters is to develop activity – that is to say, never to be short of a project, bereft of an idea, always to have something in mind, in the pipeline, with other people whom one meets out of a desire to do something.'[32] The higher the level of activity and number of projects, the higher the social rank. While the individual project remains the main element, the total set of changing projects produces a continuously expanding network. This type of network has neither sub-ordinate nor predominant positions, but only nodes with different numbers of connections. The chief task is to increase the number and quality of the connections. This networking is the foreign policy of project work:

> Hence the activity par excellence is integrating oneself into networks and exploring them, so as to put an end to isolation, and have opportunities for meeting people or associating with things, proximity to which is liable to generate a project.[33]

Time is also differently structured in the industrial city than in the projective city. The centrality of biographical coherence for career purposes
is usurped by the syncopated life rhythm of project planning, execution,
termination and the search for the next project. Life becomes a series of
temporary, discrete engagements:

> When they engage in a project, everyone concerned knows that the under-
> taking to which they are about to contribute is destined to last for a limited
> period of time – that it not only can, but must, come to an end. The prospect
> of an inevitable, desirable endpoint thus accompanies engagement with-
> out affecting enthusiasm. This is why engagement is conceived as voluntary.
> Having the option not to engage in a given project, and hence choice over
> one's projects, is a condition for the city's harmonious functioning; and this
> condition is guaranteed by the multiple activities everyone develops.[34]

The voluntary nature of project participation is countered by the pressure
to keep finding new projects. You should never be caught without one; to
exhibit such inactivity is tantamount to social death.

The 'great man in a projective city', as the predominant social role
model, possesses perfect balance and flexibility. Boltanski and Chiapello
extract from the rules of conduct adumbrated in management advice books
a catalogue of conflicting virtues contained in these qualities. Enthusiasm
and unrelenting engagement are required, but also the ability to abruptly
break off and turn to another task. The project-pursuing great man,

> (f)ar from being attached to an occupation or clinging to a qualification ... proves
> adaptable and flexible, able to switch from one situation to a very different one,
> and adjust to it; and versatile, capable of changing activity or tools, depending
> on the nature of the relationship entered into, with others or with objects.[35]

Nothing must be allowed to restrict the mobility of this 'nomad'.[36]
Yet, '[t]he great man in the projective city is not a nowhere man': 'At ease
wherever he finds himself, he also knows how to be local'. In his function
as a leader, such men do not play the superior: '[t]hey are not (hierarchical) bosses, but integrators, facilitators, an inspiration, unifiers of energies,
enhancers of life, meaning and autonomy'.[37] The ideal project leader is a
coach, mediator, manager by dint of intuition and specialist in the relevant
area all at the same time. Above all, he needs communication skills. He must
be able to arouse trust, inspire and be inspired, be open and familiar, neither
shy nor immodest, be able to resolve conflict and encourage cooperation,
distinguish relevant and irrelevant data, see opportunity lurking behind
every corner and anticipate who are going to be the right contacts to cultivate. Information capital and social capital are interdependent; you need a
large pool of contacts and must be constantly acquiring new ones in order
to access the most up-to-date knowledge: 'What all these exceptional beings

have in common is that they are in a position to explore the links with the richest opportunities, those that will extend the network furthest, which are defined largely by the distance they surmount.'[38]

This is the opposite of all those qualities which make it difficult to cultivate contacts: inhibition, intolerance, authoritarianism, lack of initiative, immobility. The 'little people' in this city are those 'who cannot be engaged, who are not employable on a project, or who prove incapable of changing projects'.[39] Living with the rhythm of project cycles demands and also fosters the type of person who can stay detached from long-term commitments. The unaffiliated, the 'streamlined',

> can root themselves only in themselves ('the self-enterprise') – the sole instance endowed with a certain permanency in a complex, uncertain and changing world. However, the quiddity that is recognizable is not the result of a pre-existing endowment, or even of a trajectory or experience. It derives from the constellation of established connections. They are themselves only because they are the links that constitute them.[40]

Boltanski and Chiapello analyse the projective city as a contemporary justification of capitalism, yet they are mistrustful of accounts of current societal change that depict it exclusively as the expansion of market mechanisms. Networks of projects are generally considered the form of social cooperation best adapted to market survival, but the world of the project also contradicts the ideal of free market competition. First, theories of market transactions imagine them occurring instantaneously and are not concerned about their duration, whereas projects always have duration, even if it is short. Second, classical economics presupposes that prices are transparently regulated by the principle of general equivalence, whereas projects are only partially visible: 'Information is not available to everyone simultaneously in its entirety, as in the ideal of pure and perfect information allowing all the participants in a market to be put on an equal footing.'[41] Third, personal affiliations are supposed to play no role in market relations, whereas project organization promises precisely to tap into the cohesive power of direct personal contact. Fourth, and finally, in the projective city information and contacts are the most important forms of capital, with the result that the products of exchange are no longer sharply distinguished from those people doing the exchanging. This applies in particular to work, which under project conditions can no longer be seen as a good separable from the person of the wage earner and codified in advance in a standard description of the job and the qualifications it requires. Boltanski and Chiapello could be summarized as saying that the new capitalism is capable of freeing market forces, while also reinforcing forms of cooperation and exchange expected to improve the participants' competitive position but which fail to follow basic market logic. In the projective city, cooperation and competition are no longer mutually exclusive, but are complementary. Succeeding in the city means finding the right way of mixing the two.

Despite the methodological and terminological differences between Boltanski und Chiapello's investigation of the legitimation of current capitalism, on the one hand, and the present analysis of liberal governmentality, on the other, there is a significant affinity between the former's ideal project worker and the entrepreneurial self. Both figures represent contemporary ways in which subjectivity is shaped, not an already existent, prevalent type. The aim of this shaping is, in connection with both figures, the attainment of activity and flexibility, both of which cannot be attained definitely but which necessitate permanent mobilization. Both see the transformations of capitalism running parallel to transformations of subjectification while not reducing subjectification to a mere effect of subjects being forced to produce economic value. Finally, both elaborate on the demands this type of subjectification imposes on people and the looming threats of failure.

The differences between the two approaches are equally apparent. Boltanski and Chiapello undertake to define the new 'spirit' of capitalism but do not inquire into the strategies it employs to put itself into practice. They describe the ideological legitimation of the projective city but forego analysis of the social and self technologies resulting from it, i.e. how the practice of project work produces the ethos of activity and how this ethos in turn translates into concrete injunctions to act. Yet there is a wealth of tools for efficient project management contained in the body of literature they base their inquiry on. Capitalism needs more than simply justifications; it also needs mechanisms for getting people to get themselves into the right shape to actively participate in it. The projective city could not exist without a project-based regime of subjectification and social cooperation. In order to be accepted as legitimate, a social order must provide convincing criteria of the good and it must train people how to act according to those criteria.

Project management

Projects need planning. Aims need to be defined, a road map drawn up, a time frame, costs and means determined, participants need selecting, motivating and their collaboration organized, there must be provision for removing unforeseen obstacles and modifying aims and means, and at the end the results must be evaluated. In the past, humans have relied on intuition and experience in undertaking all this activity, and it has worked out more or less well. Project management is the attempt to extract general principles from this intuition and experience, to find out what leads to success, what are typical problems and what are useful instruments for efficiently carrying out different types of project. It makes use of system theory, microeconomics, group therapy and organizational studies, and performs empirical testing of its concepts; it is armed with an elaborate methodology, with experts, training courses and professional standards.

It is generally agreed that project management began with one of the largest single military programmes of all time: the *Manhattan Engineering District Project* from 1941 that developed the first atom bomb. The next milestone was the Apollo programme that NASA started in 1961 with the aim of landing a human on the moon. The enormous urgency of the tasks, the scientific difficulties and diversity of institutions, researchers and engineers involved made it impossible to execute the programme with conventional organizational structures.[42] The forms of cooperation, planning and control that were tested in the project were subsequently adopted and refined by private enterprise, especially in research and development. In an early article, the *Harvard Business Review* writes: '[T]he project manager's business is to create a *product* – a piece of advance-technology hardware. The primary tool available to him is the brainpower of men who are professional specialists in diverse fields'.[43] The bias toward extremely complex ventures led to the adoption of more technical methods. Not until the 1980s did people start to realize that not only large-scale scientific and technical projects but also smaller undertakings could profit from systematic project management. It soon moved into other areas, with administration, education and NGOs installing project teams. As well as presenting the solution to the kind of 'hierarchy crisis' much discussed in Germany during the 1980s and 1990s[44] by abolishing legitimation for vertical, authoritarian power structures and thereby motivating employees, project management also promises innovation and flexibility.

With the expansion of project work, social skills have grown in importance. The key qualifications of a project manager – the ability to work with plans, cost accounting, documentation systems – are now broadened to include conducting communication with co-workers on an equal footing, conflict mediation and project presentation skills. The current literature incorporates – as well as network planning and budget programmes – creativity exercises and the fundamentals of 'theme-centred interaction' (TCI). What these soft and hard skills all have in common is the principle of indirect control. They do not stipulate in detail what to do to carry out a specific project but rather adumbrate which circumstantial factors are conducive and which obstructive. They aid in structuring and motivating project teams to nurture their capacity to independently define precise goals and attain them within the set time and budget limitations, while providing all the while for a fruitful and satisfying team experience. In sum, project management means stimulating and overseeing self-organizing processes.

This requires abstraction. Each project has its own size, shape, time and way of proceeding, while project management programmes provide phase models, flow charts, moderation techniques and group therapy typologies for application to any project at all. Projects are generalized as 'a sequential decision procedure oriented on "learning"' or as a 'problem–solving cycle' in which a *situation analysis* (what's going on?) is followed by a *goal definition* (what do we want to achieve?), a *solution search* (what are the possible solutions?), a *solution assessment* (which solutions work?), *realization* (how should the solution be achieved?) and *result control* (what was the result?). Alternately, various 'life phases' (*project definition*, *project planning*, *project execution* and *project evaluation*) are distinguished, which every project has to go through on its journey from idea to product and from problem to solution.[45]

Management demands structuring and that 'means, as we all know, breaking a system down into its component parts and registering the relations between them'.[46] In these texts, the somewhat vague entity known as the 'project' is articulated into a sequence of separate functions, making it easier to take care of the proper order and flow. There also need to be feedback loops installed to lock the elements together into what cybernetics terms a control cycle. This consists in:

> the project planning stipulating the plan values as the quota (reference value) for the project execution. The project control monitors the measured value as frequently as possible and compares it with the quota. In case of discrepancies project management either takes appropriate measures or alters the plan values. In keeping with the principles of control engineering, discrepancies can be adjusted earlier the more exactly, i.e. the more finely incremented, the controlled variables are measured.[47]

'Milestones' mark the completion of individual phases and are particularly useful 'for determining the state of operations and possible corrections'.[48]

The principle of dividing and recombining is repeated on a second, in some cases on a third and fourth, planning level. The plan is gradually fine-tuned on the principle from rough to detailed:

> The tasks at the lowest hierarchic level are referred to as work packages. These are the smallest planning units and should be capable of being disposed of and monitored on their own, clearly separated from other tasks and assigned to determined posts or persons.[49]

The 'task book' regulates the individual's assignments within the framework of the whole project, while on the level of the individual work steps 'assignment package descriptions' provide detailed 'activity descriptions, solution structures, aids, preconditions and possibly problems and risks'. Finally, a work breakdown structure provides 'the project manager with an overview of the "skeleton" of the project from an early stage on. This can be supplemented in later planning steps by "putting meat on it"'.[50]

With the help of the network planning technique, the relations itemized in the breakdown structure can be represented in graphic form and ordered in a logical sequence. This method, founded on mathematical graph theory, exists in a number of variations, mostly computer based, and was developed in the 1950s partly in connection with the US Navy's Polaris programme. It promises 'time savings of a magnitude of around 25% and cost savings around 15% ... however with extreme variance'.[51] A flow chart breaks the project down into three components: (1) *operations*: processes taking up time; (2) *events*: the emergence of defined states; and (3) *structural relations*: the interdependencies among personnel, expertise, and deadlines, as well as between individual operations. These three elements are represented as nodes and arrows; the operations and events can be represented by both depending on the case. The 'operation node network plan', for example the 'node box' contains

> first of all the process number and process denomination. Further, captions, the number or name of the work package, the processing post and directions can be inserted. The following scheduling details are provided: the length of the operation, the buffer time, as well as earliest and latest start and finish deadlines (generally in calendar dates in the final version). Also, indications of working resources and costs can be included.[52]

A net plan assists detailed time schedule planning and monitoring while leaving room for operative decisions for alternative courses of action. It also renders visible operation loops and allows probabilities and random variations to be taken into account.

Flow charts are just one of a variety of ways of modelling operating procedures. Such models standardize the organization of work by imposing a basic pattern into which the specifics of each project are inserted. In other words, these models do not stipulate a path to follow but rather map the territory:

> A project can be compared with a territory we have to negotiate our way around. The map illustrates the various aspects of this 'unknown territory'. The map is not the territory itself, but instead organizes it. Likewise, a project does not consist of phases; dividing it into phases merely provides orientation.[53]

Work breakdown structures and flow charts pre-structure how we perceive what a project is, just as cartography pre-structures how we perceive a geographical region. Indeed, a project could be defined as that undertaking which can be steered with the aid of project management. The instruments provided by project management are forged in large-scale technological undertakings and are generally deployed only by specialists. Nevertheless, they can easily be broken down for use in smaller ventures (you *can* and *should* try this at home). In a possible attempt to ingratiate itself into the affections of readers, one project management textbook explains the precedence diagram method using the example of organizing a party.[54] No matter how apparently simple a project is, it won't get off the ground without a methodical management plan.

This management aspect does not exhaust itself in structuring, calculating and controlling. To reach the finish line, projects need not only a form, they also need energy. It is not enough to arrange the tasks into a well-ordered scheme. The people carrying them out need to be cheered on, their slumbering potentials unleashed and collaborative friction reduced. Mobilizing without structuring would cast a project into ineffectual chaos, while structuring without mobilizing would send it to sleep. For this reason, the highly formalized planning and management techniques are flanked by 'soft' methods of personnel management and group work. This is taken care of by the *project team* – the social nucleus of project organization.

Project teams are a radical expression of the concept of partially autonomous group work that various manufacturers started introducing in the 1970s to combat high rates of employee fluctuation and absenteeism as well as serious product quality deficits. Batch production of items like cars remained at least indirectly linked to the steady rhythm of the assembly line and its work groups were more permanent formations. In contrast, project teams are 'temporary enterprises'; they organize their own operations, constitute autonomous profit centres and so function as schools 'for the advancement of entrepreneurial thinking'.[55] The project team consists of a limited number of members with mutually complementary skills, is assembled for a specific task and disbanded upon accomplishment. Its composition, longevity and reason for being depend entirely on this specific task. It also differs from the batch-work team in that its work is not finished at the end of the shift, but when the project aim is achieved, whenever that may be. The autonomy increases the pressure on team members, who must adjust their lives to the rhythm of the project cycles instead of that of the regular work day, and are chained together for the duration of the project:

> Project work requires on the one hand that the project group has a certain amount of autonomy; this means doing away with punch clocks, it means self-control work of work times, eliminating hierarchy within the group, self-organization of operations, room to improvise etc. On the other hand, these freedoms increase the stress potentially infinitely. This stress is then often accepted and comprehended as 'your own fault', as resulting from the 'heightened responsibility' or as a 'strenuous' but hip collective experience.[56]

Project work demands more than just the traditional work ethic virtues (in the German version: *order, diligence* and *cleanliness*) and more than just correctly fulfilling the task as described. Consequently, discipline, pecuniary incentive and promotion opportunities are insufficient for obtaining the required performance from the worker. The person in her entirety must be modified to obtain the right proportion of enthusiasm, independent initiative and creative problem solving. Careful preparation is needed in composing the team and electing leadership, and continued moderation is required to ensure the constant stress does not dampen team spirit. This elaborate planning and monitoring suggest calculability, yet the predominant management guidebooks proclaim a partnership and cooperation ethos. The key note here is *balance*, meaning teams should 'possess the right mixture of technical expertise, problem-solving skills, decision competency and communication skills between their members'. Team selection should consider 'not only skills but also the co-workers' personal peculiarities'.[57] Guides for this selection work are provided by psychological typologies like the *Myers–Briggs Type Indicator* (MBTI), which employs the dichotomies *extraversion/introversion, sensing/intuition, thinking/feeling* and *judging/perception* to distinguish personality types along the lines of preferred ways of perceiving the world and making decisions. The different types are not considered as judgements, since each one has its use in a project team.[58] 'Colourful' teams are therefore recommended: 'This admittedly makes moderating and managing the team more difficult but the qualitative performance of a "colourful" team is generally higher than that of a "monochrome" team'.[59]

The project manager should combine specialized thematic knowledge, methodological and social skills:

> Part of social competency is the ability and willingness to approach individual co-workers, listen to them, accept them as persons, and to inspire and motivate them. Further, it requires the abilities to understand and control group processes in such a way as to enable group synergistic effects by creating the conditions for the group to produce better results than would any of the members on their own.

Methodological competency involves problem-solving techniques and methods of project management; while *technical competency* implies familiarity with the tasks at hand. Decisive for integrating the different component skills is 'personality and self-leadership':

> A person is convincing when their behaviour and inner attitude are felt to be in harmony and authentic. It inspires trust and endows them with personal authority. He who will lead others must first learn to lead himself. This means, among other things, always staying on target and solution-oriented, especially in the kind of stressful situations that can arise in difficult phases of the project.[60]

Another concept recommended by numerous project management guidebooks – theme-centred interaction (TCI) – is also based on a balance principle.

In the 1950s, the psychoanalyst Ruth Cohn began developing TCI as a method of 'vital learning'.[61] According to Cohn, three factors are always present in group interaction, 'which can be imagined as the corners of a triangle: (1) *The I*, the personality; (2) *The We*, the group; (3) *The It*, the theme. This triangle is embedded in a sphere representing the environment'.[62] A group will work together happily and effectively if 'a relative, dynamic balance' subsists between the levels of I, we and the theme. This requires constant rebalancing, which is the task of the team manager. The description Cohn gives of the group leader's interventions in the discussion can easily be transferred to project team sessions:

> When the group concerns itself with the theme academically, I regard this as constructive only as long as I discover no signs of disinterest in the group, or individual participants non-involved or disturbed, and as long as no other symptoms of group disintegration emerge. Otherwise I redirect the group's attention from the theme to the person (I) or persons (We). Inversely, if the group appears to be interested only in one person or in an upsurge of various feelings in the group, and threatens to transform themselves into a therapy or sensitivity group, I throw a bridge over to the theme. In a smooth-running, experienced group such directives are less frequently needed, since the group itself develops into the guardian of the method.[63]

The balance between individual, group and theme is also supported by the two main premises: 'be your own chairperson' and 'disturbances and passionate involvements take precedence', as well as by the TCI auxiliary communication rules derived from them.[64] Rules of thumb like 'represent yourself in your statements, saying "I", not "we" or "one" … if you ask a question, say why you ask and what this question means to you [and] hold off from generalizations',[65] are intended to help the project team to concentrate on the collective task, utilizing both the cohesive force of the group and its diversity of perspectives, while not losing sight of individual needs.

There is a further aspect of TCI that makes it amenable to appropriation by project management. Cohn's basic approach, grounded in the personal growth idea of humanist psychology and employing simple guidelines, connects self-organization with a focus on the matter at hand. This makes individual needs and group cohesion important *for the sake of* the overriding collective goal. At the same time, personal growth and constructive cooperation are dependent on the group sharing a common interest. If the balance between the self, the group and the common issue works, TCI and project management both promise positive synergistic effects. If one of the three factors is lacking, the others will suffer as a consequence.

Despite the differences between the network planning technique with its flow charts and cost curves, and TCI's ethic of group moderation adopted from humanistic psychology, both follow a cybernetic model. The project manager and the team as a whole function as homeostatic regulators ensuring the 'relative, dynamic balance' of I, we and theme. Additionally, the discussion guidelines provide regular feedback that can warn of impending disturbances. These 'take precedence'; they need to be remedied or made constructive use of before they can damage the work process. In both the technical and humanistic varieties of project management, the aim is to heighten productivity by maintaining movement and avoiding standstill, idling and over-heating.

Mobility is an essential trait of another form of project management that runs obliquely to both the concepts of rational planning and the balance model of group psychology. Once again, the bestselling author Tom Peters serves as a prominent exponent. His theory of organization (or disorganization) aspires not to balance but to confusion. Instead of providing methods, he mobilizes passions: 'On the platform at his seminars (which are really rallies), he does not spout theories or present data but instead tells stories, usually parables about companies just like yours which saw the light and were saved'.[66]

The content of the gospel announced in Peters' good shepherd show, not just its form, follows the principle of leading by charisma. Peters is in possession of one whole single answer to the question of how to successfully manage a project: enthusiasm: 'Is a day in the Projects ... a full-fledged Performance? If not, is there something you can do ... n-o-w ... to enhance the excitement/theatricality of the current project ... to make it ... an act worthy of your wholesale commitment?'[67]

It is Peters' fundamental conviction that order does not need to be created; it generates and consolidates itself on its own. In fact, it does so better than is useful for enterprises in a chaotic world. The needful thing is not to maintain and optimize order; the only thing that can save us now is to imitate chaos, hence the title of one of his books: *Thriving on Chaos*.[68] Peters is convinced that to be successful you must break up the existing order again and again, making room for those creative forces. There is a threatening undertone lurking here. In fluid markets, only those enterprises that radically fluidify their operations will survive. Project teams, with their rhizomatic network connections, must provide enterprises with those discontinuity and acceleration effects needed to cope with the fractured turbulence of the market. Since collaborative groups also court the danger of petrifying and falling behind the pace of change, they should be run for a limited time only. As Peters prophesies,

[d]ynamic, short-lived project configurations will be commonplace. It will not be unusual to work on four or five project teams in a year, or a couple of teams at one time – but you will never work twice with the exact same configuration of colleagues, even in a 20-year 'career'.[69]

Project Me

Entrepreneurship is neither a definable personality trait nor merely a social status. It exists only in a disjunctive series of actions, of projects of limited duration, which are the result of social interaction in shifting actor networks.[70] The entrepreneurial self lives in a project universe. To deal with constantly new tasks and social relations, project teams and individuals need a high degree of rationalized self-control, a sense of balance and the willingness to confront the confusing and unexpected. Once it has been established that project organization is the royal road to more flexibility and initiative, it follows that the best way to conduct your own life is to project manage it. As the British sociologist Nikolas Rose has written:

> [c]ontemporary individuals are incited to live as if making a project of themselves: they are to work on their emotional world, their domestic and conjugal arrangements, their relations with employment and their techniques of sexual pleasure, to develop a 'style' of living that will maximize the worth of their existence to themselves.[71]

On this notion, the self in its relations to itself is not only plural but liquid, re-appearing in ever new confluences. The notion of patchwork identity[72] current in theories of subjectivity in the 1980s and 1990s can be adapted here in a modified form: the Project Me self is not a fabric of manifold threads interweaving to make a pattern fixed once and for all. It is a kaleidoscope forming a new image each time it is shaken. This Project Me consists of diverse projects: work, leisure, relationship, health, etc. Conducting or governing this self becomes a matter of self-managing its 'project portfolio'.

With all this improvisation and self-creation, it is not surprising that the figure of the artist as creative genius is made to serve as the model for 'Project Me'. As the author of a self-management bestseller, *Soloing: Realizing Your Life's Ambition*, writes:

> [t]he projects are the houses of art … you enter them, and you become *of* them. You become experimental, dishevelled. You begin not entirely knowing what you're looking for, only the chance to do something great …'Why should a painter work if he is not transformed by his own painting' asked French philosopher Michel Foucault. So it is for all of us who live in the projects.[73]

To meet this challenge, people are supposed to use the same kinds of technologies employed for effective and satisfying teamwork. This involves, first, detailed planning and continuous monitoring; second, negotiation between disparate personal needs; and third, enthusiasm. According to one 'Me Inc.' style advice book, it is also helpful to adopt '[t]he orientation of the classical methods of project management employed every day in business'.

Your own life can also be understood as a series of problems to be solved by following specified steps. One example of this 'permanent control by project management' can be broken down into the following tasks:

> Define your aim. Lay down an activity plan with 'milestones'. Submit yourself voluntarily to supervision. Be merciful to yourself. If the market analysis is not finished by the end of December despite all your best efforts don't throw in the towel. Now you have to quickly adapt the project plan to prevent prolonging the delay. This can mean doing some overtime at first. That will make it all the more satisfying when you reach the next milestone and have overcome the delay. Then you have definitely earned a reward (for example, a visit to the sauna followed by a back massage, a new pullover or a picnic with the family).[74]

Checklists, self-commitment agreements and personal 'annual exams' help maintain an overview of the different projects.

According to a German advice book with the compulsory Anglophonic title *Coach Yourself*, up-to-date self-management and project management are not about struggle and conquest; they call instead for negotiation skills and the ability to get all the personality components (self-management) and team members (project management) coordinated and pointing at the same target. This calls for 'ecological integration'[75] rather than selection; not an authoritarian regime with the 'head' ruling the 'gut' but rather consultation, partnership, cooperation: 'You won't reach your goals by testing your inner strength and overcoming your weaknesses, but rather by the energy that comes from running a harmonious, frictionless personality system'.[76] 'Project Me' can neither choose its co-workers nor dismiss them without notice. It has no choice but to conciliate the heterogeneous, potentially conflicting parts of itself. Moralizing would only be counterproductive. There are neither good nor bad components of personality; only good or bad teamwork among those components.

Tom Peters once again exemplifies the charismatic variant of project management. The wake-up preacher of the entrepreneurial self places his faith in the suggestive power of believing-in-yourself (of which believing in the words of Tom Peters is by implication a necessary precondition):

> The coin – the only coin – of my realm is projects ... commit yourself whole-heartedly to … the project 'life' ... [w]orking on a memorable (WOW) project. (If it's not WOW ... I'll make it WOW ... or bust trying!) […] Understand that Projects-Are-Me. *Period*. (This ain't funny: I *am* my project 'portfolio'.)[77]

In the interstices of Peters' staccato incantations, as he hacks grammar into hectic, abbreviated avowals, a different message imparts itself, sotto voce, about the fear of failure, something none of the advice literature discusses openly. The spectre of failure veritably haunts the project management literature as it does all such recipe books for happiness and success. Whatever quests the entrepreneurial self consigns to its 'project portfolio' and however cleverly and passionately it pursues them, its final success is always contingent, not least of all on the competition, all of whom are using the same tools. The tendency of the rate of profit to fall – as postulated by Marx – also applies to the use of social technologies and technologies of self. This means that everyone has to work increasingly hard to attain ever more slender competitive advantages.

Projects would not need to be managed if the results were a foregone conclusion. Risks need to be calculated precisely because they cannot be ruled out in advance. No amount of planning, controlling, balancing and inspiring can guarantee that 'Project Me' will not end up, like Defoe's projector, as a 'bankrupt'.[78]

Even bankruptcy does not release the entrepreneurial self from the logic of project making. If project management skills are needed anywhere, they are needed for coping with the financial, psychological and social consequences of this kind of failure. Debt advisors, family counsellors and labour recruitment agents are standing by to help crash victims get back on their feet, providing the personal qualities and techniques of professional project management.[79] The fact that these very tools failed to prevent the accident in the first place is not registered as an argument against them. This illustrates perhaps most clearly of all the power of the entrepreneurial idea. The concept of the 'project' has the force of an a priori principle of humans' relation to themselves – an inescapable, fundamental category within which we understand ourselves and shape ourselves.

This surrounds talk of the 'longevity' of projects with a dark existential halo. Final project termination for the larger project portfolio evoked by Tom Peters with the label 'life' is coming for everyone sooner or later. Until this time, neither absolute failure nor absolute success is possible. There are only relative, temporary failures and successes followed on their heels by the next project. And regardless of how unevenly distributed the chances are, the same maxim applies equally to everyone: *Be active! Take your life in your hands! Be your own chairperson!*

Notes

1. Friedrich Schlegel (1798/1967) 'Fragmente', in: Hans Eichner (ed.), *Kritische Friedrich-Schlegel-Ausgabe, Vol. 2: Charakteristiken und Kritiken I*, Munich: Ferdinand, pp. 165–255, here pp. 168f.
2. Cited in Pitter A. Steinbuch (1998) *Projektorganisation und Projektmanagement*, Ludwigshafen (Rheine) Schöningh: Kiehl Verlag, p. 24.
3. Vilém Flusser (2000) *From Subject to Project: Becoming Human*, London: Free Association Books.

4. Jürgen Habermas (1983) 'Modernity: An Incomplete Project', in: Hal Foster (ed.), *The Anti-Aesthetic: Essays on Postmodern Culture*, Seattle, WA: New Press, pp. 3–15.

5. Niklas Luhmann (1990) *Die Wissenschaft der Gesellschaft*, Frankfurt: Suhrkamp, p. 339; Niklas Luhmann (2012) *Theory of Society*, Stanford, CA: Stanford University Press, p. xi.

6. Joachim Matthes (1988) 'Projekte – nein, danke? Eine (un)zeitgemäße Betrachtung', in: *Zeitschrift für Soziologie*, 17, pp. 465–473, here: pp. 467f.

7. Matthes (1988) 'Projekte – nein, danke?', p. 471.

8. Luhmann (1990) *Die Wissenschaft der Gesellschaft*, p. 338.

9. Tom Peters (1999) *The Brand You 50, Or: Fifty Ways to Transform Yourself from an 'Employee' into a Brand That Shouts Distinction, Commitment, and Passion!*, New York: Knopf Doubleday, p. 43.

10. Luhmann (1990) *Die Wissenschaft der Gesellschaft*, p. 338.

11. On the historical semantics of the 'projector', see: Georg Stanitzek (1987) 'Der Projektmacher: Projektionen auf eine "unmögliche" moderne Kategorie', in: *Ästhetik & Kommunikation*, 17(65/66), pp. 135–146; Felix Klopotek (2004) 'Projekt', in: Bröckling et al. (eds), *Glossar der Gegenwart*, pp. 216–221; Markus Krajewski (2004) 'Über Projektemacher: Eine Einleitung', in: *Projektemacher*, Berlin: Kulturverlag Kadmos, pp. 7–25.

12. Daniel Defoe (1647) *An Essay Upon Projects*, pp. 33f.

13. Defoe (1647) *An Essay Upon Projects*, p. 35.

14. Klopotek (2004) 'Projekt', p. 218.

15. Stanitzek (1987) 'Der Projektmacher', p. 136.

16. Krajewski (2004) 'Über Projektemacher', pp. 19f.

17. Defoe (1647) 'The History of Projects', in: *An Essay Upon Projects*, p. 20.

18. Klopotek (2004) 'Projekt', p. 219.

19. Johann Heinrich Gottlob von Justi (1761/1970) 'Gedanken von Projecten und Projectmachern', in *Politische und Finanzschriften über wichtige Gegenstände der Staatskunst, der Kriegswissenschaften und des Cameral- und Finanzwesens, Vol. 1*, Copenhagen/Leipzig/Aalen: Rothe, pp. 256–281, here: pp. 256f.

20. Justi (1761/1970) 'Gedanken von Projecten und Projectmachern', pp. 258f.

21. Justi (1761/1970) 'Gedanken von Projecten und Projectmachern', p. 260.

22. Justi (1761/1970) 'Gedanken von Projecten und Projectmachern', p. 261.

23. Justi (1761/1970) 'Gedanken von Projecten und Projectmachern', pp. 263f.

24. Justi (1761/1970) 'Gedanken von Projecten und Projectmachern', pp. 271f.

25. Krajewski (2004) 'Über Projektemacher', p. 20.

26. Wolfgang Kraushaar (1978) 'Thesen zum Verhältnis von Alternativ- und Fluchtbewegung', in: *Autonomie oder Getto? Kontroversen über die Alternativbewegung*, Frankfurt: Neue Kritik, pp. 8–67, here: pp. 12f.

27. Bernd Leineweber and Karl-Ludwig Schibel (1978) '"Die Alternativbewegung": Ein Beitrag zu ihrer gesellschaftlichen Bedeutung und politischen Tragweite, deren Möglichkeiten und Grenzen', in: Kraushaar (ed.), *Autonomie oder Getto?*, pp. 95–128, here: p. 100.

28. Joseph Huber (1980) *Wer soll das alles ändern: Die Alternativen der Alternativbewegung*, Berlin: Rotbuch, pp. 127f.

29. Boltanski and Chiapello (2005) *The New Spirit of Capitalism*, New York: Verso.

30. Boltanski and Chiapello (2005) *The New Spirit of Capitalism*, p. 20.

31. In addition, Boltanski and Chiapello distinguish four other cities: the *inspirational city*, in which personal greatness is measured against the grade of personal inspiration, with the illuminated saint and the creative artist as role models; the *domestic city*, in which worth is contingent on a person's position in a chain of personal relations of dependency; the *reputational city*, in which worth depends on the amount of people someone is esteemed by; and the *civic city*, where that person is 'great' who expresses the general will ((2007) *The New Spirit of Capitalism* , pp. 23f.). The *city* concept is developed further in Luc Boltanski and Laurent Thévenot (2006) *On Justification: Economies of Worth*, Princeton, NJ: Princeton University Press.

32. Boltanski and Chiapello (2005) *The New Spirit of Capitalism*, p. 110.

33. Boltanski and Chiapello (2005) *The New Spirit of Capitalism*.

34. Boltanski and Chiapello (2005) *The New Spirit of Capitalism*, pp. 110f. There are evident parallels between the organization models of the projective city and the kind of anarchist notions of free association revived during and after the 1968 revolts. This confirms Boltanski and Chiapello's thesis that the new spirit of capitalism has absorbed the critique of the previous capitalist formation. The basic principles of libertarian organization theory formulated by the British anarchist Colin Ward in the 1960s would not be out of place in a management advice book from the 1990s. On Ward's model, organizations must be: '(1) voluntary, (2) functional, (3) temporary, and (4) small. They should be voluntary for obvious reasons. There is no point in our advocating individual freedom and responsibility if we are going to advocate organisations for which membership is mandatory. They should be functional and temporary precisely because permanence is one of those factors which harden the arteries of an organisation, giving it a vested interest in its own survival, in serving the interests of office-holders rather than its function. They should be small precisely because in small face-to-face groups, the bureaucratising and hierarchical tendencies inherent in organisations have least opportunity to develop' (Colin Ward (1966) 'Anarchism as a Theory of Organization', in: *Patterns of Anarchy: A Collection of Writings on the Anarchist Tradition*, New York: Anchor Books). Translated into current jargon, this is an accurate sketch of a project team.

35. Boltanski and Chiapello (2005) *The New Spirit of Capitalism*, p. 112.

36. Boltanski and Chiapello (2005) *The New Spirit of Capitalism*, p. 122.

37. Boltanski and Chiapello (2005) *The New Spirit of Capitalism*, pp. 114–115.

38. Boltanski and Chiapello (2005) *The New Spirit of Capitalism*, p. 116.

39. Boltanski and Chiapello (2005) *The New Spirit of Capitalism*, p. 119.

40. Boltanski and Chiapello (2005) *The New Spirit of Capitalism*, p. 125.

41. Boltanski and Chiapello (2005) *The New Spirit of Capitalism*, p. 130.

42. Hans-D. Litke (2004) *Projektmanagement: Methoden, Techniken, Verhaltensweisen*, Munich: Hanser, p. 23.

43. Paul O. Gaddis (1959) 'The Project Manager', in: *Harvard Business Review*, 32, May/June, pp. 89–97, here: p. 89.
44. See Peter Heintel and Ewald E. Krainz (2000) *Projektmanagement: Eine Antwort auf die Hierarchiekrise?*, Wiesbaden: Gabler, pp. 9ff.
45. See Litke (2004) *Projektmanagement*, pp. 26ff.; Manfred Burghardt (1995) *Einführung in Projektmanagement*, Munich: Publicis, pp. 11ff.; Steinbuch (1998) *Projektorganisation*, pp. 28ff. Anselm Strauss has proposed a similar schema for research in social science: (1991) 'The Articulation of Project Work: An Organizational Process', in: *Creating Sociological Awareness: Collective Images and Symbolic Representations*, New Brunswick: Transaction, pp. 99–119.
46. Litke (2004) *Projektmanagement*, p. 90.
47. Burghardt (1995) *Einführung in Projektmanagement*, p. 17.
48. Klaus Birker (1999) *Projektmanagement*, Berlin: Cornelsen Giradet, p. 36.
49. Birker (1999) *Projektmanagement*, p. 41.
50. Birker (1999) *Projektmanagement*, p. 43.
51. Günter Altrogge (1994) *Netzplantechnik*, Munich/Vienna: Oldenbourg, p. 7.
52. Altrogge (1994) *Netzplantechnik*, pp. 69ff.
53. Altrogge (1994) *Netzplantechnik*, p. 262.
54. Steinbuch (1998) *Projektorganisation*, pp. 153ff.
55. Gerold Patzak and Günter Rattay (1995) *Projektmanagement*, Vienna: Linde, p. 470.
56. Klopotek (2004) 'Projekt', p. 217.
57. Litke (2004) *Projektmanagement*, p. 182.
58. See Briggs and Myers-Briggs (1988) *Myers-Briggs Type Indicator*, Palo Alto, CA: Consulting Psychologists Press.
59. Litke (2004) *Projektmanagement*, p. 182.
60. Birker (1999) *Projektmanagement*, pp. 158f.
61. See Ruth C. Cohn (1975) *Von der Psychoanalyse zur themenzentrierten Interaktion*, Stuttgart: Klett-Cotta, pp. 110ff.
62. Cohn (1975) *Von der Psychoanalyse zur themenzentrierten Interaktion*, p. 113.
63. Cohn (1975) *Von der Psychoanalyse zur themenzentrierten Interaktion*, p. 115.
64. Cohn (1975) *Von der Psychoanalyse zur themenzentrierten Interaktion*, pp. 120ff.
65. Cohn (1975) *Von der Psychoanalyse zur themenzentrierten Interaktion*, pp. 123ff.
66. Tom Peters (1992) 'A Mess of Parables', in: *The Economist*, 5 December, cited in: Stuart Crainer (1997) *The Tom Peters Phenomenon: Corporate Man to Corporate Skunk*, Oxford: Capstone, p. 176.
67. Peters (1999) *The Brand You 50*, p. 126.
68. Tom Peters (1988) *Thriving on Chaos: Handbook for a Management Revolution*, New York: HarperCollins.
69. Tom Peters (1992) *Liberation Management*, p. 153.
70. Monica Lundgren and Johann Packendorff (2003) 'A Project-Based View of Entrepreneurship: Towards Action-Orientation, Seriality and Collectivity', in: Chris Steyaert and Daniel Hjorth (eds), *New Movements in Entrepreneurship*, Cheltenham: Edward Elgar, pp. 86–102.
71. Rose (1996) *Inventing our Selves*, p. 157.

72. On the concept of patchwork identity, see Heiner Keupp, Thomas Ahbe, Wolfgang Gmür, Renate Höfer, Beate Mitzscherlich, Wolfgang Kraus and Florian Straus (1999) *Identitätskonstruktionen: Das Patchwork der Identitäten in der Spätmoderne*, Reinbek: Rowohlt.

73. Harriet Rubin (1999) *Soloing: Realizing Your Life's Ambition*, New York: HarperCollins, pp. 114, 117.

74. Nicolette Strauss (2003) *Die andere Ich AG: Führen Sie sich selbst wie ein erfolgreiches Unternehmen*, Frankfurt: Campus-Verlag, pp. 192ff.

75. Besser-Siegmund and Siegmund (1991) *Coach Yourself*, p. 164.

76. Besser-Siegmund and Siegmund (1991) *Coach Yourself*, p. 16.

77. Peters (1999) *The Brand You 50*, pp. 42f., 6.

78. Defoe (1647) 'Of Bankrupts', in: *An Essay upon Projects*, pp. 191–227.

79. The advice book industry has already opened up this market. It delivers not only guides to success but also instructions for skilful shipwrecking. Richard Sennett's remark, 'failure is the great modern taboo. Popular literature is full of recipes for how to succeed, but largely silent about how to cope with failure' ((1998) *The Corrosion of Character*, New York: Norton, p. 189), is now outdated.

10

CONCLUSION: LINES OF FLIGHT – THE ART OF BEING DIFFERENT DIFFERENTLY

To negate a negation does not bring about its reversal; it proves, rather, that the negation was not negative enough.[1]

The interpellations of the entrepreneurial self are totalitarian. The economic imperatives it contains resolve themselves into a system of economic imperialism. Nothing escapes the command to continually self-improve for the sake of the market. There is no expression of life, the utility of which cannot be maximized, no decision that cannot be optimized, no desire or need that cannot be commodified. Even objection, refusal and transgression can be channelled into programmes promising competitive advantages, and every instance of failure just goes to show that our performance has left room for improvement. This makes living up to the entrepreneurial self a recipe for paranoia. As in the Grimm fairy tale of the hare and the hedgehog, however far you get, you always hear 'I am here already!'.

Yet the status of the entrepreneurial self is precarious. A *pure* entrepreneurial self is as impossible as a pure market. Both depend on a source they must inevitably drink dry; both are driven by a need for expansion that undermines their own existence. The entrepreneurial self's mode of existence is not that of real people; it is a hypothetical, an *as if*, a *real fiction*. It is a hypothetical with a prescriptive force, it addresses itself to us, it is the point of convergence for a whole series of social and self technologies, it is a field of force, it exerts pull, like a magnetic field, an undertow. The rationale may be internally coherent and the strategies for the shaping and conditioning of the self may be precise and effective, but they do not translate smoothly and coherently into real self-interpretations and real behaviour. The claims made for the project to create entrepreneurial selves are programmed to be falsified by experience. Since the demands cannot be finally fulfilled, all efforts are unsatisfactory and since they are ill adapted to the real world they result in unintended effects.

These slippages in the word-to-world fit, together with the preordained miscarriages and contradictions, impose limitations on the governing of the entrepreneurial self, while at the same time providing instruments to continually refine the attempt. The force generated by the interpellation of the entrepreneurial self increases when it meets resistance. For this reason, the failure of its programmes to reach their targets is not a mark of weakness but rather a necessary part of their operation. The conclusions Peter Miller and Nikolas Rose have drawn from their analyses of economic concepts of government apply equally to strategies for shaping the self on the economic model: '[G]overning is not the "realization" of a programmer's dream. The "real" always insists on the form of resistance to programming; and the programmer's world is one of constant experiment, invention, failure, critique and adjustment'.[2] Programmes for governing the entrepreneurial self do not obey the principle of rule and application but rather the cybernetic model of process monitoring, using disturbances as signals to better regulate programme functioning. There needs to be constant adjustment between the actual state of a process and its ideal state in order to cope with the risks of malfunctioning, which increase in step with growing complexity. These frictions of governing constantly steer the process by which the instruments of government are optimized.

The efficacy of the entrepreneurial interpellation, its magnetic force, resides in the difference between its character of totality and the preordained insufficiency of the response. This same gap harbours critical potential. It affords distance, an empty space for letting the motor run idle, for *going slow*. Such a critical attitude, revolving around the question, 'how not to be governed like that, by that, in the name of those principles, with such and such an objective in mind and by means of such procedures, not like that, not for that, not by them', is both the complement and the nemesis of the art of governing[3]. The entrepreneurial self cannot exist without freedom of choice (albeit a freedom imposed from without). But being compelled to make choices also provides the opportunity to choose differently, to opt out of entrepreneurial self-optimization.

Like neoliberal governmentality in general, the entrepreneurial regime is by its very nature nothing if not critical. It propagates autonomy and self-reliance, which would imply a critique of tendencies to control subjects. So how is it possible to critique a form of governing motivated by a mistrust of government? How is it possible to liberate the self from the compulsion to be entrepreneurial when 'a fundamental desire for freedom'[4] is supposed to be the engine of entrepreneurial activity? Finally, how is it possible to escape a call to action that treats everyone the same way by demanding that everyone be different?

Entrepreneurial programmes are in favour of distinction and against conformity, for transgression and against following the rules. Essentially, they demand difference. The problem for critique is now to discover how to be different but in a different way to the way being demanded. The negative component of this critique cannot adopt a stable position. Nor can the contradiction of prescribing difference as a norm for all be evaded by being even more different. No virgin territory exists outside entrepreneurial subjectivity in the depths of the self and if one did exist it would be a priori mapped out for future conquest. Accordingly, becoming fluid and leaping between multiple identities will not lead out of the trap. The variously nomadic, queer or hybrid subjects held up by post-structuralist theories like those of Gilles Deleuze, Judith Butler or Homi Bhabha may provide a kind of shape shifting that evades the remnants of the pressure to conform in a post-disciplinary society, but nevertheless do not present opposition to the neo-liberal imperative to be flexible.

Alterity is easily digested by a market capable of turning it into a unique selling point or labelling it unmarketable and taking it out of circulation altogether. One part of the art of being different differently is attempting again and again to break out of this alternative between ingestion and excretion. This art needs ever new evasive moves, must be skilful at exploiting chances, have the courage to destroy, manoeuvrability and self-will – all of which happen to also be entrepreneurial virtues. Yet it is not a question of mimesis. The art of being different differently does not merely accelerate the contest for alterity by doing alterity better than everyone else. Instead, its practitioners react with stolid indifference to the demand to be different and respond with purposeless play to the imperative to maximize utility. They are on a third path – neither the particular freedom of choice foisted on them nor the lack of freedom, but rather not being forced to choose. Their maxim is not avoidance of all decision and action, as appears to have been the fate of Melville's Bartleby, whose systematic passivity, his 'I would prefer not to',[5] finally leads to his death by starvation in prison. Being different differently can also mean preferring not to refuse oneself to death.

Critique then is not the mirror reflection of its object nor a counter-programme for a different kind of entrepreneurial self-optimization. It is the continuous effort to elude, at least for a time, all programmes. It is not an opposing force but rather turns down the field of force, interrupts the flow of energy rather than reversing it; it is a permanent diversion rather than the search for the one point of resistance. For this form of critique, there can be no advice books or coaching. Instead of establishing an opposing regime of subjectification, it is a 'de-subjectifying undertaking'.[6] Subjectification rests on procedures of education: training, shaping, straightening up. De-subjectification, on the other hand, is an activity of *education*, of leading out, seeking to overcome the *coercion to be a self*, yet without dissolving or annihilating the self[7].

This involves acting tactically rather than strategically, to employ a distinction made by Michel de Certeau. Strategic actions are 'actions which, thanks to the establishment of a place of power (the property of a proper), elaborate theoretical places (systems and totalizing discourses)', while 'a *tactic* is a calculated action determined by the absence of a proper locus'. The tactician is not the general, looking down from a higher vantage point, but rather in the middle of the battle, following her own sense of timing, her kairos, rather than a battle plan. Even when she takes the initiative, her actions are reactions:

> The space of a tactic is the space of the other. Thus it must play on and with a terrain imposed on it and organized by the law of a foreign power. It does not have the means to *keep to itself*, at a distance, in a position of withdrawal, foresight, and self-collection … This nowhere gives a tactic mobility, to be sure, but a mobility that must accept the chance offerings of the moment, and seize on the wing the possibilities that offer themselves at any given moment. It must vigilantly make use of the cracks that particular conjunctions open in the surveillance of the proprietary powers. It poaches in them. It creates surprises in them. It can be where it is least expected. It is a guileful ruse.[8]

The entrepreneurial force field can only be turned off for short periods at a time but these moments show us that it is not entirely inescapable.

Programmes and resistance, strategies and tactics belong to different types of knowledge and practice. The field of force, the call to self-mobilize, can be generated systematically but resistance cannot be planned and calculated in advance. Yet, the governmental programmes have to reckon and reckon with it in advance. There is a science of governing but not a science of not being governed. This obliges us to represent the situation in opposing ways. The technologies of the entrepreneurial self can be organized into theories, empirical tests and methods, which are susceptible to the kind of systematic reconstruction undertaken in this book. In contrast, descriptions of the art of being different differently remain anecdotal; they cannot be codified into theory. Theories are strategic; they generalize. Tactics, on the other hand, are singular; they apply to particular events.

The present book has focused on the rationale of the entrepreneurial self and on several of its key technologies. It has analysed strategies without itself adopting a stance of strategic opposition. The approach has been tactical. This is mainly due to the subject matter itself. The entrepreneurial interpellation is logically committed to limitlessness. It has no outside. At most, it has zones of differing intensity of force; it has weaker zones, where other calls superpose in varying degrees of density. A critical analysis must survey the magnetic field from within, mapping its lines of force and following them back to its sources. Critique can bring into relief the impositions and demands made on people by the regime, disclose internal contradictions between promises and delivery, but it cannot show people how to escape.

Nevertheless, the investigation would be incomplete if it did not expose the moments of inertia, turbulence and resistance that disturb the field of force, sap its energy, divert it, neutralize it, and thereby indirectly contribute to its reformation. The direction and amplitude of force depend importantly on how it meets with resistance.

This study of the entrepreneurial self concludes with a cursory glance at three examples of evasion that make use of alternative currents. Depression, irony and passive resistance are certainly not the only causes of friction in the regime of entrepreneurial subjectification. They have been presented here as anecdotal evidence and are of differing importance. None of them are suitable as models for the kind of tactical, critical practice needed to obtain a different freedom than the freedom of the market. They themselves testify both to the impossibility of truly becoming an entrepreneurial self once and for all and to the impossibility of escaping the demand to nevertheless work on becoming one.

The force of the entrepreneurial call can be weakened by its own inherent excessiveness. The entrepreneurial self is a 'weary' self.[9] The individual is always lagging behind because the demands are principally incapable of final satisfaction. She is always in danger of being eliminated because the 'categorical comparative' posed by the market maintains a permanent contest of exclusion. Since recognition is contingent on success, every failure stirs up the fear of social death. There are no stable compass points and no places of respite. As the French sociologist Alain Ehrenberg writes:

> [s]elf-control, flexibility of mind and feeling, and the capacity for action meant that each individual had to be up to the task of constantly adapting to a changing world that was losing its stable shape, becoming temporary, consisting of ebb and flow, something like a snakes-and-ladders game. The social and political game was not so easy to read any more. These institutional transformations made it seem as if each person, even the humblest and lowest of the lot, had to take on the job of *choosing* and *deciding* everything.[10]

Not everyone is in a position to withstand the pressure and no one can all of the time.

The regime produces two very different types of subjects by the same means: the clever self-optimizer and its opposite, the inadequate individual. Where activity is demanded, the inadequate individual is lethargic; when creativity is called for, it is bereft of imagination, since it is not flexible enough; instead of forging projects and networking, it withdraws from society; programmes of empowerment are like water off a duck's back to its sense of powerlessness; it is plagued by self-doubt rather than overflowing with self-confidence; it is incapable of making decisions and taking risks; instead of bursting with good humour, it is sad. In short, this negative of the entrepreneurial self is the image of clinical depression. As Ehrenberg puts it, '[i]f depression is a pathology of a consciousness that is only itself, then dependency is the pathology of a consciousness that is never enough of itself, that is never adequately filled with its identity, that is never adequately active'.[11] No amount of externally imposed empowerment can silence the condescending tone in the policeman's voice when he says, in Kafka's story, 'give it up, give it up'.

Ehrenberg, the genealogist of depression, elaborates on the way the ethos of individual responsibility, autonomy and permanent mobilization in post-disciplinary society replaces the culture of prohibition and obedience. Burnout replaces neurosis as the typical and accepted digression from the norm. Instead of wearing themselves out on the divide between will and duty like the neurotics, entrepreneurial selves just get worn out pure and simple. From this perspective, the surge of emancipation associated with the year 1968 looks like a transition from one illness to another: 'Liberation might have gotten us out of the drama of guilt and obedience, but it has taken us straight into the demands of responsibility and action. And so the weariness of depression took over from the anxiety of neuroses'.[12]

The depression-causing inability to fulfil the demands emerges as the flipside of the promise of happiness held out by the proclaimers of the entrepreneurial spirit. By directing the frustration at the state of insufficiency at themselves, the entrepreneurial aspirants are forced to affirm the tyranny of total self-responsibility. This is an expression, not of the art of being differently different, but of the coercion to be different. It was formerly possible to resolve or at least relax psychic conflicts by compromising between desire and reality. This new feeling of insufficiency, however, is chronic. The usual therapies promise not to resolve the crisis but to ameliorate or cushion the symptoms by means of psychic maintenance work. This is one of the main reasons why medication has come to replace the psychoanalytic procedures of *remembering*, *repeating* and *working through*. Those driven to despair by the imperative to self-optimize can be kept under its sway by pharmacological adjustment.[13]

Dependency is closely allied to depression. Both are symptoms of the inability to cope with pressure. The usual clinical approach is to treat dependence or addiction less as an individual pathology or as the psychophysical effect of a drug than as a relationship problem. Being dependent means being unable to live without some particular thing. Society has nothing against people having connections and employing aids, but they should be capable of getting off them at any time, and if they are not they will be seen as lacking the independence needed to cope with life. The addict helps to prop up the entrepreneurial self as an ideal role model by showing us what it looks like to fail.

If depression, exhaustion and addiction are the dark side of the entrepreneurial self, irony is its compensatory other. Depression's inertia weakens the magnetic force because the self itself is weakened. Ironic distance mean-while generates turbulence. The ironist is well aware of the laws governing the market and the inherently paradoxical demands it makes. She knows what is being imposed upon her and she says it, pushing the facts of the matter to their illogical conclusion, exposing as absurd what she cannot otherwise change.

The comic artist Scott Adams, inventor of Dilbert, that minimalist icon of the new economy, has concisely summarized this approach:

> The world has become so complicated that we're all bluffing our way through the business day, hoping that we'll not be unmasked for the boobs that we really are. I see the world as a massively absurd endeavour, populated by people who struggle every minute to rationalize the silly things they do ... We rarely recognize our own idiocies, yet we can clearly identify the idiocies of others. That's the central tension of business: We expect others to act ration-ally even though we are irrational. It's useless to expect rational behaviour from the people you work with, or anybody else for that matter. If you can come to peace with the fact that you're surrounded by idiots, you'll realize that resistance is futile, your tension will dissipate, and you can sit back and have a good laugh at the expense of others.[14]

For a time, Dilbert cartoons could be found on almost all office walls and Adams' books have become standard reading for MBA courses. This shows how many people recognize their own mirror image in Dilbert, who func-tions clearly as an everyman. The comics operate on the principle 'But he doesn't have anything on!' and, as in *The Emperor's New Clothes*, the utter-ance does not cause the emperor's power to collapse: he 'shivered, for he was certain that they were right; but he thought: "I must bear it until the pro-cession is over." And he walked even more proudly, and the two gentlemen of the imperial bedchamber went on carrying the train that wasn't there'.[15] In our democratic times, Dilbert fans function as populace and emperor in one person, assuring each other they have seen through the rituals they themselves are continually performing, using irony as a vent. Nodding at the cartoon hanging on the wall above the desk with the knowing smile that says 'that's the way it is' ensures that it stays the way it is.

There may exist a way of laughing – especially laughing at oneself – that doesn't exhaust itself in compensation. The sort of ironic distance exemplified by Dilbert may give rise to the determination to leave the entrepreneurial self behind. And even if it fails to, what can be said against looking into the derisive mirror for temporary relief? Only when I see insanity and idiocy everywhere do I fall for the trick of abstract negation, affirming and embracing the rationale I am actually trying to hold at arm's length.

The entrepreneurial self differs from the regime of discipline by invoking the congruity of self-realization and economic success, desire and duty. But as such it remains at heart, like discipline, a programme of hard work.

What has changed decisively is the object of zeal: the way abilities are put to work, how work is justified to the worker and who gives the commands. The ethos of increasing productivity remains. You cannot optimize utility by sitting around doing nothing. Would this not suggest praise of idleness as a reaction to the entrepreneurial mode of being governed? Would not the 'Ne travaillez jamais!' daubed by Situationist Guy Debord[16] on some Parisian masonry be an appropriate motto for the artists of being different differently? Could laziness be the model of a practice of de-subjectification fit to elide the entrepreneurial self?

In the 1990s, a Berlin group calling themselves *The Happy Unemployed* (*Die Glücklichen Arbeitslosen*) staged a number of actions including the issuing of 'laziness papers'.[17] Their circular, the *Müßiggängster* (*Gangsters of Idleness*, a play on the words gangster and *Müßiggang*, meaning indulgence in idleness), attacked common-sense assumptions about the unemployed:

> If the unemployed are unhappy, then not because they are without work but because they have no money. Therefore, we should no longer speak of 'people without work', but only of 'people without money'; we should no longer speak of 'jobseekers' but only of 'moneyseekers'. Then we will be representing the state of things clearly.[18]

The *Gangsters of Idleness* consequently demanded the unconditional and indefinite remuneration of non-labour without 'reintegration measures'. The social utility of faineance, they attest, is beyond doubt:

> What happens when a concern announces that it will eliminate a certain number of jobs? Everyone at the stock exchange praises the courageous measure, shares go up and the balance sheets soon show the corresponding profits. In this way the unemployed produce more profit than their former co-workers. It would be logical to give thanks to the unemployed for contributing more to economic growth than anyone else.[19]

The group was not attempting to make a contribution to debates on an unconditional basic income. They were interested neither in 'prefabricated mental architectures in which people will be obliged to settle whether they like it or not',[20] nor in 'critique of the system', nor in the rhetoric of class struggle. Instead, they were on a 'search for unclear resources', creating 'Without Me Incs.', 'Alliances for Simulation', operating on the principle that, 'you pretend to create jobs and we pretend to work', extolling 'creative passivity' and specializing in 'propaganda by deed, misdeed and above all by no deed at all'.[21]

Apart from occasional romantic lapses (as when citing 'the intensive social life of pre-capitalist traditions' in non-Western cultures with their 'economy of mutuality'[22]), the happy unemployed were performing a practical, experimental critique of entrepreneurial rationale and its work ethic, while refusing to elaborate on feasible alternatives or grand utopias:

> The utopian draughts exact plans for a putatively ideal construction and expects the world to pour itself into this mould. The happy unemployed is rather a topist, tinkering with places and things already there. He is not constructing a system but rather looking for opportunities to improve his environment.[23]

In other words, the *Happy Unemployed* were tacticians rather than strategists. Their role models, 'even if only metaphorically', were eastern martial arts such as Nèijiā, 'based exclusively on two principles: non–action and using the opponent's mistakes', or Aikido with its principle of 'evading again and again until the attacker enters a position in which his balance can be broken with minimal effort'.[24] Alternately, the *Gangsters of Idleness* professed allegiance to the 'healthy opportunism' of the 'glider tactic':

> Instead of doggedly fixing on a single focus, different social winds are taken as welcome opportunities. The decisive thing is not the object of the activity (it could be a banquet, swap circles, group sex, discussion salons, rioting or gardening), but rather whether or not it affords an increase in communication.[25]

Their sanguine hedonism placed the *Happy Unemployed* at equidistance from the pedantic tedium of the social sciences, from neo–liberal mobilization rhetoric, social work empowerment jargon and late Marxian theories of everything. The gangsters also evaded classification as an especially trippy variant of 'fun culture' and repeatedly deflected appropriation attempts by the media, achieving this in the end by dropping the whole endeavour – an exemplary tactical move.

Since then however, doing nothing has itself become a marketable commodity. With more and more people without job prospects, there has been a boom in advice books promising the absence of wealth and success. Some examples bear titles like: *Bonjour Laziness: Why Hard Work Doesn't Pay*,[26] *Starting Small: On the Advantages of Not Having Permanent Employment*[27] and *The Elegant Art of Impoverishment*.[28] When the work ethic erodes because no work is available, then idleness also loses its subversive edge. The entrepreneurial regime updates itself in cynical recommendations in the style of *Downsize Me Inc.* in order to survive the crisis. The 'superfluous' members of the market society should learn humility, tighten their belts, and reinterpret austerity as a gentle art of simple living – especially since they have no choice.[29] This is an old tune: happy is he who accepts the inevitable. The new twist is that even accepting the inevitable needs to be learnt and trained.

The passive activism practised by the *Happy Unemployed*, their 'busy doing nothing', does not lead to a programme of resistance against the entrepreneurial self. The exponents were well aware of the contingent historical and geographical enabling conditions when they wrote: 'In 1995 it was relatively easy to live in Berlin without work'. They were also aware of the resulting limited life expectancy of the lazy gangster, who in any case was 'intended more as a literary figure à la Candide than as a real existence'. In the introduction to a text anthology, the group states its aim clearly: 'It was about making an absence visible, making present – for a short time only – a realm beyond the workplace'. The author adds: 'even repetition becomes destructive ... There is not much to say about being happily unemployed and we do not want to become tedious'.[30]

Ephemeral presentation of the absent may seem a negligible way to disturb the entrepreneurial field of force, but even this is a difficult enough task. The art of being different differently consists perhaps precisely in this embrace of the ephemeral; in stopping at the right moment and restarting elsewhere.

Notes

1. Theodor W. Adorno (1966/2007) *Negative Dialectics*, New York: Routledge, pp. 159f.
2. Miller and Rose (1990) 'Governing Economic Life', p. 14.
3. Foucault (1997) 'What is Critique?', p. 44.
4. Tara J. Fenwick (2002) 'Transgressive Desires: New Enterprising Selves in the New Capitalism', in: *Work, Employment and Society*, 16(4), pp. 703–723, here: pp. 711f.
5. See Herman Melville (1967) 'Bartleby the Scrivener', in: *Billy Budd, Sailor and Other Stories*, Harmondsworth: Penguin, pp. 57–99.
6. Michel Foucault (1991) *Remarks on Marx: Conversations with Ducio Trombadori*, New York: Semiotext(e), p. 31.
7. See Jan Masschelein (2004) '"Je viens de voir, je viens d'entendre": Erfahrungen im Niemandsland', in Ricken and Rieger-Ladich (eds), *Michel Foucault: Pädagogische Lektüren*, Wiesbaden: Springer-Verlag, p. 95–115.
8. Michel de Certeau (1984) *The Practice of Everyday Life*, Oakland, CA: University of California Press, pp. 38, 37.
9. See Alain Ehrenberg (2010) *The Weariness of the Self: Diagnosing the History of Depression in the Contemporary Age*, Montreal: McGill-Queen's University Press.
10. Ehrenberg (2010) *The Weariness of the Self*, p. 185.
11. Ehrenberg (2010) *The Weariness of the Self*, p. 221.
12. Ehrenberg (2010) *The Weariness of the Self*, p. 229.
13. See Peter D. Kramer (1994) *Listening to Prozac*, London: Fourth Estate; Carl Elliott (2003) *Better than Well: American Medicine meets the American Dream*, New York: W. W. Norton.
14. Scott Adams (1996) *The Dilbert Principle: A Cubicle's-Eye View of Bosses, Meetings, Management Fads and Other Workplace Afflictions*, New York: Boxtree, pp. 6f.
15. Hans Christian Andersen (1983) *The Complete Fairy Tales and Stories*, New York: Anchor, p. 81.

16. See Guy Debord (1958) 'Théorie de la dérive', in *Internationale Situationniste, #2*, Paris, December. (Engl: *Situationist International Anthology*, ed. and trans. by Ken Knabb, Berkeley, 2006.)
17. Several of the group's texts are anthologized in Guillaume Paoli (ed.) (2002) *Mehr Zuckerbrot, weniger Peitsche: Aufrufe, Manifeste und Faulheitspapiere der Glücklichen Arbeitslosen*, Berlin: Edition Tiamat; further texts can be found at: http://guillaumepaoli.de/muessiggangster/ [18.01.2015].
18. Die Glücklichen Arbeitslosen (1996/2002) 'Auf der Suche nach unklaren Ressourcen', in: Paoli (ed.), *Mehr Zuckerbrot, weniger Peitsche*, pp. 30–45, here: p. 35.
19. 'Die Glücklichen Arbeitslosen (1996/2002) Auf der Suche.
20. Guillaume Paoli (2002) 'Wer hat Angst vor der freien Zeit', in: Paoli (ed.), *Mehr Zuckerbrot, weniger Peitsche*, pp. 172–182, here: p. 173.
21. See Die Glücklichen Arbeitslosen (1996/2002) 'Ohne mich-AG', in: Paoli (ed.), *Mehr Zuckerbrot, weniger Peitsche*, pp. 62–71; 'Bündnis für Simulation', in: Paoli (ed.), *Mehr Zuckerbrot, weniger Peitsche*, pp. 49f.; 'Für die Ausdehnung des Sommerlochs! Für die kreative Passivität!', in: Paoli (ed.), *Mehr Zuckerbrot, weniger Peitsche*, pp. 83–85; Guillaume Paoli, 'Aussteigen für Einsteiger: Eine Einführung', in: Paoli (ed.), *Mehr Zuckerbrot, weniger Peitsche*, pp. 7–27, here: p. 21.
22. Die Glücklichen Arbeitslosen (1996/2002) 'Auf der Suche', pp. 43f.
23. Die Glücklichen Arbeitslosen (1996/2002) 'Auf der Suche', p. 40.
24. Paoli (2002) 'Aussteigen für Einsteiger', pp. 25f.
25. Paoli (2002) 'Aussteigen für Einsteiger', p. 25.
26. Corinne Maier (2005) *Bonjour Laziness: Why Hard Work Doesn't Pay*, New York: Pantheon Books. This bestseller is addressed not at the unemployed but rather at stressed average employees in the middle echelons, to whom the author gives rather middle-class advice on how to make things more comfortable in the niches of company life: 'Avoid operational ("hands-on") positions like the plague. The ideal is to be "sidelined": these non-productive, often interde-partmental, posts effect nothing, and are subject to no management pressure' (p. 120). She has a low opinion of absenteeism or re-appropriation: 'It's pointless trying to change the system. By opposing it, you merely reinforce it, entrench it further. Of course, you can indulge in anarchic behaviour, such as phone calls to the office to say that you're ill, or adopt the manifesto 'Steal from work because work steals from you'. But as for fully fledged revolt, that was OK for the radicals of the 1970s, but look what they turned into (the bosses)' (p. 119).
27. Achim Schwarze (2005) *Kleine Brötchen: Von den Vorzügen, ohne feste Anstellung zu sein*, Munich: Taschenbuch.
28. Alexander von Schönburg (2005) *Die Kunst stilvollen Verarmens: Wie man ohne Geld reich wird*, Berlin: Rowohlt.
29. See Werner Tiki Küstenmacher and Lothar J. Seiwert (2004) *How to Simplify Your Life: Seven Practical Steps to Letting Go of Your Burdens and Living a Happier Life*, New York: McGraw-Hill.
30. Paoli (2002) 'Aussteigen für Einsteiger', pp. 8f., 21f.

BIBLIOGRAPHY

Adams, Robert (1996) *Social Work and Empowerment*, Houndmills: Palgrave Macmillan.

Adams, Robert (1991) *Protests by Pupils: Empowerment, Schooling and the State*, Basingstoke: Falmer.

Adams, Scott (1996) *The Dilbert Principle: A Cubicle's-Eye View of Bosses, Meetings, Management Fads and Other Workplace Afflictions*, New York: Boxtree.

Adorno, Theodor W. (1966/2007) *Negative Dialectics*, New York: Routledge.

Agamben, Giorgio (1998) *Homo Sacer: Sovereign Power and Bare Life*, Stanford, CA: Stanford University Press.

Albert, Robert S. and Runko, Mark A. (1999) 'A History of Research on Creativity', in: Robert J. Steinberg (ed.), *Handbook of Creativity*, Cambridge: Cambridge University Press, pp. 16–31.

Alchian, Armen A. and Demsetz, Harold (1972) 'Production, Information Cost, and Economic Organization', in: *American Economic Review*, 62, pp. 777–795.

Alinsky, Saul D. (1971) *Rules for Radicals: A Practical Primer for Realistic Radicals*, New York: Vintage.

Althusser, Louis (1971) *Lenin and Philosophy and Other Essays*, London: New Left Books.

Altrogge, Günter (1994) *Netzplantechnik*, Munich: Oldenbourg.

Amabile, Teresa (1981) *The Social Psychology of Creativity*, New York: Springer.

Andersen, Hans Christian (1983) *The Complete Fairy Tales and Stories*, New York: Anchor.

Antonovsky, Aaron (1987) *Unraveling The Mystery of Health – How People Manage Stress and Stay Well*, San Francisco: Jossey-Bass.

Antonovsky, Aaron (1989) 'Die salutogenetische Perspektive: Zu einer neuen Sicht von Gesundheit und Krankheit', in: *Meducs*, 2, pp. 51–57.

Antonovsky, Aaron (1993) 'Gesundheitsforschung versus Krankheitsforschung', in: Alexa Franke and Michael Broda (eds), *Psychosomatische Gesundheit: Versuch einer Abkehr vom Pathogenese-Konzept*, Tübingen: DGVT-Verlag, pp. 3–14.

Atkinson, Lynn (1988) *Power and Empowerment: The Power Principle*, Las Vegas: New Falcon.

Bachrach, Peter and Botwinick, Aryeh (1992) *Power and Empowerment: A Radical Theory of Participatory Democracy*, Philadelphia: Temple University Press.

Baecker, Dirk (1999) *Die Form des Unternehmens*, Frankfurt: Suhrkamp.

Baethge, Martin (1991) 'Arbeit, Vergesellschaftung, Identität: Zur zunehmenden normativen Subjektivierung der Arbeit', in: *Soziale Welt*, 42, pp. 6–19.

Baistow, Karen (1995) 'Liberation and Regulation? Some Paradoxes of Empowerment', in: *Critical Social Policy*, 15(42), pp. 34–46.

Bandler, Richard (1985) *Using Your Brain – For a Change: Neuro-Linguistic Programming*, Moab, UT: Real People Press.

Bandura, Albert (1977) 'Self Efficacy: Toward a Unifying Theory of Behavioral Change', in: *Psychological Review*, 84, pp. 191–215.

Bandura, Albert (1997) *Self Efficacy: The Exercise of Control*, New York: Worth.

Batliwala, Srilatha (1994) 'The Meaning of Women's Empowerment: New Concepts from Action', in: Gita Sen, Adrienne Germain and Lincoln C. Chen (eds), *Population Policies Reconsidered: Health, Empowerment, and Rights*, Boston: Harvard University Press, pp. 127–138.

Beck, Ulrich (1992) *Risk Society: Towards a New Modernity*, London: Sage.

Beck, Ulrich (1993) *Die Erfindung des Politischen: Zu einer Theorie reflexiver Modernisierung*, Frankfurt: Suhrkamp.

Becker, Gary S. (1976) *The Economic Approach to Human Behavior*, Chicago: University of Chicago Press.

Becker, Gary S. (1993) Economic Imperialism [Interview], in: *Religion & Liberty*, 3.2, www.acton.org/pub/religion-liberty/volume-3-number-2/economic-imperialism (15.03.2015).

Becker, Gary S. (1997) 'The Economic Way of Looking at Life', Nobel Lecture, December 1992, in: *Nobel Lectures, Economics 1991–1995*, ed. Torsten Persson, Singapore: World Scientific Publishing.

Beckert, Jens (2002) *Beyond the Market: The Social Foundations of Economic Efficiency*, Princeton, NJ: Princeton University Press.

Bellah, Robert N., Madsen, Richard, Tipton, Steven M., Sullivan, William M. and Swidler, Ann (1991) *The Good Society*, New York: Vintage.

Bengel, Jürgen, Strittmatter, Regine and Willmann, Hildegard (1998) *Was erhält Menschen gesund? Antonovskys Modell der Salutogenese: Diskussionsstand und Stellenwert*, Cologne: BZgA (Forschung und Praxis der Gesundheitsförderung, Bd. 6).

Berger, Peter L. and Neuhaus, Richard John (1977) *To Empower People: The Role of Mediating Structures in Public Policy*, Washington, DC: American Enterprise Institute for Public Policy Research.

Besser-Siegmund, Cora and Siegmund, Harry (1991) *Coach Yourself.* (Persönlichkeitskultur für Führungskräfte), Düsseldorf: ECON-Verlag.

Birker, Klaus (1999) *Projektmanagement*, Berlin: Cornelsen Giradet.

Blanchard, Kenneth, Carlos, John P. and Randolph, Alan (1999) *The 3 Keys to Empowerment: Release the Power within People for Astonishing Results*, Oakland, CA: Berrett-Koehler.

Blanchard, Kenneth, Carlos, John P. and Randolph, Alan (2001) *Empowerment Takes More than a Minute*, Oakland, CA: Berrett-Koehler.

Block, Peter (1987) *The Empowered Manager: Positive Political Skills at Work*, San Francisco: Jossey-Bass.

Block, Peter (1997) *Entfesselte Mitarbeiter: Demokratische Prinzipien für die radikale Neugestaltung der Unternehmensführung*, Stuttgart: Schäffer-Poeschel.

Bologna, Sergio (1997/2006) *Die Zerstörung der Mittelschichten: Thesen zur neuen Selbständigkeit*, Graz/Vienna: Nausner and Nausner.

Boltanski, Luc and Chiapello, Ève (2005) *The New Spirit of Capitalism*, New York: Verso.

Boltanski, Luc, Chiapello, Ève and Thévenot, Laurent (2006) *On Justification: Economies of Worth*, Princeton, NJ: Princeton University Press.

Bono, Edward de (1970) *Lateral Thinking: Creativity Step by Step*, New York: Harper & Row.

Bonß, Wolfgang, Keupp, Heiner and Koenen, Elmar (1984) 'Das Ende des Belastungsdiskurses? Zur subjektiven und gesellschaftlichen Bedeutung von Arbeitslosigkeit', in: Wolfgang Bonß and Rolf G. Heinze (eds), *Arbeitslosigkeit in der Arbeitsgesellschaft*, Frankfurt: Suhrkamp, pp. 143–188.

Bookman, Ann and Morgan, Sandra (eds) (1988) *Women and the Politics of Empowerment*, Philadelphia: Temple University Press.

Boutillier, Sophie and Uzunidis, Dimitri (1999) *La Légende de l'entrepreneur*, Paris: Syros.

Boutillier, Sophie and Uzunidis, Dimitri (2006) *L'aventure des entrepreneurs*, Paris: Group Studyrama.

Brandes, Fritz (1998) 'Profitabler werden mit zufriedenen Kunden', in: *Frankfurter Allgemeine Zeitung, Blick durch die Wirtschaft*, 6 May.

Branz, Manuela (2005) 'Gelungenes Scheitern. Scheitern in der Postmoderne', in: *Kunstforum International*, 174, Jan.–Mar., pp. 262–267.

Brentano, Lujo von (1907) *Der Unternehmer: Vortrag gehalten am 3. Januar 1907 in der Volkswirtschaftlichen Gesellschaft in Berlin*, Berlin: Verlag von Leonhard Simion.

Brickman, Philip, Rabinowitz, Vita Carulli, Karuza Jr, Jurgis, Coates, Dan, Cohn, Ellen and Kidder, Louise (1982) 'Models of Helping and Coping' (1982) 'Models of Helping and Coping', in: *American Psychologist*, 37(4), pp. 368–384.

Bridges, William (1998) *Creating You & Co.: Learn to Think Like the CEO of Your Own Career*, Cambridge, MA: DaCapo.

Bridges, William (1994) *JobShift: How to Prosper in a Workplace Without Jobs*, New York: DaCapo.

Briggs, Katharine C. and Briggs Myers, Isabel (1988) *Type Indicator*, Palo Alto, CA: Consulting Psychologists Press.

Bröckling, Ulrich (2000) 'Totale Mobilmachung. Menschenführung im Qualitäts- und Selbstmanagement', in: Ulrich Bröckling, Susanne Krasmann and Thomas Lemke (eds), *Gouvernementalität der Gegenwart*, Frankfurt: Suhrkamp, pp. 131–167.

Bröckling, Ulrich (2002) 'Diktat des Komparativs: Zur Anthropologie des "unternehmerischen Selbst"', in: Ulrich Bröckling and Eva Horn (eds), *Anthropologie der Arbeit*, Tübingen: Gunter Narr Verlag, pp. 157–173.

Bröckling, Ulrich (2002) 'Jeder könnte, aber nicht alle können: Konturen des unternehmerischen Selbst', in: *Mittelweg 36*, 11(4), pp. 6–26.

Bröckling, Ulrich (2003) 'Bakunin Consulting, Inc.: Anarchismus, Management und die Kunst, nicht regiert zu werden', in: Marion von Osten (ed.), *Norm der Abweichung*, Zürich: Springer, pp. 19–38.

Bröckling, Ulrich (2003) 'Das demokratisierte Panopticon: Subjektivierung und Kontrolle im 360° Feedback', in: Axel Honneth and Martin Saar (eds), *Michel Foucault: Zwischenbilanz einer Rezeption. Frankfurter Foucault Konferenz 2001*, Frankfurt: Suhrkamp, pp. 77–93.

Bröckling, Ulrich (2003) 'You are not Responsible for Being Down, but you are Responsible for Getting Up: Über Empowerment', in: *Leviathan*, 31, pp. 323–344.

Bröckling, Ulrich (2004) 'Über Kreativität: Ein Brainstorming', in: Ulrich Bröckling, Axel T. Paul and Stefan Kaufmann (eds), *Vernunft – Entwicklung – Leben: Schlüsselbegriffe der Moderne*, Munich: Wilhelm Fink, pp. 235–243.

Bröckling, Ulrich (2004) 'Empowerment', 'Kontrakt', 'Kreativität', 'Mediation', 'Prävention', 'Unternehmer', in: Ulrich Bröckling, Susanne Krasmann and

Thomas Lemke (eds), *Glossar der Gegenwart*, Frankfurt: Suhrkamp, pp. 55–62, 132–138, 139–144, 159–166, 210–215, 271–276.

Bröckling, Ulrich (2005) 'Gendering the Enterprising Self: Subjectification Programs and Gender Differences in Guides to Success', in: *Distinktion: Scandinavian Journal for Social Theory*, Oct., pp. 7–25.

Bröckling, Ulrich (2005) 'Projektwelten: Anatomie einer Vergesellschaftungsform', in: *Leviathan*, 33, pp. 364–383.

Bröckling, Ulrich (2006) 'Und ... wie war ich? Über Feedback', in: *Mittelweg 36*, 15(2), pp. 27–44.

Bröckling, Ulrich (2007) Regime des Selbst. Ein Forschungsprogramm', in: Thorsten Bonacker and Andreas Reckwitz (eds), *Kulturen der Moderne. Soziologische Perspektiven der Gegenwart*, Frankfurt: Suhrkamp, pp. 119–139.

Bröckling, Ulrich (2010) 'Human Economy, Human Capital: A Critique of Biopolitical Economy', in: Ulrich Bröckling, Susanne Krasmann and Thomas Lemke (eds), *Governmentality: Current Issues and Future Challenges*, New York: Routledge, pp. 247–268.

Bröckling, Ulrich and Horn, Eva (eds) (2002) *Anthropologie der Arbeit*, Tübingen: Gunter Narr.

Bröckling, Ulrich, Bühler, Benjamin, Hahn, Marcus, Schöning, Matthias and Weinberg, Manfred (eds) (2004) *Disziplinen des Lebens: Zwischen Anthropologie, Literatur und Politik*, Tübingen: Gunter Narr.

Bröckling, Ulrich, Krasmann, Susanne and Lemke, Thomas (eds) (2000) *Gouvernementalität der Gegenwart*, Frankfurt: Suhrkamp.

Bröckling, Ulrich, Krasmann, Susanne and Lemke, Thomas (eds) (2004) *Glossar der Gegenwart*, Frankfurt: Suhrkamp.

Bröckling, Ulrich, Krasmann, Susanne and Lemke, Thomas (eds) (2012) *Governmentality: Current Issues and Future Challenges* (2nd edition), New York: Routledge.

Buchanan, James M. and Tullock, Gordon (1962) *The Calculus of Consent: Logical Foundations of Constitutional Democracy*, Ann Arbor, MI: The University of Michigan Press.

Buchanan, James M. (1975) *The Limits of Liberty: Between Anarchy and Leviathan*, Chicago: University of Chicago Press.

Buchanan, James M. (1975) 'A Contractarian Paradigm for Applying Economic Theory', in: *The American Economic Review*, LXV, pp. 225–230.

Buchanan, James M. (1963/4) 'What Should Economists Do?', in: *The Southern Economic Journal*, XXX(3), pp. 213–222.

Bude, Heinz (1997) 'Der Unternehmer als Revolutionär der Wirtschaft', in: *Merkur*, 51(582/3), Special Issue: 'Kapitalismus als Schicksal? Zur Politik der Entgrenzung', pp. 866–876.

Bühner, Rolf von (1993) *Der Mitarbeiter im Total Quality Management*, Düsseldorf: VDI-Verlag.

Burchell, Graham (1996) 'Liberal Government and Techniques of the Self', in: Andrew Barry, Thomas Osborne and Nikolas Rose (eds), *Foucault and Political Reason: Liberalism, Neo-liberalism and Rationalities of Government*, London: University of Chicago Press, pp. 19–36.

Burghardt, Manfred (1995) *Einführung in Projektmanagement*, Munich: Publicis.

Burnham, James (1941) *The Managerial Revolution*, New York: Penguin.

Burrows, Roger (ed.) (1991) *Deciphering the Enterprising Culture*, London: Cengage.

Butler, Judith (1997) *The Psychic Life of Power: Theories in Subjection*, Stanford, CA: Stanford University Press.

Butler, Judith (2003) 'Noch einmal: Körper und Macht', in: Axel Honneth and Martin Saar (eds), *Michel Foucault: Zwischenbilanz einer Rezeption*, Frankfurt: Suhrkamp, pp. 52–67.

Buzan, Tony (2002) *How to Mind Map: The Ultimate Thinking Tool That Will Change Your Life*, London: Thorsons.

Camp, Robert C. (1989) *Benchmarking: The Search for Industry Best Practices That Lead to Superior Performance*, Milwaukee: Quality Press.

Casson, Mark (1982) *The Entrepreneur: An Economic Theory*, Oxford: Wiley-Blackwell.

Casson, Mark (2000) *Enterprise and Leadership*, Cheltenham: Edward Elgar.

Certeau, Michel de (1984) *The Practice of Everyday Life*, Berkeley, CA: University of California Press.

Chell, Elizabeth, Haworth, Jean and Brearly, Sally (1991) *The Entrepreneurial Personality: Concepts, Cases and Categories*, London/New York: Cengage.

Cleaver, Frances (1999) 'Paradoxes of Participation: Questioning Participatory Approaches to Development', in: *Journal of International Development*, 11, pp. 597–612.

Coase, Ronald H. (1937) 'The Nature of the Firm', in: *Economica*, 4, pp. 386–405.

Cohn, Ruth C. (1975) *Von der Psychoanalyse zur themenzentrierten Interaktion*, Stuttgart: Klett-Cotta.

Conger, Jay A. and Kanungo, Rabindrah N. (1988) 'The Empowerment Process: Integrating Theory and Practice', in: *Academy of Management Review*, 13, pp. 471–482.

Cooke, Bill and Kothari, Uma (eds) (2001) *Participation: The New Tyranny?*, London/New York: Zed Books.

Crainer, Stuart (1997) *The Tom Peters Phenomenon: Corporate Man to Corporate Skunk*, Oxford: Capstone.

Cruikshank, Barbara (1999) *The Will to Empower: Democratic Citizens and Other Subjects*, Ithaca, NY: Cornell University Press.

Crutchfield, Richard S. (1962) 'Conformity and Creative Thinking' in: Howard E. Gruber, Glenn Terrel and Michael Wertheimer (eds), *Contemporary Approaches to Creative Thinking*, New York: Atherton Press, pp. 120–140.

Csikszentmihalyi, Mihaly (1996) *Creativity: The Psychology of Discovery and Invention*, New York: Harper.

Dean, Mitchell (1999) *Governmentality: Power and Rule in Modern Society*, London: Sage.

Defoe, Daniel (1647) *An Essay Upon Projects*, London.

Deleuze, Gilles (1988) *Foucault*, Minneapolis: University of Minnesota Press.

Deleuze, Gilles (1992) *Postscript on the Societies of Control*, Oct., 59, Winter, pp. 3–7.

DeLillo, Don (2003) *Cosmopolis*, New York: Picador.

Deutschmann, Christoph (2001) 'Die Gesellschaftskritik der Industriesoziologie – ein Anachronismus', in: *Leviathan*, 29, pp. 58–69.

Diemer, Regina von (1994) 'Motivation', in: Walter Masing (ed.), *Handbuch Qualitätsmanagement*, Munich: Hanser Fachbuchverlag, pp. 1061–1074.

Donabedian, Avedis (1980) *The Definition of Quality and Approaches to its Assessment*, Ann Arbor, MI: Health Administration Press.

Donabedian, Avedis and Salaman, Graeme (1992) 'The Cult(ure) of the Customer', in: *Journal of Management Studies*, 29, pp. 615–633.

Duesenberry, James (1960) 'Comment on "An Economic Analysis of Fertility"', in: The Universities' National Bureau Commitee for Economic Research (ed.),

Demographic and Economic Change in Developed Countries, Princeton, NJ: Princeton University Press.

du Gay, Paul (1996) *Consumption and Identity at Work*, London: Sage.

du Gay, Paul (2000) 'Enterprise and its Futures: A Response to Fournier and Grey', in: *Organization*, 7, pp. 165–183.

Durkheim, Emile (1893/1933) *The Division of Labor in Society*, New York: Free Press.

Edwards, Mark R. and Ewen, Ann J. (1996) *360° Feedback: The Powerful New Model for Employee Assessment and Performance Improvement*, New York: AMACOM.

Ehrenberg, Alain (2010) *The Weariness of the Self: Diagnosing the History of Depression in the Contemporary Age*, Montreal: McGill–Queen's University Press.

Elliott, Carl (2003) *Better than Well: American Medicine Meets the American Dream*, New York: W.W. Norton.

Elster, John (1986) 'Introduction', in: *The Multiple Self*, Cambridge: Cambridge University Press, pp. 1–34.

Emerson, Ralph Waldo (1841/1983) 'Self-reliance', in: *Essays and Lectures*, New York: Library of America, pp. 257–282.

Erikson, Erik H. (1980) *Identity and the Life Cycle*, New York: Norton.

Eucken, Walter (1959) *Grundsätze der Wirtschaftspolitik*, Hamburg: Rowohlt.

Ewald, François (1986) *L'Etat-Providence*, Part 1, Paris: Grasset.

Fawcett, Stephen B., Seekins, Tom, Whang, Paula L., Muiu, Charles and Suarez de Balcazar, Yolanda (1984) 'Creating and Using Social Technologies for Community Empowerment', in: *Prevention in Human Services*, 3(2/3), Special Issue: 'Studies in Empowerment', pp. 145–171.

Fenwick, Tara J. (2002) 'Transgressive Desires: New Enterprising Selves in the New Capitalism', in: *Work, Employment and Society*, 16(4), pp. 703–723.

Florida, Richard (2002) *The Rise of the Creative Class*, New York: Basic Books (p/b edition 2004).

Florida, Richard (2005) *Cities and the Creative Class*, New York: Psychology Press.

Florida, Richard (2005) *The Flight of the Creative Class: The New Global Competition for Talent*, New York: Collins.

Flusser, Vilém (2000) *From Subject to Project: Becoming Human*, London: Free Association Books.

Foucault, Michel (1977) *Discipline and Punish*, New York: Vintage Books.

Foucault, Michel (1981) 'Omnes et Singulatim: Towards a Criticism of "Political Reason"', in: Sterling M. McMurrin (ed.), *The Tanner Lectures on Human Values II*, Salt Lake City: University of Utah Press/Cambridge University Press, pp. 225–254.

Foucault, Michel (1983) 'Subject and Power', in: Hubert L. Dreyfus and Paul Rabinow, *Michel Foucault: Beyond Structuralism and Hermeneutics*, Chicago: University of Chicago Press, pp. 208–226.

Foucault, Michel (1983) 'On the Genealogy of Ethics: An Overview of Work in Progress', in: Hubert L. Dreyfus and Paul Rabinow, *Michel Foucault: Beyond Structuralism and Hermeneutics*, Chicago: University of Chicago Press, pp. 229–253.

Foucault, Michel (1984) 'What is Enlightenment?', in: Paul Rabinow (ed.), *The Foucault Reader*, New York: Penguin, pp. 32–50.

Foucault, Michel (1988) 'Technologies of the Self', in: Luther H. Martin, Huck Gutman and Patrick H. Hutton (eds), *Technologies of the Self*, Amherst, MA: University of Massachusetts Press, pp. 16–49.

Foucault, Michel (1990) *The Use of Pleasure*, New York: Vintage.

Foucault, Michel (1991) *Remarks on Marx: Conversations with Ducio Trombadori*, New York: Semiotext(e).

Foucault, Michel (1994) 'The Ethics of the Concern for Self as a Practice of Freedom' (interview with H. Becker, R. Fornet-Betancourt and A. Gomez-Müller, 20 January 1984), in: *Ethics, Subjectivity and Truth: The Essential Works of Michel Foucault 1954–1984*, Vol. 1, New York: Allen Lane, pp. 281–301.

Foucault, Michel (1997) 'What is Critique?', in: Sylvère Lotringer and Lysa Hochroth (eds), *The Politics of Truth*, New York: Semiotext(e), pp. 41–81.

Foucault, Michel (2003) *Society Must be Defended: Lectures at the College de France (1975–76)*, New York: Penguin.

Foucault, Michel (2009) *Security, Territory, Population: Lectures at the Collège de France 1977–1978*, New York: Palgrave Macmillan.

Foucault, Michel (2010) *The Birth of Biopolitics: Lectures at the Collège de France, 1978–1979*, New York: Palgrave Macmillan.

Fournier, Valérie and Grey, Christopher (1999) '"Too Much, Too Little and Too Often": A Critique of du Gay's Analysis of Enterprise', in: *Organization*, 6, pp. 107–128.

Frank, Thomas and Weiland, Matt (eds) (1997) *Commodify Your Dissent: Salvos from the Baffler*, New York: W.W. Norton & Co.

Frehr, Hans-Ulrich (1993) *Total Quality Management*, Munich: Hanser.

Freire, Paulo (2005) *Pedagogy of the Oppressed*, London: A&C Black.

Freire, Paulo (2013) *Education for Critical Consciousness*, London: A&C Black.

Freud, Sigmund (1964) *The Standard Edition of the Complete Psychological Works of Sigmund Freud*, Vol. XXII, London: W.W. Norton.

Friedman, David (1989) *The Machinery of Freedom: Guide to a Radical Capitalism*, La Salle, IL: University of Chicago Press.

Friedman, David (1996) *Hidden Order: The Economics of Everyday Life*, New York: Harper Business.

Friedman, Milton (1962) *Capitalism and Freedom*, Chicago: University of Chicago Press.

Friedmann, John (1992) *Empowerment: The Politics of Alternative Development*, Cambridge, MA: Blackwell.

Fuchs, Peter (1997) 'Adressabilität als Grundbegriff der soziologischen System-theorie', in: *Soziale Systeme*, 3, pp. 57–79.

Furubotn, Eirik G. and Richter, Rudolf (2005) *Institutions and Economic Theory: The Contribution of the New Institutional Economics* (2nd edition), Ann Arbor, MI: University of Michigan Press.

Gaddis, Paul O. (1959) 'The Project Manager', in: *Harvard Business Review*, 32, May/June, pp. 89–97.

Galton, Francis (1869) *Hereditary Genius*, New York: D. Appleton & Co.

Gardiner, P. D., Wongrassamee, S., Simmons, J. E. L. and Gardiner, P. D. (2003) 'Performance Measurement Tools: The Scorecard and the EFQM Excellence Model', in: *Measuring Business Excellence* 7(1), pp. 14–29.

Garvin, David A. (1984) 'What does "Product Quality" Really Mean?', in: *Sloan Management Review*, 26, pp. 25–43.

Gergen, Christopher and Vanourek, Gregg (2008) *Life Entrepreneurs: Ordinary People Creating Extraordinary Lives*, San Francisco, CA: John Wiley & Sons.

Giddens, Anthony (1991) *Modernity and Self-identity: Self and Society in the Late Modern Age*, Stanford, CA: Polity Press.

Goffman, Erving (1967) *Interaction Ritual: Essays on Face-to-Face Behavior*, New York: Pantheon.

Goffman, Erving (1971) *Relations in Public: Microstudies of the Public Order*, New York: Allen Lane.

Goffman, Erving (1971) *The Presentation of Self in Everyday Life*, Harmondsworth: Penguin.

Goffman, Erving (1974) *Frame Analysis: An Essay on the Organization of Experience*, Boston: Northeastern University Press.

Gordon, Colin (1991) 'Governmental Rationality: An Introduction', in: Graham Burchell, Colin Gordon and Peter Miller (eds), *The Foucault Effect: Studies in Governmentality*, Chicago: University of Chicago Press, pp. 1–51.

Gordon, Thomas (1970) *Parent Effectiveness Training: The Proven Program for Raising Responsible Children*, New York: Three Rivers Press.

Gordon, William J. J. (1961) *Synectics: The Development of Creative Capacity*, New York: Harper & Row.

Granovetter, Mark (1985) 'Economic Action and Social Structure: The Problem of Embeddedness', in: *American Journal of Sociology*, 91, pp. 481–510.

Granovetter, Mark (1990) 'Entrepreneurship, Development and the Emergence of Firms', *Wissenschaftszentrum für Sozialforschung Berlin, Forschungsschwerpunkt Arbeitsmarkt und Beschäftigung*, discussion paper FS I 90-2, April.

Gray, John N. (1986) *Hayek on Liberty* (2nd edition), New York: Wiley-Blackwell.

Groys, Boris (2014) *On the New*, New York: Verso.

Gruber, Judith and Trickett, Edison J. (1987) 'Can We Empower Others? The Paradox of Empowerment in the Govering of an Alternative Public School', in: *American Journal of Community Psychology*, 15, pp. 353–371.

Guilford, Joy Paul (1967) 'Creativity: Yesterday, Today, and Tomorrow', in: *The Journal of Creative Behavior*, 1, pp. 3–14.

Guilford, Joy Paul (1950) 'Creativity', in: *The American Psychologist*, 5(9), pp. 444–454.

Guler, Isin, Guillén, Mauro F. and Macpherson, John M. (2002) 'Global Competition, Institutions, and the Diffusion of Organizational Practices: The International Spread of ISO 9000 Quality Certificates', in: *Administrative Science Quarterly*, 47(2), pp. 207–232.

Habermas, Jürgen (1983) 'Modernity: An Incomplete Project', in: Hal Foster (ed.), *The Anti-Aesthetic Essays on Postmodern Culture*, Seattle, WA: New Press, pp. 3–15.

Hacking, Ian (1986) 'Making up People', in: Thomas C. Heller, Morton Sosna and David E. Wellbery (eds), *Reconstructing Individualism: Autonomy, Individuality, and the Self in Western Thought*, Stanford, CA: Stanford University Press, pp. 222–236.

Hacking, Ian (1986) 'Self-improvement', in: David Couzens Hoy (ed.), *Foucault: A Critical Reader*, Oxford/New York: Wiley, pp. 235–240.

Hacking, Ian (1995) *Rewriting the Soul*, Princeton, NJ: Princeton University Press.

Hacking, Ian (2004) 'Between Michel Foucault and Erving Goffman: Between Discourse in the Abstract and Face-to-Face Interaction', in: *Economy and Society*, 33, pp. 277–302.

Händler, Ernst-Wilhelm (2002) *Wenn wir sterben*, Frankfurt: Suhrkamp.

Hannah-Moffat, Kelly (2000) 'Prisons that Empower: Neo-liberal Governance in Canadian Women's Prisons', in: *British Journal of Criminology*, 40, pp. 510–531.

Hayek, Friedrich August von (1939) 'Freedom and the Economic System', *Public Policy Pamphlet*, No. 29, (ed. Harry D. Gideonse), Chicago: University of Chicago Press.

Hayek, Friedrich August von (1944/1971) *The Road to Serfdom*, London: Routledge.

Hayek, Friedrich August von (1960) *The Constitution of Liberty*, London: University of Chicago Press.

Hayek, Friedrich August von (1963/1994) 'Wirtschaft, Wissenschaft und Politik', in: *Freiburger Studien*, Tübingen: Mohr Siebeck, pp. 1–17.

Hayek, Friedrich August von (1967/69) 'Principles of a Liberal Social Order', *Studies in Philosophy, Politics and Economics*, London: Routledge, pp. 160–177.

Hayek, Friedrich August von (1982) *Law, Legislation and Liberty*, London: Routledge.

Hayek, Friedrich August von (1996) *Die Anmaßung von Wissen: Neue Freiburger Studien*, Tübingen: Mohr Siebeck.

Hayek, Friedrich August von (2001) *Wirtschaft, Wissenschaft und Politik: Aufsätze zur Wirtschaftspolitik (Gesammelte Schriften in deutscher Sprache, Abt. A: Aufsätze, Bd. 6)*, Tübingen: Mohr Siebeck.

Hayek, Friedrich August von (2002) 'Competition as a Discovery Procedure', in: *The Quarterly Journal of Austrian Economics*, 5(3), pp. 9–23.

Hayek, Friedrich August von (2014) 'The Meaning of Competion', in: *The Market and Other Orders: The Collected Works of F. A. Hayek, Vol. XV*, Chicago: University of Chicago Press, pp. 105–116.

Hébert, Robert F. and Link, Albert N. (1988) *The Entrepreneur: Mainstream Views and Radical Critiques* (2nd edition), New York: Praeger.

Heelas, Paul and Morris, Paul (eds) (1992) *The Values of the Enterprise Culture: The Moral Debate*, London: Routledge.

Heiner, Maja (1996) 'Evaluation zwischen Qualifizierung, Qualitätsentwicklung und Qualitätssicherung', in: *Qualitätsentwicklung durch Evaluation*, Freiburg: Lambertus, pp. 20–47.

Heintel, Peter and Krainz, Ewald E. (2000) *Projektmanagement: Eine Antwort auf die Hierarchiekrise?*, Wiesbaden: Gabler.

Henkel, Heiko and Stirrat, Roderick (eds) (2001) 'Participation as Spiritual Duty; Empowerment as Secular Subjection', in: Bill Cooke and Uma Kothari (eds), *Participation: The New Tyranny*, London: Zed Books, pp. 168–184.

Hentig, Hartmut von (2000) *Kreativität: Hohe Erwartungen an einen schwachen Begriff*, Weinheim/Basel: Beltz.

Herriger, Norbert (1997) *Empowerment in der Sozialen Arbeit: Eine Einführung*, Stuttgart: W. Kohlhammer.

Heward, Christine and Bunwaree, Sheila (eds) (1999) *Gender, Education, and Development: Beyond Access to Empowerment*, London/New York: Zed Books.

Hill Collins, Patricia (2000) *Black Feminist Thought: Knowledge, Consciousness, and the Politics of Empowerment*, New York: Psychology Press.

Hindess, Barry (1997) 'A Society Governed by Contract', in: Glyn Davis, Barbara Sullivan and Anna Yeatman (eds), *The New Contractualism*, Melbourne: Macmillan, pp. 14–26.

Hjorth, Daniel (2003) *Rewriting Entrepreneurship for a New Perspective on Organisational Creativity*, Copenhagen: Samfundslitterature Press.

Hoffmann, Heinz (1980) *Kreativitätstechniken für Manager*, Munich: Moderne Industrie.

Holmer Nadesan, Majia (2003) 'Engineering the Entrepreneurial Infant: Brain Science, Infant Development Toys, and Governmentality', in: *Cultural Studies*, 16, pp. 401–432.

Honneth, Axel (1995) *Struggle for Recognition: The Moral Grammar of Social Conflict*, Cambridge: Polity.

Howkins, John (2001) *The Creative Economy: How People Make Money from Ideas*, New York: Allen Lane.

Huber, Joseph (1980) *Wer soll das alles ändern: Die Alternativen der Alternativbewegung*, Berlin: Rotbuch.

Huizinga, Jakob (1950) *Homo Ludens: a Study of the Play-Element in Culture*, Boston, MA: The Beacon Press.

Hutter, Michael and Teubner, Gunther (1994) 'Der Gesellschaft fette Beute. *Homo juridicus* und *homo oeconomicus* als kommunikationserhaltende Fiktionen', in: Peter Fuchs and Andreas Göbel (eds), *Der Mensch – das Medium der Gesellschaft*, Frankfurt: Suhrkamp, pp. 110–145.

Imai, Masaaki (1992) *Kaizen*, Munich: Hanser.

Jaeger, Hans (1990) Artikel 'Unternehmer', in: Otto Brunner, Werner Conze and Reinhart Koselleck (eds), *Geschichtliche Grundbegriffe: Historisches Lexikon zur politisch-sozialen Sprache in Deutschland*, Vol. 6, Stuttgart, pp. 707–732.

Joas, Hans (1996) *The Creativity of Action*, Chicago, IL: University of Chicago Press.

Justi, Johann Heinrich Gottlob von (1761/1970) 'Gedanken von Projecten und Projectmachern', in: *Politische und Finanzschriften über wichtige Gegenstände der Staatskunst, der Kriegswissenschaften und des Cameral- und Finanzwesens*, Vol. 1, Copenhagen/Leipzig/Aalen: Rothen, pp. 256–281.

Kafka, Franz (1983) 'Give it up!', in: *The Complete Stories*, New York: Penguin.

Kahn, Si (1982) *Organizing: A Guide to Grassroots Leaders*, New York: McGraw-Hill.

Karlöf, Bengt and Östblom, Svante (1994) *Das Benchmarking Konzept: Wegweiser zur Spitzenleistung in Qualität und Produktivität*, Munich: Vahlen.

Kastner, Michael (1999) *Syn-Egoismus: Nachhaltiger Erfolg durch soziale Kompetenz*, Freiburg: Herder.

Katz, Richard (1984) 'Empowerment and Synergy: "Expanding the Community's Healing Resources"', in: *Prevention in Human Services*, 3(2/3), Special Issue: Studies in Empowerment, pp. 201–226.

Kersting, Wolfgang (1994) *Die politische Philosophie des Gesellschaftsvertrags*, Darmstadt: Auflage.

Kets de Vries, Manfred F. R. (1977) 'The Entrepreneurial Personality: A Person at the Crossroads', in: *The Journal of Management Studies*, 14, pp. 34–57.

Keupp, Heiner, Ahbe, Thomas, Gmür, Wolfgang, Höfer, Renate, Mitzscherlich, Beate Kraus, Wolfgang and Straus, Florian (1999) *Identitätskonstruktionen: Das Patchwork der Identitäten in der Spätmoderne*, Reinbek: Rowohlt.

Keynes, John Maynard (1936) *The General Theory of Employment, Interest and Money*, London: Macmillan.

Kieffer, Charles H. (1984) 'Citizen Empowerment: A Developmental Perspective', in: *Prevention in Human Services*, 3(2/3), Special Issue: Studies in Empowerment, pp. 9–36.

Kierkegaard, Søren (1849/1941) *The Sickness Unto Death*, Princeton, NJ: Princeton University Press.

Kirchgässner, Gebhard (2010) *Homo Oeconomicus: The Economic Model of Behaviour and its Applications in Economics and Other Social Sciences*, New York: Springer.

Kirzner, Israel M. (1973) *Competition and Entrepreneurship*, Chicago: University of Chicago Press.

Kirzner, Israel M. (1979) *Perception, Opportunity and Profit: Studies in the Theory of Entrepreneurship*, Chicago: University of Chicago Press.

Klopotek, Felix, 'Projekt', in: Bröckling, Krasmann and Lemke (eds), *Glossar der Gegenwart*, Frankfurt: Suhrkamp, pp. 216–221.

Knabb, Ken (ed.) (2006) *Situationist International Anthology*, Berkeley, CA: Bureau of Public Secrets.

Knight, Frank H. (1921/1964) *Risk, Uncertainty, and Profit*, New York: Augustus M. Kelley.

Knight, Frank H. (1942) 'Profit and Entrepreneurial Functions', in: *The Journal of Economic History*, 2, pp. 126–132.

Kobasa, Suzanne C. (1979) 'Stressful Life Events, Personality and Health: An Inquiry into Hardiness', in: *Journal of Personality and Social Psychology*, 37, pp. 1–11.

Kobasa, Suzanne C. (1982) 'The Hardy Personality: Toward a Social Psychology of Stress and Health', in: Glenn S. Sanders and Jerry Suls (eds), *Social Psychology of Health and Illness*, Hillsdale, NJ: Erlbaum, pp. 3–32.

Kocyba, Hermann (1999) 'Das aktivierte Subjekt: Mit post-tayloristischen Formen der Arbeit ändert sich auch die moderne Berufsidee', in: *Frankfurter Rundschau*, 28 September.

Kommission für Zukunftsfragen Bayern-Sachsen (ed.) (1997) *Erwerbstätigkeit und Arbeitslosigkeit in Deutschland: Entwicklung, Ursachen und Maßnahmen, Teil III – Maßnahmen zur Verbesserung der Beschäftigungslage*, Bonn, www.bayern.de/wirtschaftsstandort/zukunftsfragen/ (13.10.2005).

Koppermann, Heiner (1996) 'Empowerment: Schlummernde Potentiale wecken', in: Buchner, Dietrich and Lasko, Wolf W., *Vorsprung im Wettbewerb: Ganzheitliche Veränderungen, Netzwerke, Synergie, Empowerment, Coaching. Das Veränderungshandbuch von Winner's Edge*, Wiesbaden: Gabler, pp. 291–306.

Krajewski, Markus (2004) 'Über Projektemacher: Eine Einleitung', in: *Projektemacher*, Berlin: Kulturverlag Kadmos, pp. 7–25.

Kramer, Peter D. (1994) *Listening to Prozac*, London: Fourth Estate.

Kraushaar, Wolfgang (1978) 'Thesen zum Verhältnis von Alternativ- und Flucht-bewegung', in: *Autonomie oder Getto? Kontroversen über die Alternativbewegung*, Frankfurt: Verlag Neue Kritik, pp. 8–67.

Kreuz, Werner (1994) 'Benchmarking: Voraussetzung für den Erfolg von TQM', in: Achim Töpfer and Armin Mehdorn (eds), *Besser – Schneller – Schlanker: TQM-Konzepte in der Unternehmenspraxis*, Neuwied: Luchterhand, pp. 83–108.

Kris, Ernst (1952) *Psychoanalytic Explorations in Art*, New York: IUP.

Kropotkin, Peter (1926) *The Conquest of Bread*, New York: Vanguard Press.

Kropotkin, Peter (2000) 'Grenzen der Vermarktlichung: Die Mythen um unterne-hmerisch handelnde Mitarbeiter', in: *WSI-Mitteilungen*, 53, pp. 818–828.

Küstenmacher, Werner Tiki and Seiwert, Lothar J. (2004) *How to Simplify Your Life: Seven Practical Steps to Letting Go of Your Burdens and Living a Happier Life*, New York: McGraw-Hill.

Lange-Eichbaum, Wilhelm (1931) *The Problem of Genius*, London: K. Paul, Trench, Trubner & Company.

Lavoie, Don (1991) 'The Discovery and Interpretation of Profit Opportunities: Culture and the Kirznerian Entrepreneur', in: Brigitte Berger (ed.), *The Culture of Entrepreneurship*, San Francisco: ICS Press, pp. 33–51.

Lazear, Edward P. (2000) 'Economic Imperialism', in: *Quarterly Journal of Economics*, 115(1), pp. 99–146.

Lazzarato, Maurizio (1996) 'Immaterial Labour', in: *Radical Thought in Italy: A Potential Politics*, Minneapolis: University of Minnesota Press.

Lazzarato, Maurizio (2012) *The Making of the Indebted Man: Essay On the Neoliberal Condition*, Los Angels: Semiotext(e).

Lazzarato, Maurizio (2015) *Governing by Debt*, South Pasadena, CA: Semiotext(e).

Leineweber, Bernd and Schibel, Karl-Ludwig (1978) '"Die Alternativbewegung": Ein Beitrag zu ihrer gesellschaftlichen Bedeutung und politischen Tragweite, deren Möglichkeiten und Grenzen', in: Wolfgang Kraushaar (ed.), *Autonomie oder Getto? Kontroversen über die Alternativbewegung*, Frankfurt: Verlag Neue Kritik, pp. 95–128.

Lemke, Thomas (1997) *Eine Kritik der politischen Vernunft: Foucaults Analyse der modernen Gouvernementalität*, Berlin: Argument.

Lemke, Thomas (2001) '"The Birth of Biopolitics": Michel Foucault's Lecture at the Collège de France on Neo-liberal Governmentality', in: *Economy and Society*, 30, pp. 190–207.

Lemke, Thomas, Krasmann, Susanne and Bröckling, Ulrich (2000) 'Gouvernementalität, Neoliberalismus, Selbsttechnologien: Eine Einleitung', in: Bröckling, Krasmann and Lemke (eds), *Gouvernementalität der Gegenwart*, Frankfurt: Suhrkamp, pp. 7–40.

DeLillo, Don (2003) *Cosmopolis*, New York: Simon & Schuster.

Lepage, Henri (1982) *Tomorrow, Capitalism: The Economics of Economic Freedom*, La Salle, IL: Open Court.

Lichterman, Paul (1992) 'Self-help Reading as a Thin Culture', in: *Media, Culture and Society*, 14, pp. 421–447.

Link, Jürgen (1997) *Versuch über den Normalismus: Wie Normalität produziert wird*, Opladen: Vandenhoeck & Ruprecht.

Litke, Hans-D. (2004) *Projektmanagement: Methoden, Techniken, Verhaltensweisen*, Munich: Hanser.

Lombroso, Cesare (1891) *The Man of Genius*, London: Scott.

Luhmann, Niklas (1980) 'Gesellschaftliche Struktur und semantische Tradition', in: *Gesellschaftsstruktur und Semantik: Studien zur Wissenssoziologie der modernen Gesellschaft*, Vol. 1, Frankfurt: Suhrkamp, pp. 9–71.

Luhmann, Niklas (1989) 'Individuum, Individualität, Individualismus', in: *Gesellschaftsstruktur und Semantik: Studien zur Wissenssoziologie der modernen Gesellschaft*, Vol. 3, Frankfurt: Suhrkamp, pp. 149–258.

Luhmann, Niklas (1990) *Die Wissenschaft der Gesellschaft*, Frankfurt: Suhrkamp.

Luhmann, Niklas (1993) *Risk: A Sociological Theory*, New York: De Gruyter.

Luhmann, Niklas (2012) *Theory of Society*, Stanford, CA: Stanford University Press.

Lukes, Steven (1968) 'Methodological Individualism Reconsidered', *British Journal of Sociology*, 19, pp. 119–129.

Lundgren, Monica and Packendorff, Johann (2003) 'A Project-based View of Entrepreneurship: Towards Action-Orientation, Seriality and Collectivity', in:

Chris Steyaert and Daniel Hjorth (eds), *New Movements in Entrepreneurship*, Cheltenham/Northampton, MA: Edward Elgar, pp. 86–102.

MacKinnon, Donald W. (1965) 'Personality and the Realization of Creative Potential', in: *American Psychologist*, 20(4), pp. 273–281.

Maier, Corinne (2005) *Bonjour Laziness: Why Hard Work Doesn't Pay*, New York: Pantheon Books.

Maine, Henry Sumner (1861) *Ancient Law: Its Connection with the Early History and its Relations to Modern Ideas*, London: John Murray.

Makropoulos, Michael (1997) *Modernität und Kontingenz*, Munich: Fink.

Malpass, Jeff and Wickham, Gary (1995) 'Governance and Failure: On the Limits of Sociology', in: *Australian and New Zealand Journal of Sociology*, 31(3), pp. 37–50.

Marris, Peter and Rein, Martin (1967) *Dilemmas of Social Reform: Poverty and Community Action in the United States*, Chicago: Transaction.

Martin, Luther H., Gutman, Huck and Hutton, Patrick H. (eds) (1988) *Technologies of the Self*, Amherst, MA: University of Massachusetts Press.

Martinelli, Alberto (1994) 'Entrepreneurship and Management', in: Neil J. Smelser and Richard Swedberg (eds), *The Handbook of Economic Sociology*, Princeton, NJ: Princeton University Press, pp. 476–503.

Marx, Karl (1996) *Capital*, Vol. 1, Washington, DC: International Pub.

Maslow, Abraham H. (1970) *Motivation and Personality* (2nd edition), New York: Harper & Row.

Masschelein, Jan (2004) '"Je viens de voir, je viens d'entendre": Erfahrungen im Niemandsland', in: Ricken and Rieger-Ladich (eds), *Michel Foucault: Pädagogische Lektüren*, Wiesbaden: Springer-Verlag, pp. 95–115.

Masschelein, Jan and Simons, Maarten (2005) *Globale Immunität oder Eine kleine Kartographie des europäischen Bildungsraums*, Zurich: Diaphanes.

Matthes, Joachim (1988) 'Projekte – nein, danke? Eine (un)zeitgemäße Betrachtung', in: *Zeitschrift für Soziologie*, 17, pp. 465–473.

McArdle, Louise, Rowlinson, Michael, Procter, Stephen, Hassard, John and Forrester, Paul (1995) 'Total Quality Management and Participation: Employee Empowerment, or the Enhancement of Exploitation', in: Adrian Wilkinson and Hugh Willmott (eds), *Making Quality Critical: New Perspectives on Organizational Change*, London: Routledge, pp. 156–172.

McClelland, David C. (1987) 'Characteristics of Successful Entrepreneurs', in: *Journal of Creative Behavior*, 21, pp. 219–233.

McClelland, David C. (1972) *The Achievement Motive*, New York: John Wiley.

McClelland, David C. (1961) *The Achieving Society*, Princeton, NJ: Van Nostrand.

McKenzie, Richard B. and Tullock, Gordon (1978) *The New World of Economics: Explorations into the Human Experience*, Homewood, IL: Richard D. Irwin.

McRobbie, Angela (2001) '"Everyone is Creative": Artists as New Economy Pioneers?', in: *Open Democracy*, pp. 119–132, www.opendemocracy.net/node/652.

McRobbie, Angela (1998) *British Fashion Design: Rag Trade or Image Industry?* London: Routledge.

Mead, George H. (1934/1962) *Mind, Self, and Society from the Standpoint of a Social Behaviorist*, Chicago: University of Chicago Press.

Melville, Herman (1967) 'Bartleby the Scrivener', in: *Billy Budd, Sailor and Other Stories*, Harmondsworth: Penguin, pp. 57–99.

Ménard, Claude (2000) 'Enforcement Procedures and Governance Structures: What Relationship?', in: *Institutions, Contracts and Organizations: Perspectives from New Institutional Economics*, Cheltenham: Edward Elgar, pp. 234–253.

Miller, Peter and Rose, Nikolas (1995) 'Production, Identity, and Democracy', in: *Theory and Society*, 25, pp. 427–467.

Miller, Peter and Rose, Nikolas (1990) 'Governing Economic Life', in: *Economy and Society*, 19, pp. 1–31.

Mises, Ludwig von (1996) *Human Action* (4th edition), San Francisco: Fox & Wilkes.

Moldaschl, Manfred F. and Sauer, Dieter (2000) 'Internalisierung des Marktes: Zur neuen Dialektik von Kooperation und Herrschaft', in: Heiner Minssen (ed.), *Begrenzte Entgrenzungen: Wandlungen von Organisation und Arbeit*, Berlin: Edition Sigma, pp. 205–224.

Moldaschl, Manfred F., Sauer, Dieter and Voß, G. Günter (eds) (2002) *Subjektivierung von Arbeit*, Munich: Hampp.

Morris, Paul (1991) 'Freeing the Spirit of Enterprise: The Genesis and Development of the Concept of Enterprise Culture', in: Russell Keat and Nicholas Abercrombie (eds), *Enterprise Culture*, London/New York: Routledge, pp. 21–37.

Narayan, Deepa (ed.) (2002) *Empowerment and Poverty Reduction: A Sourcebook*, Washington, DC: World Bank Publications.

Neubeiser, Marie-Louise (1992) *Management Coaching*, Düsseldorf: Orell-Füssili.

Neuberger, Oswald (2000) *Das 360° Feedback: Alle fragen? Alles sehen? Alles sagen?*, Munich: Rainer Hampp.

Neumeier, Rudolf (1997) *Qualitätsmanagement für Dienstleister*, unpublished seminar document from the TÜV Akademie Hessen.

Nietzsche, Friedrich (2013) *Human, All Too Human: A Book for Free Spirits*, Auckland: Create Space.

O'Malley, Pat (2000) 'Uncertain Subjects: Risks, Liberalism and Contract', in: *Economy and Society*, 29, pp. 460–484.

O'Malley, Pat (2004) *Risk, Uncertainty and Government*, London: Routledge-Cavendish.

Odiorne, George S. (1965) *Management by Objectives: A System of Managerial Leadership*, New York: Pitman.

Oess, Attila (1994) 'Total Quality Management (TQM): Eine ganzheitliche Unternehmensphilosophie', in: Stauss (ed.), *Qualitätsmanagement und Zertifizierung*, pp. 199–222.

Opitz, Sven (2004) *Gouvernementalität im Postfordismus: Macht, Wissen und Techniken des Selbst im Feld unternehmerischer Rationalität*, Hamburg: Argument.

Osborn, Alex F. (1953) *Applied Imagination: Principles and Procedures of Creative Thinking*, New York: Charles Scribners and Sons.

Osborne, David and Gaebler, Ted (1992) *Reinventing Government: How the Entrepreneurial Spirit is Transforming the Public Sector*, Reading, MA: Prentice Hall.

Osborne, Thomas (2001) 'Techniken und Subjekte: Von den "Governmentality Studies" zu den "Studies of Governmentality"', in: *Demokratie. Arbeit. Selbst: Analysen liberal-demokratischer Gesellschaften im Anschluss an Michel Foucault, Mitteilungen des Instituts für Wissenschaft und Kunst Wien*, 56(2/3), pp. 12–16.

Osborne, Thomas (2003) 'Against "Creativity": A Philistine Rant', in: *Economy and Society*, 32, pp. 507–525.

Pankofer, Sabine (2000) 'Empowerment: eine Einführung', in: Tilly Miller and Sabine Pankofer (eds), *Empowerment konkret! Handlungsentwürfe und Reflexionen aus der psychosozialen Praxis*, Stuttgart: Lucius and Lucius, pp. 7–22.

Paoli, Guillaume (ed.) (2002) *Mehr Zuckerbrot, weniger Peitsche: Aufrufe, Manifeste und Faulheitspapiere der Glücklichen Arbeitslosen*, Berlin: Edition Tiamat.

Parsons, Ruth J. (1991) 'Empowerment: Purpose and Practice Principle in Social Work', in: *Social Work with Groups*, 14(2), pp. 7–21.

Parsons, Talcott and Smelser, Neil J. (1956) *Economy and Society*, London: Routledge.

Pateman, Carol (1988) *The Sexual Contract*, Stanford, CA: Stanford University Press.

Patzak, Gerold and Rattay, Günter (1955) *Projektmanagement*, Vienna: Linde.

Peach, Robert W. (1995) *The ISO 9000 Handbook*. Scarborough, ON: CEEM Information Services.

Peters, Thomas J. and Waterman, Robert H. (1982) *In Search of Excellence: Lessons from America's Best-Run Companies*, New York: Warner.

Peters, Tom (1988) *Thriving on Chaos: Handbook for a Management Revolution*, New York: HarperCollins.

Peters, Tom (1992) *Liberation Management: Necessary Disorganization for the Nanosecond Nineties*, New York: Alfred A. Knopf.

Peters, Tom (1999) *The Brand You 50: Fifty Ways to Transform Yourself from an 'Employee' into a Brand That Shouts Distinction, Commitment, and Passion!*, New York: Knopf Doubleday.

Peters, Tom (2004) 'Brand You Survival Kit', in: *Fast Company*, issue 83, June, p. 95, http://pf.fastcompany.com/magazine/83/playbook.html (12.05.2005).

Pies, Ingo (1998) 'Theoretische Grundlagen demokratischer Wirtschafts- und Gesellschaftspolitik – Der Beitrag Gary Beckers', in: Ingo Pies and Martin Leschke (eds), *Gary Beckers ökonomischer Imperialismus*, Tübingen: Mohr Siebeck, pp. 1–29.

Pies, Ingo (1996) 'Theoretische Grundlagen demokratischer Wirtschafts- und Gesellschaftspolitik – Der Beitrag James Buchanans', in: Ingo Pies and Martin Leschke (eds), *James Buchanans konstitutionelle Ökonomik*, Tübingen: Mohr Siebeck, pp. 1–18.

Pinchot, Gifford III (1985) *Intrapreneuring: Why You Don't Have to Leave the Corporation to Become an Entrepreneur*, New York: Joanna Cotler.

Plato (1966) *Laws* (trans. A. E. Taylor), in: Edith Hamilton and Huntington Cairns (eds), *Collected Dialogues of Plato* (4th edition), New York: Pantheon.

Plehwe, Dieter, Walpen, Bernhard and Neunhöffer, Gisela (eds) (2006) *Neoliberal Hegemony: A Global Critique*, New York: Routledge.

Plessner, Hellmuth (1985) *Die Stufen des Organischen und der Mensch* (3rd edition), Berlin: Walter de Gruyter.

Pongratz, Hans. J. and Voß, Günter G. (1997) 'Fremdorganisierte Selbstorganisation', in: *Zeitschrift für Personalforschung*, 7, pp. 30–53.

Pongratz, Hans J. and Voß, G. Günter (2003) *Arbeitskraftunternehmer: Erwerbsorientierungen in entgrenzten Arbeitsformen*, Berlin: Auflage (Forschung aus der Hans-Böckler-Stiftung, Bd. 47).

Pongratz, Hans. J. and Voß, Günter G. (2003) 'From Employee to "Entreployee": Towards a "Self-entrepreneurial" Work Force?', in: *Concepts and Transformation*, 8(3), pp. 239–254.

Popitz, Heinrich (1997) *Wege der Kreativität*, Tübingen: Mohr Siebeck.

Potterfield, Thomas A. (1999) *The Business of Employee Empowerment: Democracy and Ideology in the Workplace*, Westport, CT: Greenwood.

Poulsen, Margo Hildreth (1975) 'Anarchy is a Learning Environment', in: *Journal of Creative Behavior*, 9, pp. 131–136.

Power, Michael (1994) *The Audit Explosion*, London: Demos.

Power, Michael (1994) 'The Audit Society', in: Anthony G. Hopwood and Peter Miller (eds), *Accounting as Social and Institutional Practice*, Cambridge: Cambridge University Press, pp. 299–316.

Power, Michael (1997) *The Audit Society: Rituals of Verification*, Oxford: Oxford University Press.

Praag, C. Mirjam van (1999) 'Some Classic Views on Entrepreneurship', in: *The Economist*, 147, pp. 311–335.

Preiser, Siegfried (1976) *Kreativitätsforschung*, Darmstat: Wissenschafftliche Buchegesellschaft.

Prilleltensky, Isaac (1994) 'Empowerment in Mainstream Psychology: Legitimacy, Obstacles, and Possibilities', in: *Canadian Psychology (Psychologie canadienne)*, 35(4), pp. 358–375.

Proudhon, Pierre-Joseph (2004) *General Idea of the Revolution in the Nineteenth Century*, New York: University Press of the Pacific.

Putnam, Robert (2000) *Bowling Alone: The Collapse and Revival of American Community*, New York: Simon & Schuster.

Quaghebeur, Kerlijn (2006) 'Pathways of Participation: A critical exploration of participation as a dominant learning perspective in the world of development cooperation', dissertation, Katholieke Universiteit, Leuven.

Radnitzky, Gerard and Bernholz, Peter (eds) (1987) *Economic Imperialism: The Economic Approach Applied Outside the Field of Economics*, New York: Pwpa.

Randolph, W. Alan (1994–5) 'Navigating the Journey to Empowerment', in: *Organizational Dynamics*, 23(4), pp. 19–31.

Raphael, Lutz (1996) 'Die Verwissenschaftlichung des Sozialen als methodische und konzeptionelle Herausforderung für eine Sozialgeschichte des 20. Jahrhunderts', in: *Geschichte und Gesellschaft*, 22, pp. 165–193.

Rappaport, Julian (1981) '"In Praise of Paradox": A Social Policy of Empowerment over Prevention', in: *American Journal of Community Psychology*, 9, pp. 1–25.

Rappaport, Julian (1985–6) 'The Power of Empowerment Language', in: *Social Policy*, 16(2), pp. 15–21.

Rappaport, Julian (1987) 'Terms of Empowerment/Exemplars of Prevention: Toward a Theory for Community Psychology', in: *American Journal of Community Psychology*, 15, pp. 121–148.

Reagan, Ronald (1985) 'Why this is an Entrepreneurial Age', in: *Journal of Business Venturing*, 1, pp. 1–4.

Reckwitz, Andreas (2006) *Das hybride Subjekt: Eine Theorie der Subjektkulturen von der bürgerlichen Moderne zur Postmoderne*, Weilerswist: Velbrück.

Redlich, Fritz (1949) 'The Origin of the Concepts of "Entrepreneur" and "Creative Entrepreneur"', in: *Explorations in Entrepreneurial History*, 1(2), pp. 1–7.

Redlich, Fritz (1949) 'The Business Leader in Theory and Reality', in: *American Journal of Economics and Sociology*, 8(3), pp. 223–237.

Redlich, Fritz (1959) 'Entrepreneurial Typology', in: *Weltwirtschaftliches Archiv*, 82, pp. 150–168.

Rentmeister, Josef (2000) 'Fünf Fragen an Josef Rentmeister, Mitglied der Geschäftsführung, Cisco Systems Deutschland GmbH', in: *ULA Nachrichten: Zeitschrift für Führungskräfte der Deutschen Wirtschaft*, No. 5/6, June, p. 2.

Ricken, Norbert (2004) 'Die Macht der Macht – Rückfragen an Michel Foucault', in: Ricken and Rieger-Ladich (eds), *Michel Foucault: Pädagogische Lektüren*, Wiesbaden: Springer, pp. 119–143.

Ricken, Norbert and Rieger-Ladich, Markus (eds) (2004), *Michel Foucault. Pädagogische Lektüren*, Wiesbaden: Springer.

Rico, Gabriele L. (2000) *Writing the Natural Way*, New York: Tarcher/Putnam.

Riger, Stephanie (1993) 'What's Wrong with Empowerment?', in: *American Journal of Community Psychology*, 21, pp. 279–292.

Rimke, Heidi Marie (2000) 'Governing Citizens through Self-help Literature', in: *Cultural Studies*, 14, pp. 61–78.

Rogers, Carl R. (1959) 'Toward a Theory of Creativity', in: Harold A. Anderson (ed.), *Creativity and its Cultivation*, New York: Harper & Row, pp. 69–82.

Röpke, Wilhelm (1950) *Ist die deutsche Wirtschaftspolitik richtig? Analyse und Kritik*, Stuttgart [reproduced in: Wolfgang Stützel et al. (eds) (1981) *Grundtexte zur Sozialen Marktwirtschaft: Zeugnisse aus zweihundert Jahren ordnungspolitischer Diskussion*, Stuttgart/New York: Gustav Fischer, pp. 49–62].

Rose, Nikolas (1992) 'Governing the Enterprising Self', in: Paul Heelas and Paul Morris (eds), *The Values of the Enterprise Culture: The Moral Debate*, London: Routledge, pp. 141–164.

Rose, Nikolas (1996) *Inventing Our Selves: Psychology, Power, and Personhood*, Cambridge: Cambridge University Press.

Rothbard, Murray N. (1962) *Man, Economy, and State*, 2 vols, Princeton, NJ: D. Van Nostrand.

Rothbard, Murray N. (1970/2004) 'Power and Market', in: *Man, Economy, and the State with Power and Market*, Auburn, AL: Nash Pub, pp. 1047–1369.

Rothbard, Murray N. (1978) *For a New Liberty: The Libertarian Manifesto*, New York: Macmillan.

Rothbard, Murray N. (1982) *Ethics of Liberty*, Atlantic Highlands, NJ: Humanities Press.

Rotter, Julian B. (1966) 'General Expectancies for Internal versus External Control of Reinforcement', in: *Psychological Monographs*, 80, No. 609.

Rubenson, Daniel L. and Runco, Mark A. (1992) 'The Psychoeconomic Approach to Creativity', in: *New Ideas in Psychology*, 10, pp. 131–147.

Rubin, Harriet (1999) *Soloing: Realizing Your Life's Ambition*, New York: Harper Collins.

Rüstow, Alexander von (1945/2001) *Das Versagen des Wirtschaftsliberalismus*, Marburg: Europa-Verlag.

Schildknecht, Rolf (1992) *Total Quality Management*, Frankfurt: Campus.

Schiller, Friedrich (1795/1902) 'On the Aesthetic Education of Man' (letter 15), in: *Aesthetical and Philosophical Essays, Vol. I*, Boston: Robertson, Ashford and Bentley.

Schlegel, Friedrich (1798/1967) 'Fragmente', in: Hans Eichner (ed.), *Kritische Friedrich Schlegel Ausgabe, Vol. 2: Charakteristiken und Kritiken I*, Munich: Schöningh, pp. 165–255.

Schönburg, Alexander von (2005) *Die Kunst stilvollen Verarmens: Wie man ohne Geld reich wird*, Berlin: Rowohlt.

Schönhuth, Michael and Kievelitz, Uwe (1994) *Participatory Learning Approaches: Rapid Rural Appraisal/Participatory Appraisal – An Introductory Guide*, Rossdorf: TZ-Verlag.

Schultz, Theodore W. (1975) 'The Value of the Ability to Deal with Disequilibria', in: *The Journal of Economic Literature*, XIII, pp. 827–846.

Schultz, Theodore W. (1980) 'Investment in Entrepreneurial Ability', in: *Scandinavian Journal of Economics*, 82, pp. 437–448.

Schultz, Theodore W. (1982) *Investing in People: The Economics of Population Quality*, Berkeley, CA: University of California Press.

Schumpeter, Joseph A. (1926) *Theorie der wirtschaftlichen Entwicklung* (2nd edition), Leipzig: Duncker & Humblot.

Schumpeter, Joseph A. (1928) 'Unternehmer', in: Ludwig Elster, Adolf Weber and Friedrich Wieser (eds), *Handwörterbuch der Staatswissenschaften, Vol. 8* (4th edition), Jena, pp. 476–487.

Schumpeter, Joseph A. (1949/1991) 'Economic Theory and Entrepreneurial History', in: Richard V. Clemence (ed.), *Essays on Entrepreneurs, Innovations, Business Cycles, and the Evolution of Capitalism*, New Brunswick: Transaction, pp. 253–271.

Schumpeter, Joseph A. (1976) *Capitalism, Socialism and Democracy*, London: Harper.

Schwarze, Achim (2005) *Kleine Brötchen: Von den Vorzügen, ohne feste Anstellung zu sein*, Munich: Taschenbuch.

Scott, Cynthia D. and Jaffe, Dennis T. (1995) *Empowerment – mehr Kompetenzen den Mitarbeitern: So steigern Sie Motivation, Effizienz und Ergebnisse*, Vienna: Ueberreuter.

Seligman, Martin E. P. (1975) *Learned Helplessness: On Depression, Development and Death*, San Francisco: W. H. Freeman.

Sennett, Richard (1998) *The Corrosion of Character*, New York: Norton.

Simmel, Georg (1917/1984) *Grundfragen der Soziologie* (4th edition), Berlin/New York: Walter de Gruyter.

Simon, Barbara Levy (1994) *The Empowerment Tradition in American Social Work: A History*, New York: Columbia University Press.

Simon, Herbert A. (1972) 'Theories of Bounded Rationality', in: Charles B. McGuire and Roy Radner (eds), *Decision and Organization: A Vol. in Honor of Jacob Marschak*, Amsterdam: North-Holland Pub, pp. 161–176.

Smith, John F., Fawcett, Stephen B. and Balcazar, Fabricio E. (1991) 'Behaviour Analysis of Social Action Constructs: The Case of Empowerment', in: *Behaviour Change*, 8, pp. 4–9.

Solomon, Barbara Bryant (1976) *Black Empowerment: Social Work in Oppressed Communities*, New York: Columbia University Press.

Sombart, Werner (1909) 'Der kapitalistische Unternehmer', in: *Archiv für Sozialwissenschaft und Sozialpolitik*, 29, pp. 689–758.

Sombart, Werner (1915) *The Quintessence of Capitalism: A Study of the History and Psychology of the Modern Business Man*, New York: E. P. Dutton.

Sondermann, Jochen P. (1994) 'Instrumente des Total Quality Management', in: Stauss, *Qualitätsmanagement und Zertifizierung*, Wiesbaden: Gabler, pp. 223–253.

Spencer, Herbert (1900) *Principles of Sociology, Vol. 2*, New York: D. Appleton & Co.

Stanitzek, Georg (1987) 'Der Projektmacher: Projektionen auf eine "unmögliche" moderne Kategorie', in: *Ästhetik & Kommunikation*, 17(65/66), pp. 135–146.

Stark, Wolfgang (1996) *Empowerment: Neue Handlungskompetenzen in der psychosozialen Praxis*, Freiburg: Lambertus.

Stauss, Bernd (ed.) (1994) *Qualitätsmanagement und Zertifizierung*, Wiesbaden: Gabler.

Steinbuch, Pitter A. (1998) *Projektorganisation und Projektmanagement*, Ludwigshafen (Rhein): Kiehl Verlag.

Sternberg, Robert J. and Lubart, Todd L. (1991) 'An Investment Theory of Creativity and its Development', in: *Human Development*, 34, pp. 1–31.

Sternberg, Robert J. and Lubart, Todd L. (1992) 'Buy Low and Sell High: An Investment Approach to Creativity', in: *Current Directions in Psychological Science*, 1, pp. 1–5.

Sternberg, Robert J. and Lubart, Todd L. (1995) *Defying the Crowd: Cultivating Creativity in a Culture of Conformity*, New York: Free Press.

Sternberg, Robert J. and Lubart, Todd L. (1996) 'Investing in Creativity', in: *American Psychologist*, 51, pp. 677–688.

Strauss, Anselm (1991) 'The Articulation of Project Work: An Organizational Process', in: *Creating Sociological Awareness: Collective Images and Symbolic Representations*, New Brunswick, NJ: Transaction, pp. 99–119.

Strauss, Nicolette (2003) *Die andere Ich AG: Führen Sie sich selbst wie ein erfolgreiches Unternehmen*, Frankfurt: Campus-Verlag.

Swift, Carolyn and Levin, Gloria (1987) 'Empowerment: An Emerging Mental Health Technology', in: *Journal of Primary Prevention*, 8(1/2), pp. 71–94.

Taylor, Irving A. (1975) 'A Retrospective View of Creativity Investigation', in: Irving A. Taylor and Jacob W. Getzels (eds), *Perspectives in Creativity*, Chicago: Transaction, pp. 1–36.

Tellmann, Ute (2003) 'The Truth of the Market', in: *Distinktion: Scandinavian Journal for Social Theory*, 7, pp. 49–63.

Temin, Peter (1991) 'Entrepreneurs and Managers', in: Patrice Higonnet, David S. Landes and Henry Rosovsky (eds), *Favorites of Fortune: Technology, Growth, and Economic Development since the Industrial Revolution*, Cambridge, MA: Harvard University Press, pp. 339–355.

Teubner, Gunther (1992) 'Die vielköpfige Hydra: Netzwerke als kollektive Akteure höherer Ordnung', in: Wolfgang Krohn and Günter Küppers (eds), *Emergenz: Die Entstehung von Ordnung, Organisation und Bedeutung*, Frankfurt: Suhrkamp, pp. 189–216.

Teubner, Gunther (1997) 'Im blinden Fleck der Systeme: Die Hybridisierung des Vertrages', in: *Soziale Systeme*, 3, pp. 313–326.

Teubner, Gunther (1998) 'Vertragswelten: Das Recht in der Fragmentierung von Private Governance Regimes', in: *Rechtshistorisches Journal*, 17, pp. 234–265.

Thibaud, Paul (1985) 'The Triumph of the Entrepreneur', in: *Telos*, Nr. 64, Summer, pp. 134–140 [original: 'Le triomphe de l'entrepreneur', in: *Esprit*, Dec. 1984, pp. 101–110].

Thomas, Kenneth W. and Velthouse, Betty A. (1990) 'Cognitive Elements of Empowerment: An "Interpretative" Model of Intrinsic Task Motivation', in: *Academy of Management Review*, 15, pp. 666–681.

Thönneßen, Johannes (1999) 'Mitarbeiter beurteilen ihre Chefs – das Beispiel Bayer', in: *Harvard Businessmanager*, 5, pp. 99–106.

Töpfer, Armin and Mehdorn, Achim (eds) (1995) *Total Quality Management*, Neuwied: Luchterhand.

Townley, Barbara (1995) '"Know Thyself": Self-awareness, Self-formation and Managing', in: *Organization*, 2, pp. 271–289.

Townley, Barbara (1998) 'Beyond Good and Evil: Depth and Division in the Management of Human Resources', in: Alan McKinlay and Ken Starkey (eds), *Foucault, Management and Organization Theory*, London: Sage, pp. 191–210.

Trendbüro (ed.) (2001) *Duden Wörterbuch der New Economy*, Mannheim: Bibliographisches Institut.

Tuckman, Alan (1995) 'Ideology, Quality and TQM', in: Adrian Wilkinson and Hugh Wilmott (eds), *Making Quality Critical*, London: Routledge, pp. 54–81.

Udehn, Lars (2002) *Methodological Individualism: Background, History and Meaning*, New York: Routledge.

Ulmann, Gisela (ed.) (1973) 'Einleitung: Psychologische Kreativitätsforschung', in: *Kreativitätsforschung*, Cologne: Kiepenheuer and Witsch, pp. 11–22.

Valverde, Mariana (1996) '"Despotism" and Ethical Liberal Governance', in: *Economy and Society*, 25, pp. 357–372.

Virno, Paolo (2004) *A Grammar of Multitude*, Los Angeles/New York: Semiotext(e).

Voehl, Frank, Jackson, Peter and Ashton, David (1994) *ISO 9000: An Implementation Guide for Small to Mid-Sized Businesses*, Boca Raton, FL: St Lucie Press.

Voß, G. Günter and Pongratz, Hans J. (1998) 'Der Arbeitskraftunternehmer: Eine neue Grundform der Ware Arbeitskraft?', in: *Kölner Zeitschrift für Soziologie und Sozialpsychologie*, 50, pp. 131–158.

Wabner, Rolf (1997) *Selbstmanagement: Werden Sie zum Unternehmer Ihres Lebens*, Niedernhausen/Ts: Falken.

Wallas, Graham (1926) *The Art of Thought*, New York: Watts.

Ward, Colin (1966) 'Anarchism as a Theory of Organization', in: Leonard I. Krimerman and Lewis Perry (eds), *Patterns of Anarchy: A Collection of Writings on the Anarchist Tradition*, New York: Anchor Books.

Weber, Max (1946) 'Science as Vocation', in: H. H. Gerth and C. Wright Mills (eds), *From Max Weber: Essays in Sociology,* New York: Routledge.

Weber, Max (1949) '"Objectivity" in Social Science and Social Policy', in: *Methodology of Social Sciences* (trans./ed. Edward Shils and Henry Finch), Glencoe, IL: Free Press, pp. 49–112.

Weber, Max (1978) *Economy and Society*, Berkeley, CA: University of California Press.

Weick, Ann, Rapp, Charles, Sullivan, W. Patrick and Kisthardt, Walter (1989) 'A Strength Perspective for Social Work Practice', in: *Social Work*, July, pp. 350–354.

Wertheimer, Max (1945) *Productive Thinking*, New York: Harper.

Whyte, William H. (1956) *The Organization Man*, New York: Clarion.

Wilkinson, Adrian and Wilmott, Hugh (eds) (1995) 'Introduction', in: *Making Quality Critical*, London: Routledge, pp. 1–32.

Wildenmann, Bernd (2000) *Professionell führen: Empowerment für Manager, die mit weniger Mitarbeitern mehr leisten müssen* (5th edition), Neuwied: Kriftel: Luchterhand.

Wilkinson, Adrian and Wilmott, Hugh (eds) (1995) *Making Quality Critical: New Perspectives on Organizational Change*, London: Routledge.

Williamson, Oliver E. (1985) *The Economic Institutions of Capitalism: Firms, Markets, Relational Contracting*, New York: Free Press.

Wolf, Harald (1999) *Arbeit und Autonomie: Ein Versuch über Widersprüche und Metamorphosen kapitalistischer Produktion*, Münster: Verlag Westfälisches Dampfboot.

Worell, Judith and Remer, Pam (1992) *Feminist Perspectives in Therapy: An Empowerment Model for Women*, Chichester: John Wiley & Sons.

Wörnle, Kirsten (2002) 'Unterricht mit Schulvertrag', in: *Badische Zeitung*, 2 October, p. 19.

Yeatman, Anna (1995) 'Interpreting Contemporary Contractualism', in: Jonathan Boston (ed.), *The State Under Contract*, Wellington: Paul & Co Pub Consortium, pp. 124–139.

Yeatman, Anna (1997) 'Contract, Status and Personhood', in: Glyn Davis, Barbara Sullivan and Anna Yeatman (eds), *The New Contractualism*, Melbourne: Palgrave Macmillan, pp. 39–56.

Zilsel, Edgar (1926) *Die Entstehung des Geniebegriffs*, Tübingen: JCB Mohr.

Zilsel, Edgar (1918) *Die Geniereligion: Ein kritischer Versuch über das moderne Persönlichkeitsideal*, Vienna: Braumüller.

Zimmerman, Marc A. (1990) 'Toward a Theory of Learned Hopefulness: A Structural Model Analysis of Participation and Empowerment', in: *Journal of Research in Personality*, 24, pp. 71–86.

Zimmerman, Marc A. (2000) 'Empowerment Theory: Psychological, Organizational and Community Levels of Analysis', in: Julian Rappaport and Edward Seidman (eds), *Handbook of Community Psychology*, New York: Springer, pp. 43–63.

AUTHOR INDEX

SUBJECT INDEX